Designing a
Prosocial Classroom

T0339343

A NORTON PROFESSIONAL BOOK

Designing a Prosocial Classroom

FOSTERING COLLABORATION

IN STUDENTS FROM PRE-K–12

WITH THE CURRICULUM YOU ALREADY USE

Christi Bergin

W. W. NORTON & COMPANY

Independent Publishers Since 1923

New York ■ London

Note to Readers: Models and/or techniques described in this volume are illustrative or are included for general informational purposes only; neither the publisher nor the author(s) can guarantee the efficacy or appropriateness of any particular recommendation in every circumstance.

Copyright © 2018 by Christi Bergin

All rights reserved
Printed in the United States of America
First Edition

For information about permission to reproduce selections from this book, write to
Permissions, W. W. Norton & Company, Inc., 500 Fifth Avenue, New York, NY 10110

For information about special discounts for bulk purchases, please contact
W. W. Norton Special Sales at specialsales@wwnorton.com or 800-233-4830

Manufacturing by Maple Press
Book design by Vicki Fischman
Production manager: Christine Critelli

Library of Congress Cataloging-in-Publication Data

Names: Bergin, Christi Ann Crosby, author.
Title: Designing a prosocial classroom : fostering collaboration in students
from preK-12 with the curriculum you already use / Christi Bergin.
Description: New York : W.W. Norton & Company, [2018] | Includes bibliographical references.
Identifiers: LCCN 2017060272 | ISBN 9780393711981 (pbk.)
Subjects: LCSH: Behavior modification. | Affective education. | Classroom environment. |
Teacher-student relationships. | Group work in education.
Classification: LCC LB1060.2 .B47 2018 | DDC 371.102/4—dc23
LC record available at https://lccn.loc.gov/2017060272

W. W. Norton & Company, Inc., 500 Fifth Avenue, New York, N.Y. 10110
www.wwnorton.com

W. W. Norton & Company Ltd., 15 Carlisle Street, London W1D 3BS

1 2 3 4 5 6 7 8 9 0

This book is dedicated to you, for caring enough to create a classroom where children thrive.

CONTENTS

Designing a
Prosocial Classroom

INTRODUCTION

As a professor, my expertise is in how to promote kindness, compassion, and integrity in children. I have often been asked by teachers, including my former students who are practicing teachers, to write a "how to" book for teachers. Recently a director of a professional development agency told me:

> *We spend months showing teachers how to create fantastic, problem-based, hands-on, inquiry-oriented, team-centered lessons using technology. Their districts invest heavily in this professional development and in purchasing the technology. We do a good job helping teachers design lessons that will prepare students for 21st-century work.*
>
> *Yet, when we follow up, we find that many of the teachers are not teaching these kinds of lessons. We ask, "Why?" The teachers say they tried, but those types of lessons make huge demands on students to get along with each other, and their students don't share, cooperate, or help each other enough. Can you teach the teachers how to help their students learn to be kinder and cooperate with each other—to smooth implementation of their problem-based, team-centered lessons?*

This book is a response to requests like this. Before writing, I surveyed teachers, asking what they would like in a book. Their responses were:

- **Keep it short**; I am too busy to read a long book! (This was the most overwhelming response.)

- **Make it useful;** I want to be able to implement what I read immediately in my classroom.

- **Make it research-based;** I want to know that there is evidence to support my teaching.

To honor these requests, I've done my best to distill a complex research literature into a succinct set of tools that I hope you find genuinely useful.

What is a Prosocial Classroom?

The term *prosocial* behavior was coined as the antonym to *antisocial* behavior. Antisocial behavior disrupts the functioning of society. This is a broad definition that can include any behavior that is aversive, annoying, or harmful to others. It includes aggression, bullying, substance abuse, and delinquency (e.g., breaking the law, truancy, vandalism). In contrast, prosocial behavior is behavior that supports the functioning of society. This is also a broad definition that can include any behavior that benefits others or promotes harmonious relationships (Denham, Mason, & Couchoud, 1995; Eisenberg et al., 1996; Eisenberg & Miller, 1987; Fabes, Carlo, Kupanoff, & Laible, 1999; Hay, 1994; Naparstek, 1990). Simply put, *prosocial* refers to positive interactions and *antisocial* to negative interactions regarding others. Some psychologists refer to them as "moving toward" others and "moving against" others.

❝ Prosocial behavior is voluntary behavior that benefits others or promotes harmonious relationships.❞

A key point is that prosocial and antisocial refer to quality, not quantity, of interactions with others. Some people mistakenly use the term antisocial to mean asocial, nonsocial, or introverted and the term prosocial to mean outgoing, but this is not correct. You probably know an antisocial person who is outgoing (e.g., think of some politicians), and a prosocial person who is quiet and a little introverted (e.g., Beth March in *Little Women*, or Neville Longbottom in *Harry Potter*). What identifies a person as prosocial or antisocial is the nature of their interactions with others—kindly or destructive—not how much they interact with others.

Prosocial behavior overlaps with morality. Moral behavior refers to abiding by obligatory, universal laws in order to do what is just and right. Prosocial behavior is morality writ large, but goes beyond it. For example, behaving honestly is both moral and prosocial. However, complimenting another person is not a moral issue involving questions of justice or right versus wrong, but it is prosocial.

Prosocial behavior also includes altruism, but goes beyond it. Altruism is a type of prosocial behavior that benefits someone else *at the expense of the self, such as giving up time, fun, or money.* For example, when you give up personal time to tutor a student or help a struggling colleague with lesson plans, you are being altruistic. Prosocial behavior can be altruistic, but it can also include behaviors with little cost to self, such as a warm greeting or simply saying, "Thank you." Thus, prosocial behavior is a broader concept than morality or altruism.

Prosocial behavior can also sometimes be assertive or paternalistic. Have you ever pulled a toddler away from the edge of a pool even though the toddler wanted to get in the pool? Have you ever made your students do something they did not want to do for their benefit (e.g., revise an essay, or eat their vegetables before dessert)? Probably several times a day! Even 5-year-olds do this. If they are told that chocolate will make another child sick, but the child asks for chocolate, they are likely to give the child fruit snacks instead (A. Martin, Lin, & Olson, 2016). (They will not give carrots instead. Their paternalism has limits!) Prosocial behavior is about genuinely benefitting others, not just doing what others want you to do.

Non-Cognitive Skills and Socioemotional Learning

Prosocial behavior is part of the *non-cognitive* skills that the U.S. Department of Education (ED) has recently made a priority for research. It is part of ED's college-and-career-ready push. This is because, as I'll discuss in Chapter 2, non-cognitive skills may be more important for your students' success in school than are cognitive skills. That covers the *college ready* dimension, but what about the *career ready* dimension? In a survey asking employers what skills they value, employers emphasized social skills such as ability to collaborate with others, listen actively, manage interpersonal conflicts, and show respect for others (Savitz-Romer, Rowan-Kenyon, Zhangg, & Fancsali, 2014). In another study, hundreds of employers ranked non-cognitive skills as more important than cognitive skills for workplace success (Casner-Lotto & Barrington, 2006). Thus, when you help your students develop these skills, you are helping them become successful well beyond your classroom doors.

Non-cognitive skills refer to things like turning in your homework on time, persistence, organization, communication, getting along with others in your study group, having a good attitude, and obeying the teacher. In contrast, cognitive skills refer to the kinds of things measured on achievement tests, such as the ability to solve an algebra equation or fluently read a text.

The term non-cognitive is dreadful, not only because something so important should not be defined by what it is not, but also because getting along with others and self-control can require a lot of cognition (e.g., reasoning, problem-solving, and pondering). They've also been called *soft skills*, which is just as inappropriate a term, since such skills can be very hard, both hard to develop and hard to enact. Nevertheless, one positive is the word *skill*, which implies they can be taught and are not simply traits you are born with or not. The purpose of this book is to give you the tools you need to teach important non-cognitive skills to your students, regardless of the level of skills they may bring with them to your classroom.

You may have heard the term SEL, or social-emotional learning. SEL is a subgroup of non-cognitive skills. One prominent organization, the *Collaborative for Academic, Social, and Emotional Learning* (or CASEL), defines SEL as comprised of five core competencies: (1) self-management, (2) self-awareness, (3) responsible decision making, (4) social awareness, and (5) relationship skills. Some researchers divide these into intrapersonal and interpersonal skills. Intrapersonal skills would include skills such as self-control, setting goals, and growth mindset. Interpersonal skills would include skills such as getting along with others or prosocial behavior (Domitrovich, Durlak, Staley, & Weissberg, 2017; Osher et al., 2016). Both non-cognitive skills and SEL are huge, everything-but-the-kitchen-sink concepts. Prosocial behavior is one important piece of these larger concepts that is increasingly

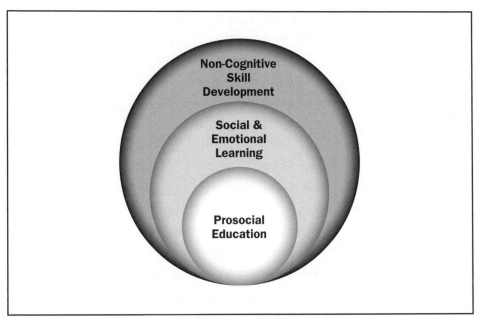

Figure 0.1 Relationship of Prosocial Education to SEL and Non-Cognitive Skills

becoming used in education circles (see Figure 0.1). In Chapter 1, we'll look more closely at what kinds of prosocial behaviors you might expect from your students at school.

The Organization of this Book

This book is divided into two parts. **Part 1: What is Prosocial Behavior and Why Does it Matter?** has two chapters and explains *why* it is important to increase prosocial behavior among your students to address twin goals: first, to raise your students' academic achievement, and second, to improve their happiness and your own level of enjoyment of teaching. In *Chapter 1: What is Prosocial Behavior?* you will learn what prosocial education is and the policy changes that are fueling the new movement in prosocial education. In *Chapter 2: Prosocial Behavior Increases Your Students' Learning*, you will learn how and why prosocial behavior predicts your students' academic achievement and social success at school. You will also learn how promoting prosocial behavior may help narrow the achievement gap.

Part 2: What Specific Approaches Create More Prosocial Classrooms? has four chapters and moves to the *how* of reaching those goals and presents the tools you need to promote prosocial behavior among your students. While you could take a programmatic (curriculum add-on) approach, this book takes an interactional approach (teaching practices that occur as part of the regular curriculum) so that *using these research-based tools will not add to your already full curriculum.*

In *Chapter 3: Discipline: Key to Teaching Empathy and Values*, you will learn about the types of discipline, particularly victim-centered discipline, that promote empathy and prosocial behavior. Even well-meaning teachers can undermine prosocial behavior by using power-assertive discipline, so it is important to know how to replace it with more constructive discipline. In *Chapter 4: Practice, Modeling, and Reinforcement Build Prosocial Habits*, you will learn about the importance of your students' having prosocial models and opportunity to practice prosocial behavior, both during daily classroom activities (e.g., helping another child pick up spilled papers) and during service learning (e.g., volunteering in the community). I will discuss under what conditions preaching kindness and praising prosocial behavior works and when rewards can backfire. In *Chapter 5: Positive Teacher-Student Relationships*, you will learn that teacher-student relationships are foundational to prosocial behavior and how you can establish positive relationships with your students. Finally, in *Chapter 6: Emotionally Upbeat Classrooms*, you will learn how positive and negative emotions affect students' prosocial behavior and learning. You will acquire the tools to help students manage their emotions effectively and read others' emotions so they can respond with compassion.

Each chapter is interspersed with authentic classroom vignettes, positive and negative, as well as text boxes highlighting key concepts. In addition, each chapter ends with a brief review of research about how the same tools that increase prosocial behavior may simultaneously reduce antisocial behavior. At the conclusion of this book, in the appendix, you will find a case study for review and discussion of the tools you have learned throughout Part 2.

How to Use This Book as a
Professional Development Resource

This book is designed to help you develop skill in promoting prosocial behavior among students. Skill development takes deliberate practice. Consider starting small, and then plan to grow and expand your abilities. Discuss what is happening in your classroom with supportive colleagues, raising concerns and solutions (Osher et al., 2016). You might consider videotaping yourself teaching, and then watching for areas to improve. Occasionally review this book, as you monitor and evaluate your success.

Note that in some situations, it is best to consult or seek help for the student from other professionals. Discussions of such instances is flagged with an icon in the margin of the text, like the one beside this paragraph.

Research on the effectiveness of teachers' professional development finds that in order to actually improve your teaching practices and improve student outcomes you need to periodically reflect on and discuss with others your experiences, thoughts, and feelings so that you can step out of ongoing stresses and problem solve effectively. Therefore, at the conclusion of each chapter, you will find a "For Reflection and Discussion" box. These are designed to help you with personal reflection as well as to promote discussion within a peer learning group of colleagues in your school or district.

PART 1

WHAT IS PROSOCIAL BEHAVIOR AND WHY DOES IT MATTER?

Think about your students.

- Do each of them experience kindness from their classmates regularly?

- Does the amount of kindness they receive from their classmates affect how much they learn?

This section will help you answer these questions. Before we dive in, let's listen to what one high school teacher said about students' behavior:

> *Students' misbehavior has really increased. When I was in high school I never saw a single episode of the kinds of things I now deal with daily as a teacher—conflicts, arguments, defiance, and some of my students even have criminal records.*

Would you agree with this teacher's perspective? Unfortunately, research suggests she is correct. Scientists measured the same behaviors of 7- to 16-year-olds in 1976 and again a generation later in 1999, using carefully matched samples for gender, age, socioeconomic status, and ethnicity. They found that children had become more anxious, depressed, withdrawn, aggressive, and inattentive. The increase in children's misbehavior and distress was small, but significant. Of particular concern, more children reached levels of problem behavior that are classified as clinical, meaning they merit a diagnosis and need intervention (Achenbach, Dumenci, & Rescorla, 2003). The change was not limited to a single group; it occurred for both boys and girls, and poor to rich kids.

Ironically, over the same decades there has been an increase in jobs that require teamwork with people who are different from ourselves as we solve complex problems in the workplace. Many would argue that ability to get along well with others in teamwork is an essential 21st-century work skill; it is an important asset for students doing group work in your classroom as well. Success in school requires not only academic skills, but also prosocial, responsible behavior. In fact, studies have found that social skills may be more important than intelligence or education for your students' long-term life success.

Due to the growing recognition of the importance of the ability to get along well with others, the U.S. Department of Education has begun to emphasize the development of social skills at school. The 2012 Race-to-the-Top grants gave bonus points to states if part of their school improvement plans included programs to improve students' social skills. The 2015 Every Student Succeeds Act (ESSA) requires states to include non-academic factors in how they gauge school success.[1] Soon, the National Assessment of Educational Progress—a test of students in grades 4, 8, and 12 commonly known as the nation's report card—will include questions about students' social-emotional skills.

All 50 states have standards for preschools that include promoting social skills, and they are beginning to adopt similar standards for K–12 students as well. For example, one of Illinois state school standards is that students will "use . . . interpersonal skills to establish and maintain positive relationships" (Dusenbury, Zadrazil, Mart, & Weissberg, 2011). Many school districts have mission statements that claim the school promotes students' social skills; perhaps your district does. In addition, many teacher evaluation systems include measures of how well teachers promote social skills (CASEL, 2013). For example, one of the teaching practices that Missouri teachers may be evaluated on is their use of "strategies that promote social competence" in students (see Missouri's Network for Educator Effectiveness).

This is wonderful! For too long, schools have focused attention and resources on addressing negative behaviors, especially bullying, but have not focused as much on promoting positive social skills. However, as with any change, some teachers may feel hesitant. You might think, "I have enough to do to teach the subject areas. Now I have to teach social skills as well!?" The good news is that prosocial behavior is changeable, and that change endures over time (Domitrovich et al., 2017). It is not difficult to promote positive social skills in your students without adding content to your curriculum. This book is designed to give you the tools you need to be successful. The great added bonus is that if you use these tools, you'll find that it is actually much easier to teach the subject areas as well (see Chapter 2).

CHAPTER 1

What is Prosocial Behavior?

In an elementary classroom, the children are gathered on a rug at the front of the room while the teacher reads to them. Jake keeps talking to and bothering other students, so the teacher tells Jake to go to his desk to sit. Jake is unable to stay put at his desk, so the teacher tells him to go sit in the Safe Seat. Jake becomes upset and tears well in his eyes, but he starts walking toward the Safe Seat. Lauralee pops up and goes to Jake, gives him a hug and tells him it will be OK. Jake is a little surprised, but calms down and stays in the seat until the teacher tells him he can go back to his table.

Later, as students transition to different stations, Lauralee asks a few of them what they are working on and how they are doing. If they look sad, she gives them a hug. She offers to help a few students with their work. Sometimes the teacher has to remind Lauralee to focus on her own work, but she seems to get it done well and on time.

Then a student takes a ruler from another student. Lauralee steps into the altercation to tell him to give the ruler back, and to instead ask politely if he can borrow it. He does!

Lauralee consistently says "Please" and "Thank you." She smiles at each classmate that she passes. They smile back and seem to have their spirits lifted by her smile. When the class goes outside to recess, Lauralee is just as warm and friendly with students who are in other classes. She asks them how they are, what they are doing, smiles at them, and hugs those who seem to need it.

Lauralee helps, comforts, confronts wrong-doers and is polite. These are all prosocial behaviors. I encourage you to add the term *prosocial* to your vocabulary. It is an academic term, which at first might feel pedantic, yet it is genuinely useful. As a teacher, you know that use of academic language enhances and shapes thinking (DiCerbo, Anstrom, Baker, & Rivera, 2014; Snow, Lawrence, & White, 2010). In fact, the Common Core Standards and Next Generation Science Standards have renewed attention to teaching academic language. This is because academic language allows you to communicate, and to reason and problem-solve, with greater precision. The same is true of the term prosocial. Using the term will help you create a common language that aligns with research and shared understanding with your colleagues. In turn, that will help you problem-solve how to increase your students' prosocial behavior. You could make do with terms like *nice* and *kind* in some situations, but there is more to prosocial behavior than merely being nice. In fact, prosocial behavior can involve assertiveness and confronting others, which many would not necessarily characterize as nice. In the introduction, you learned that prosocial behavior is a broad concept including any behavior that benefits others or promotes harmonious relationships. It is about the quality, not quantity, of interactions with others. It is a vital part of the larger concepts of non-cognitive skills and social-emotional learning. Prosocial behavior includes kindness, compassion, collaboration, teamwork, and cooperation, but none of these behaviors alone encompasses prosocial behavior.

What Types of Prosocial Behavior Might You See at School?

Is Lauralee's behavior typical? Colleagues and I interviewed several groups of 6th graders and asked them, *What kinds of things do your classmates do that are positively social? Can you name the most positively social classmate you have, and tell us why you think that person is positively social?* (Bergin, Talley, & Hamer, 2003). We wanted to give voice to the students themselves, because prosocial behavior is often subtle, and not always observed by adults. (Lauralee's teacher will see some of her prosocial behavior, but not all of it.) The groups we interviewed were quite diverse; they were from subsidized housing, working-class, and well-to-do neighborhoods and came from different ethnic communities. These are the kinds of prosocial behaviors they said their 6th grade classmates engaged in using their own examples (in order, with the most frequently mentioned first):

1. **Standing up for others and confronting wrongdoers** (e.g., counter a rumor someone is spreading, or stop someone from putting another person down, defend someone who is being made fun of, stick up for a substitute who is being treated badly, talk a friend out of doing something wrong)

2. **Providing emotional support to others** (e.g., help someone who is down feel better, or "be there" when needed)

3. **Helping others develop skills** (e.g., give tips on how to play basketball, or explain math to someone, coach a boy on how to talk to girls, or a friend on how to resolve conflict)

4. **Complimenting and encouraging others** (e.g., say "You can do it!," "Try again!," "You're doing well!," and point out strengths, rather than weaknesses)

5. **Including others** (e.g., sit by or befriend someone who is alone, be nice even to people one doesn't like, make people feel free to "be themselves" and still be liked, be willing to come over and play even if there isn't anything to do)

6. **Physically helping others** (e.g., mow the neighbor's lawn, help a kid who fell down)

7. **Making others smile and laugh** (e.g., smile kindly at others, turn put-downs into a joke, entertain others)

8. **Making peace** (e.g., try to get others to stop fighting, settle conflict)

9. **Sharing** (e.g., share lunch money or pizza)

10. **Avoiding fights and calming others** (e.g., ignore taunting, disagree in a kind and gentle way, never yell)

11. **Keeping confidences** (e.g., not tell secrets)

12. **Providing community service** (e.g., run for student office or volunteer in the community)

13. **Being honest** (e.g., not cheat, pay back debts)

14. **Avoiding hurting others** (e.g., say jokes are funny when they are corny, not bother the weird kid, change the subject when others are making fun of someone)

15. **Admitting mistakes and apologizing** (e.g., after making a mistake, not get mad, but say "I'll do better next time," apologize after doing something bad)

16. **Avoiding bragging and being a good sport** (e.g., not show off grades, or think one's self is better than everybody, not hog the points and the glory)

In another study, colleagues and I asked the same thing of teachers and parents of 2-year-olds and 5-year-olds (Bergin, Bergin, & French, 1995). Although the children were much younger than the 6th graders, similar behaviors were nominated for the most prosocial young child these adults knew. Other studies have found similar prosocial behaviors in elementary-age students to 18-year-olds (Caldarella & Merrell, 1997; Greener & Crick, 1999; Paulus, 2014). Lauralee's prosocial behaviors are among the most commonly nominated.

As you can see from this list, the prosocial behaviors students said their classmates engage in are quite varied. They include politeness and gratitude, such as saying, "Thank you" to acknowledge others' good deeds. They include behaviors that are part of the realm of morality, such as being honest. They also include assertiveness, such as standing up for victims (e.g., Lauralee telling her classmate to give the ruler back). Clearly, prosocial students are not passive. However, prosocial behaviors also include humility, such as apologizing and giving in to avoid unnecessary fights. What these behaviors have in common is that they all benefit others and promote harmonious relationships with others.

Most of these behaviors won't surprise you once you understand what is prosocial behavior. However, making others smile or laugh with their humor (number 7 in the list above) might not seem to fit with the others. This is a behavior that teachers tend to be divided on. Let's briefly look at humor in the classroom.

Humor in the Classroom

Teachers are divided on humor because some view it as disruptive or inappropriate. It is true that humor can be antisocial, involving jokes that are disparaging or disgusting. There is no place for such humor in school. It is also true that students' humor can derail a lesson. In middle school, students who are particularly humorous do tend to call out, be out of their seats, be off task, and interact with others more often because they are active and social children. However, by high school, those same students have developed more skill at complying with classroom norms while still making others smile and laugh (Fabrizi & Pollio, 1987). Nevertheless, humorous teens are more likely to occasionally misbehave than more socially withdrawn teens (Sletta, Sobstad, & Valas, 1995). This may be why some secondary teachers shut down humor in their classrooms. Research suggests that teacher- and student-generated humor is about two to three times more common in elementary than secondary school (Banas, Dunbar, Rodriguez, & Liu, 2010; Fabrizi & Pollio, 1987; McGhee, 2013).

On the other hand, research shows that prosocial humor enhances learning (Banas et al., 2010; D. M. Martin, Preiss, Gayle, & Allen, 2006). How does it do this? Humor mentally refreshes, recharges attention, promotes creativity, and increases students' motivation for learning. Let's see how this works in a middle school class:

> *In a 7th grade honors algebra class, the teacher wrote a problem on the SMART board. She asked the students to use their calculators to find the solution. After a few minutes she called out, "Joseph, what does your calculator say?" Joseph promptly replied with a deadpan face, "Battery low. Suggest replacement." Both the teacher and students laughed. This class is in the oldest school building in the city. It is overcrowded and*

> *insufferably hot on the third floor. Yet, the ambiance is pleasant because the students often use humor, but not in destructive ways (Bergin & Bergin, 2015, p. 362).*

In Chapter 6, you'll delve more deeply into how positive emotions, which are central to school climate, promote learning.

Humor serves other important functions as well (Fitzsimmons & McKenzie, 2003). It strengthens relationships, lifts the mood of the class, smooths over socially awkward situations, and helps students cope with stress (Dowling, 2013). It can also help resolve conflict or "put others in their place" in a non-confrontational way that allows everyone to save face. It is even healing. *Reader's Digest* (one of the nation's most widely read periodicals) has had a regular feature for over 80 years called, "Laughter is the Best Medicine" that receives a whopping 10,000 pieces of mail each month. During the feature's 80-year run, science has confirmed that indeed laughter does boost health in a variety of ways.

It's no surprise that humorous students are better liked by classmates and teachers. When humor is used to make others feel good, it is a key part of prosocial behavior. Let's see how it played out in a high school class:

> *Trevor is brushing tears aside during class. The teacher notices and asks him to step out in the hallway to find out what is going on. Trevor tells the teacher that another boy, Mitch, had been surreptitiously punching Trevor throughout class when the teacher wasn't watching. Mitch is a bully. Trevor is worried about what will happen after school. Evan then steps out of the class and comforts Trevor. Evan jokes with Trevor until Trevor is calm and ready to go back into the class.*

Evan was deliberately using his humor skills to make Trevor feel better. In a study of thousands of elementary and secondary students, those who were identified as well-liked leaders were also described as having a sense of humor

(Zeller, Vannatta, Schafer, & Noll, 2003). Our research, and that of others, has also found that prosocial exemplars are often described as using humor to help others feel happier. For example, two researchers asked 4th through 6th graders to write a response to the question "*What do boys/girls do when they want to be nice to someone?*" Among the most common responses was "uses humor," along with some of the same prosocial behaviors listed above, such as being inclusive, sharing, avoiding hurting others, and making peace (Greener & Crick, 1999). Thus, using humor is an important component of being prosocial and creating a positive classroom climate.

How Much Prosocial Behavior is Normal?

In this section you will learn what prosocial behavior is normal for preschool and school-age children. Even if you teach high school, you will find it useful to learn about prosocial babies because it will give you insight into the benevolent nature that your students were born with, whether or not that nature is currently obvious. In fact, you can think of this book as a tool to help you magnify your students' in-born tendency to be prosocial. There is considerable research on the prosocial behavior of very young children, so let's begin there.

Babies to Preschoolers

A preschool teacher once told me that "everybody knows" little children cannot be prosocial. Her perspective is common because in college teachers are steeped in Piagetian theory which asserts that preschoolers are egocentric. She couldn't be more wrong. Babies come into the world willing to be quite benevolent and other-centered. Babies share with others as early as 8 months. By 12 months sharing is so universal that if babies do not share, it is a red flag for potential developmental problems such as autism (Eisenberg, Fabes, & Spinrad, 2006; Warneken, 2015).

You could argue that sharing in infants is just a reflex that does not have prosocial intent. But research shows us that even before babies are mobile or able to help others themselves, they are actually surprised when they see others not helping those in need, suggesting they understand benevolent intent and expect it from others. How do we know this? Infants' look longer at inexplicable events, so looking patterns are a common way scientists study infants' expectations and understanding of the world around them. For example, in one experiment researchers showed babies (9 to 18 months old) a video of two cartoon characters with balls. One character was able to reach the ball, but the other character was not. When a third character entered the scene, an eye-tracking device showed that the babies looked to the character who needed help reaching the ball and then back at the new character; they were anticipating the new character to help the one in need (Köster, Ohmer, Nguyen, & Kärtner, 2016). In half the videos, the new character gave the ball to the character that needed help (expected event), but in half the videos gave the ball to the character that did not need help (unexpected event). When this happened, infants stared longer at the unexpected event, indicating they were perplexed by the lack of helpful behavior.

As infants grow into toddlers, they will help others themselves. You may notice that they spontaneously help others, such as fetching the dust pan when you are sweeping or picking up something you dropped. One experiment showed that they are so motivated to be helpful that they will leave their own play and climb over obstacles to help others (Warneken & Tomasello, 2009).[2]

Toddlers are also compassionate and will try to cheer up someone who is crying (Dunfield & Kuhlmeier, 2013). You've probably experienced this first-hand; when you were upset you may have had a child bring you their own favorite blankie, bottle, or stuffed animal, or just climb into your lap for a hug. Almost all (90%) 2-year-olds will pat, hug, or try to comfort a child who is crying or upset (Baillargeon et al., 2011). Researchers have verified this in different cultures by shamelessly faking distress. For example, in one study with toddlers in Berlin and Delhi (two very different cultures) an adult began sobbing when her teddy bear's arm fell off. The toddlers, who didn't know the bear was rigged, would bring her another toy or hug her (Kärtner, Keller, & Chaudhary, 2010). Toddlers can show a remarkable level of sensitivity to others, even when they don't sob. In another study, an actor was mean to another adult by tearing up her picture. The victim showed no emotion, yet the toddlers understood that this was a distressing experience and gave the victim, an adult stranger, a balloon to cheer her up (Vaish, Carpenter, & Tomasello, 2009).

Of course, toddlers have a dual nature; they demand, snatch, hit, bite, and declare, "It's mine!" In fact, there is a decline in sharing as babies become toddlers because self-interest starts to become manifest. They figure out that if they give their cookie away, they won't have one. They also begin to learn that prosocial behavior can be a tool to get what they want in social interactions: "You can have the blue balloon, if I get the yellow one." They start to become more discriminating about who they are prosocial toward, sharing with family and friends, or someone who has shared with them, rather than just anyone (Dunfield & Kuhlmeier, 2010; A. Martin & Olson, 2015). They also become more judicious. For example, 3-year-olds do not show concern for others who cry over things that do not really justify tears (Hepach, Vaish, & Tomasello, 2013). They would show concern if you whimpered after getting your fingers caught in a closing cupboard, but not if you whimpered after getting your sleeve caught.

Still, babies and preschoolers have extensive prosocial repertoires and are ready to be prosocial. They are like little judges, meting out justice and fairness. For example, most are egalitarian about sharing treats if you have them work on a task together to earn the treat (Warneken, Lohse, Melis, & Tomasello, 2011). So what happens as they enter school?

School-Age Children

School-age children are more skilled at prosocial behavior compared to younger children. For example, they become better at reassuring peers, comforting others who are upset, and cheering sad peers up (Saarni, 1999). They become more genuinely helpful to those who need assistance. They also become better at figuring out how to collaborate. For example, in laboratory experiments where children play "winner-takes-all" games, school-age children can figure out that they should take turns winning. They let the other child win in one round, then they win in the next round. There may be short-term loss during their turn, but there is long-term gain if they take turns winning (Melis, Grocke, Kalbitz, & Tomasello, 2016). Preschoolers are unlikely to cooperate like this. School-age children also override strict equity with generosity. For example, in laboratory experiments, they will give more of their prize winnings to another child than to themselves if the other child is needy in some way (McGuigan, Fisher, & Glasgow, 2016; Shaw, Choshen-Hillel, & Caruso, 2016). Preschoolers are unlikely to do this; they want strict equity or give themselves more. Because of these increased prosocial skills, by the time they are 6 to 8 years of age, children are given caretaking responsibilities of younger children in many cultures across the world (Whiting, 1983).

Teenagers are even more skilled. When they were 3 years old they might have brought a toy to crying peers to cheer them up, but in their teens they can help them try to control their emotions in more sophisticated ways, such as helping a friend think about the problem from a different perspective: "I know you wanted to make it to states, but since you didn't qualify you'll have more time to skateboard!" Or they might joke a friend into feeling better, as Evan did with Trevor. Teenagers are able to help their peers and families in many ways, such as helping with homework, negotiating compromises to conflict, or helping with chores (Bergin et al., 2003).

The Great Puzzle: Why Aren't Teenagers Pillars of Kindness?

Despite this increased skill, as children get older they do not necessarily behave prosocially more often. In a British study, teachers of 5- to 16-year-olds were asked to rate whether their students engaged in five prosocial behaviors over the past 6 months: considerate of other people's feelings; shares readily with other children; helps if someone is hurt, upset or feeling ill; kind to younger children; often volunteers to help others' (Scourfield, John, Martin, & McGuffin, 2004). There was no correlation with age, although there was a tendency for children over age 11 to be rated as <u>less</u> prosocial.

Other studies have found that children are less prosocial with age. My colleagues and I asked over 3,400 students from 4th grade to 12th grade how often their classmates engaged in eight prosocial behaviors: (1) stand up for others, (2) provide emotional support and comfort, (3) help others develop skills, (4) compliment and encourage, (5) are inclusive and friendly, (6) provide physical assistance, (7) make others smile or laugh, and (8) help settle conflicts. We combined their answers across the eight prosocial behaviors and plotted the average by grade level. Figure 1.2 shows the results. Notice the dramatic drop-off from elementary school to the transition to middle school in 6th grade. The nadir of prosocial behavior is 10th grade, with an uptick beginning in 11th grade. (On a side note, I showed these results to a group of high school students in a different district. Their response was, "We could've told you that without the study. Everyone knows It sucks to be in 10th grade." Hmm. Perhaps you should pass this book on to all the 10th grade teachers

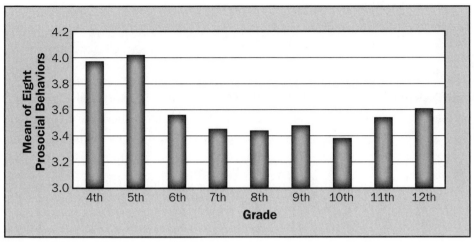

Figure 1.1 Prosocial Behavior by Grade

you know.) This was a single, although large, study; we don't know how common this pattern is, but other studies have also found a decrease in prosocial behavior into early adolescence that may be followed by a rebound as children emerge into young adulthood (Carlo, Padilla-Walker, & Nielson, 2015; Eisenberg et al., 2006). This suggests that students like Lauralee may get less prosocial with age.

This trend in decreased prosocial behaviour is puzzling. Think of the countless times you have told your students to be kind and polite: "Let's take turns." "Share with your neighbor." "Say please and thank you." "Help him out." "We include everyone." "Say you are sorry." Multiply your efforts by all the prosocial lessons from their other teachers, their parents, their pastors, and the whole village that is conspiring to grow children into prosocial citizens. Given that babies are nearly universally benevolent, and that they have these positive forces shaping their prosocial behavior, you might expect that by the time they reach adolescence all teenagers are prosocial superheroes. High schools should be utopias of kindliness. Why aren't they?

There are forces within children that push them towards less prosocial behavior. With age, children are better at controlling their own emotional response to others' distress. This helps them suppress their innate impulse to help others, so that prosocial behavior becomes more of a choice than an impulse. They also become more attuned to social groups, so that they are increasingly selective, behaving prosocially primarily with those who are like them and belong to their social circle (van Rijsewijk, Dijkstra, Pattiselanno, Steglich, & Veenstra, 2016; Warneken & Tomasello, 2009). They become more aware of the costs of prosocial behavior and more motivated to protect their self-interests. Research on reasoning abilities in teens shows that the "What's in it for me?" attitude, or what psychologists call hedonistic prosocial reasoning, may *increase* for some adolescents. This continues into adulthood. This may surprise you, but in laboratory experiments where adults earn real money and then have the opportunity to share it with others, they share *less* when they think about it in a slow, rational way. They share *more* when they are forced to respond very quickly, in an intuitive way (Rand, 2016). Thus, as children become more rational into adolescence and adulthood, their self-interest may increasingly override their prosocial nature.

❝ Some people believe that young children are self-centered and less prosocial compared to teens. Research suggests this is not true, but with the right tools you can help your students become more prosocial.**❞**

There are also forces outside the child that push them toward less prosocial behavior. One of these forces is antisocial role models at home, school, and in the media (e.g., books, movies, videogames). Another force is adults who train children to inhibit their natural prosocial behaviors—including well-meaning teachers. For example, they may tell children it is the teacher's job to take care of others, not theirs, and that being helpful is disruptive to class. In Chapter 4 I'll discuss how you can avoid unintentionally inhibiting your students' prosocial behavior in this way.

Let's look at how forces can work toward promoting or inhibiting prosocial behavior in two different students, as told by their teachers:

> **Case 1.** *After misbehaving, a challenging student, M, left class without permission and slammed the door as he left. I called his mother because I thought she'd like to know what was going on, but she didn't. She answered the phone, shouting at me "What? I don't have time to listen*

to you snitch on my son!" (Apparently her son had already called her about the incident). She clearly did not see herself as working with me to help M develop better behavior. After that, I understood where M's aggression came from and realized that he would not learn prosocial behavior from his mother.

Case 2. *After misbehaving, I asked D to take home a note about his behavior and have his parents sign it, then return it to me the next day. The next day D handed me a paper that clearly had a fake signature. I asked him about it, and he lied that it was his mother's signature. I emailed his parents and immediately got replies from both, who expressed disappointment with D's dishonesty. At the end of the school day, his father was standing in the hallway. We had an impromptu conference with D about the importance of honesty. His father told him that his parents and teachers wanted the best for him, and D genuinely apologized. I was impressed (and so was D) that his father thought a lesson on honesty was important enough to leave work for, rather than waiting until evening.*

M has an antisocial role model in the home and D has a prosocial role model directing D toward becoming a moral citizen. The behavior of both sets of parents is affected by their own values and situations; in her defense, it is possible that M's mother was coping with toxic levels of stress that D's parents were not. Nevertheless, the point is that while all children have forces acting on them toward both prosocial and antisocial behavior, the scale tips more toward prosocial behavior for some children. Children like both M and D need your help to become more prosocial, but M may need it even more than D. This book will give you the tools to help them both.

Which Students are Nicer Than Others?

Regardless of their age, some children are more prosocial than others. Let's explore whether gender matters, and whether you can make a difference in how prosocial your students become.

Are Girls Nicer Than Boys?

The following old 19th-century rhyme conveys a bias that has carried through culture today. Songs, cartoons, and even baby shower announcements feature this nursery rhyme:

What are little boys made of?	*What are little girls made of?*
Snips and snails And puppy-dogs' tails	Sugar and spice And everything nice

When researchers ask teachers or students, *Who is nice to others?* girls are more likely than boys to be nominated. Most studies, although not all, find that people tend to report girls as more prosocial than boys, and they do so as early as preschool and on through high school (e.g., Caprara, Barbaranelli, & Pastorelli, 2001; Carlo, Samper, Malonda, Tur-Porcar, & Davis, 2016; Davidov & Grusec, 2006; Pagani, Tremblay, Vitaro, Boulerice, & McDuff, 2001; van Rijsewijk et al., 2016).

Is this bias unjustified, or are girls really more prosocial than boys? It could be bias due to a reaction toward boys' greater aggression. The most robust gender difference in child development is that boys are more aggressive than girls. As early as infancy and toddlerhood, boys are more likely to grab, push, shove, hit, bite, and express anger than girls (Alink et al., 2006; Baillargeon et al., 2007; Hay et al., 2014). During the school years the gender gap in antisocial behavior widens; by high school, on average, boys are more aggressive, delinquent, and disruptive in class (Autor, Figlio, Karbownik, Roth, & Wasserman, 2015; Ho, Bluestein, & Jenkins, 2008; Xie, Drabick, & Chen, 2011). This is true for rich and poor children, and children from very different countries (Joussemet et al., 2008; Lansford et al., 2012). There is a "mean girls" stereotype that while boys are more physically aggressive, girls are more likely to be socially aggressive, meaning that they spread malicious rumors or pointedly exclude others. This is a myth. It is true that when girls are aggressive, they are more likely to be aggressive in social rather than physical ways (Ettekal & Ladd, 2015; Putallaz et al., 2007). However, boys, overall, are more aggressive in all ways, including social ways (Card, Stucky, Sawalani, & Little, 2008; Lansford et al., 2012). Although this gender difference in aggression is real, teachers tend to exaggerate it, rating boys as even more aggressive than they are (Pellegrini, 2011). This bias, and boys' real aggressiveness, may lead people to report them as less prosocial than they are.

It could also be bias due to differences in the kinds of prosocial behaviors that boys and girls engage in, with girls' style of prosocial behavior more widely recognized. In our focus groups of 6th graders, prosocial boys were more likely to be described as providing physical assistance to others and sharing—overt kinds of prosocial behavior. Prosocial girls were more likely to be described as compassionately caring, soothing others' feelings, keeping confidences, and being inclusive—relational kinds of prosocial behavior (Bergin et al., 2003). Other researchers have found similar results, with girls behaving more compassionately than boys as early as toddlerhood (e.g., Baillargeon et al., 2011; Carlo et al., 2016). In some cultures, rescuing is often thought of as men's role, and nurturing as women's, yet both are important forms of prosocial behavior. Lauralee gave sad peers hugs, whereas Evan joked his sad friend into feeling better. Although both were nurturing, compassionate behaviors, Lauralee's prosocial behavior may have been more obvious to others than Evan's.

Individual Differences Among Students

Not only may there be gender differences in prosocial behavior, but there are also individual differences. That is, some girls are more prosocial than other girls, and some boys are more prosocial than other boys of the same age. Above, you learned that the impulse to help and share is nearly universal among toddlers. Even before age 2, individual differences in prosocial behavior emerge and can be measured (Baillargeon et al., 2011). The forces that shape a child toward greater or lesser prosocial behavior are already having an effect in the first 16 months of life.

The toddlers who are more prosocial than their age-mates tend to be more prosocial in multiple ways. For example, they are more likely to share, help someone pick up crayons, and recognize and cheer up someone that is sad (Newton, Thompson, & Goodman, 2016). This is remarkable given that different prosocial behaviors may require different skills and motivation, yet what seems to distinguish prosocial toddlers is a general prosocial orientation.

Although this is a very young age, these emerging differences are surprisingly stable across time (e.g., Baillargeon et al., 2011; Romano, Babchishin, Pagani, & Kohen, 2010; Vaish et al., 2009). That is, 3-year-olds who are above average in prosocial behavior tend to become 15-year-olds who are above average in prosocial behavior. Amazingly, one study even found that how much preschoolers shared predicted how prosocial they were in their early 30s (Eisenberg, Hofer, Sulik, & Liew, 2014). Think about all the experiences those children had across three decades that could have turned them in different directions, yet for the most part the children who were more prosocial in preschool remained the more prosocial as adults. The same is true of antisocial behavior; aggression is one of our most stable attributes. This means that in the case above, M was probably less prosocial and more aggressive than his classmates even in preschool. Children tend to begin to specialize as nice kids (or not) very early.

Preschoolers Are an Exception

One important caveat to this notion that children specialize early toward prosocial or antisocial behavior is that highly social, outgoing preschoolers may be both prosocial and aggressive. Preschoolers (ages 2 to 4 years) tend to be the most aggressive of all ages; their aggression diminishes substantially by kindergarten (Vlachou, Andreou, Botsoglou, & Didaskalou, 2011). Their aggression is of a special kind: They mostly engage in what is called *instrumental aggression*. This means that they snatch, hit, and grab because they want something, rather than because they want to hurt someone. Children might shove others in order to get their paint brush, swing, or building block, but not because they are malicious toward others. This is an important difference. Such instrumental (rather than hostile) aggression does not portend later behavior problems (Hay, Castle, & Davies, 2000). As preschoolers gain in language and social skills, they can start to ask for the paint brush, swing, or building block, rather than snatch it. Until these skills develop, *preschoolers who are highly prosocial are often highly aggressive as well.* They are likely to share as well as to snatch (Hay, 2009). Since I come from a science background, I like to use the analogy of molecules to explain this. Most preschoolers are like molecules in a liquid; they vibrate, move about, and slide past each other. In contrast, highly social preschoolers are like molecules in a gas who vibrate a lot and move freely at high speeds. They have more collisions with other molecules, or more interactions than other children, some of which are bound to be positive and some of which are bound to be negative until their social skills are better developed. By school age, children tend to specialize, tilting more towards consistent prosocial or antisocial behavior in their interactions with others.

So how do you know if you should be worried about a preschooler's aggressive behavior? Watch for two things. First, there should be a high ratio of positive to negative behaviors. That is, you want to see *more* prosocial compared to aggressive behavior. Second, determine what kind of aggression is occurring. You may see a 3-year-old shove another in the stomach as a way of saying "Hey! Pay attention to me! I want to play with you!" and look baffled when the other child objects to being shoved. If it is clear that this is a good-hearted child with no malicious intent, then mild instruction on better ways to invite others to play is all that is needed (but plan to have to repeat this instruction until the new skills are mastered). If you continue to be concerned because you believe a child is on an aggressive developmental pathway rather than a prosocial one, following the strategies outlined in Part 2 of this book will help you redirect that pathway. Do this as early as possible, because aggression becomes stable at an early age and is increasingly difficult to change, although even aggressive adolescents will benefit from the strategies you will learn in this book.

Why Are Some Students Prosocial but Others Are Antisocial?

At this point you may be left with an unsettling question: If children begin to specialize as nice kids (or not) very early, and these differences are stable, can one teacher make a difference, especially later in their lives? The resounding answer is yes, you can make a difference.

To help you understand this, let's begin with a discussion of whether these differences in prosocial behavior are inborn, or the result of experience. It is logical to assume that because these differences emerge within the first few years of life they may be genetically programmed into children. In our current culture, genes are given a great deal more credit for the way children develop than they may deserve.

Do Genes or Experience Matter?

Scientists determine the extent to which genes contribute to a particular trait (e.g., alcoholism, aggression, extroversion, risk-taking, shyness) through comparing siblings with different degrees of genetic and child-rearing similarity or comparing adopted children with their biological or adoptive parents or siblings. They use a mathematical formula to parse out the percentage of similarity between individuals within a population that is due to genes versus environment. The portion ascribed to genes is known as the *heritability index* or h^2. This classic approach to studying genetic propensity for behavior finds that roughly 20% to 60% of many traits are heritable, although it varies by trait (Bouchard, 2004; Polderman et al., 2015; Saudino & Micalizzi, 2015; Turkheimer, Pettersson, & Horn, 2014). Not surprisingly, this approach finds a modest genetic component to prosocial behavior (A. M. Gregory, Light-Häusermann, Rijsdijk, & Eley, 2009).

Some scientists are very critical of this classic approach to studying the contribution of genes to behavior because it cannot separate out the role of experience. Parents pass on their genes to their children, but they also pass on the children's environment in multiple ways. For example, prosocial parents may pass on prosocial genes, but also model prosocial behavior and create a loving home atmosphere. Which is influencing the child, genes or the environment? Furthermore, now that the human genome has been mapped, there is an all-out race to identify which genes are responsible for which attributes, and that race is not going well. Typically, scientists find that specific genes only contribute perhaps 1% to 3% of the variation in a population on a specific trait, like prosocial behavior. The huge gap between heritability indices (e.g., of 20–60%) and genetic identification (e.g., of 3%) is currently a scientific mystery with its own name: *missing heritability* (Manuck & McCaffery, 2014). Three other major findings of modern genetics also cast doubt on a strong role for genes in prosocial behavior:

1. You have remarkably few genes that are free to vary. You share almost all your genes with apes and all other human beings; only about 1% of genes are free to create differences between one person and another (Bjorklund & Pellegrini, 2000; N. A Johnson, Smith, Pobiner, & Schrein, 2012; Quartz & Sejnowski,

2002). The function of genes is to specify the building of pro-
teins, not to dictate specific behavior. If genes had to specify
minute aspects of complex human behavior, you'd need a
larger genome. One scientist said that you'd have to drag your
genome behind you in a suitcase. So how are we so diverse and
adaptable? Instead, the human brain's architecture is designed
to be remarkably sensitive to input from your environment.

2. Experience actually alters genes. Genes are like books in
   a library, they have no influence on you if they are not read
   (Champagne & Mashoodh, 2009). Experience can determine
   whether, and which, genes are read. This is called *epigenetics*.
   For example, a student like M who has a hostile mother lives
   with chronic stress, which causes chemicals to bind to his
   genes in a way that alters the expression of those genes. This
   could explain why he is aggressive. Remarkably, these epigen-
   etic changes can be passed on to your children and grandchil-
   dren (Meaney, 2010).

3. You tend to only develop a trait when genetic predisposition
   combines with an environment that promotes the trait (e.g.,
   Davies, Cicchetti, & Hentges, 2015; Kim-Cohen & Gold, 2009;
   Wiebe et al., 2009). That is, both the gene and your envrion-
   ment must work in tandem to produce a trait.

Still, many parents believe their children's traits are genetically driven
because one child is so different from another. They insist that because both
children have the same parents and are growing up in the same family, this
is proof that their differences must be genetically driven. This is not a good
argument for two reasons. First, no two children grow up in the same family.
A second child is born into a very different family from a first child; there are
different factors acting on each child, the parents have changed over time, and
siblings are powerful influences on each other. Second, parents' comparison
of their children tends to be based on a narrow frame of reference—their own
children—rather than a broad comparison with many children. This is why
teachers (who experience many children) tend to view siblings as more alike

than do their parents (who experience fewer children). Because within-family comparisons are rampant, children take on specialized niches within the family (e.g., *he's the shy one and I'm the bold one* or *she's the messy one and I'm the neat one*) which can strongly shape their personalities. These are environmental, not genetic, influences.

The bottom line is that genes don't determine traits, but rather interact with experience to shape who a child becomes (Bronfenbrenner & Ceci, 1994). Even if we were able to identify genes that determine whether a specific child becomes prosocial or not, the contribution of that gene is likely to be very small, and whether specific children become more or less prosocial depends primarily on their experience (Paulus, 2014; Van Ryzin et al., 2015). Furthermore, research has found that a person's *agreeableness* (a personality trait that refers to people who are warm, kind, thoughtful of others, helpful, and cooperative) is not very heritable, but rather is strongly influenced by the quality of the family environment (e.g., Bokhorst et al., 2003; Ganiban, Saudino, Ulbricht, Neiderhiser, & Reiss, 2008). This suggests that prosocial students are shaped by their experiences, rather than born that way (Laursen, Pulkkinen, & Adams, 2002).

This is important and great news! It means that even when children have a slight genetic push toward problem behavior, a positive environment can derail that effect. If teachers intervene and provide a supportive relationship with the at-risk child, the child is likely to develop in a positive way (Kim-Cohen & Gold, 2009).

Can You Make a Difference?

You can influence children's prosocial behavior while they are in your classroom. Students who are not very prosocial in other settings may become more prosocial in your classroom. One study found that some high school students were cooperative and engaged while in one teacher's classroom, but in another teacher's classroom misbehaved to the point they were suspended (A. Gregory & Ripski, 2008). The same student can behave quite differently depending on the situation. You have probably heard about a study conducted in 1971 at Stanford University known as the *Prison Experiment* that showed dramatic change in behavior. Twenty male students were randomly assigned to be either inmates or guards at a fake prison in the base-ment of the psychology building. The *guards* had agreeable and healthy personalities, but after a few days they had become cruel to the *inmates* and the study had to be terminated. Since then, many studies have shown that behavior is to some extent situation-dependent (Mischel, Shoda, & Mendoza-Denton, 2002). Personality is not a simple collection of traits (e.g., "He is prosocial"), but rather a series of *if . . . then scenarios*. For example, if a child is treated respectfully, then he is cooperative, but if he is shamed, then he is aggressive or withdrawn. The situation dictates the *if* conditions, and the personality dictates the *then* responses. This book will help you create the conditions that promote greater prosocial behavior among your students while they are in your classroom regardless of how prosocial they are in other classrooms or settings.

You can also influence children's prosocial behavior well beyond your classroom as you help them learn better responses to a wider set of condi-tions. While you learned above that individual differences in prosocial behav-ior emerge at a very young age, and these tend to be stable into middle age, keep in mind that research pertains to people as a group, not individuals. That is, while prosocial young children are *more likely* to become prosocial adults, not *all* prosocial children will do so, and other children who were not prosocial may become more so. Research is about probability, not certainty. Individuals can change—that is the purpose of psychotherapy—although it becomes more difficult with age. One 25-year veteran teacher, Mrs. Wentz,[3] helped Josh change. She said that Josh, a 6th grader, was the most difficult to manage student she'd had in her career. Josh was often involved in conflict at school that required police presence and suspensions. His home life was toxic and he seemed to just be getting worse. Clearly the interventions at the school were not working for Josh, so Mrs. Wentz decided to implement the practices you'll learn in this book. Within a few months Mrs. Wentz and Josh had a positive relationship. Josh began to hang out in her classroom between classes, cooperate with classmates, and make learning progress (Bergin & Bergin, 2015). Change is possible even for seemingly recalcitrant students. Part 2 of this book will help you engineer the experiences your students need to become more prosocial.

NOTE ABOUT AGGRESSIVE STUDENTS

You may be reading this book because you have a problematic student you want help with. Whenever I attend gatherings with teachers and they find out that I am a developmental psychologist specializing in children's social-emotional well-being, they invariably grab my arm with excitement and say "I need to talk to you!" Then they rush through a tangled story that might go something like this: "I have this student, Joey, who has been removed from his mother's custody because of her drug use, but he loves her and is worried about her, and has been placed in the custody of his father, who is a mean man and he hates him, won't even call him dad, and is so angry that he is acting out in school, disrupting learning of other students, the vice principal has suspended him and says one more time and he is out . . . (pause for air) . . . I don't know how to handle him in the classroom. What should I do?"

I usually start with "What does his counselor say?" but I know that almost a third of the children in this country attend rural schools, many of whom do not have specialized counseling staff to help. Therefore, regular classroom teachers need tools to help antisocial students. This book will help. Although I focus on promoting prosocial behavior, the strategies you will learn will also reduce antisocial behavior. Interestingly, strategies and programs aimed at reducing bad behavior do not necessarily increase good behavior (because students don't learn more productive replacement behavior), but the reverse is true. Strategies aimed at increasing prosocial behavior also reduce antisocial behavior. This is why prosocial education is important. I'll conclude subsequent chapters with information about how to reduce antisocial behavior while increasing prosocial behavior. You may not move a Joey all the way to a Lauralee, but you can move him enough closer to change his developmental path toward becoming a happier and more productive community member.

FOR REFLECTION AND DISCUSSION

What kinds of prosocial behaviors have you witnessed among your students, from small, daily acts to big, infrequent acts?

Think about all the students in your class. Which one would you nominate as the most prosocial student in the class? What behaviors does this student engage in that led you to nominate him or her? (Is this student male or female? Might gender have biased your nomination?) Would your students nominate the same student(s)? Might there be highly prosocial students you are overlooking because they are quietly kind?

Reflect on humor in your classroom, whether teacher or student generated. Would you characterize it as too much, not enough, or just right? Have you seen it serve prosocial purposes among your students?

Have you taught different grade levels? Does the chart on age trends (Figure 1.2) fit with your experience or not? If not, why do you think that is?

Before reading Part 2, reflect on what strategies you already use to promote prosocial behavior in your students. At the end of your reading, refer back to your list and reevaluate.

CHAPTER 2

Prosocial Behavior Increases Your Students' Learning

> *In a middle school classroom, Mrs. Koztin says "We have some activities to help you learn about sources of heat. Get into your new work groups. Make sure your pencils are sharp." Students begin to move around the room to join their group. Some students kindly offer to sharpen others' pencils. Sophie goes to sharpen pencils, and returns to find her chair missing. She shouts, "Hey! Who took my chair?" A boy replies, "I did. Sorry. Here you go."*

Mrs. Koztin is a teacher known for promoting prosocial behavior. In just a short visit to her classroom, I witnessed several incidents of prosocial behavior. In addition, incidents that could have escalated, like taking someone's chair, did not. The overall tone of the classroom was one of cooperation and support from one student to another. In an era in which standardized test scores seem to be the most important factor in how teachers and schools are judged, does it matter whether your classroom, like Mrs. Koztin's, is an oasis of kindness or not? Let's see what the research says.

Does Prosocial Behavior Enhance Academic Achievement?

Prosocial behavior is worth cultivating for its own sake. You and your students will be happier in classrooms with prosocial others. However, given the pressure you face to show that your students are learning academic content, it is important to point out that prosocial behavior predicts those all-important standardized test scores.

As early as preschool, the more prosocial children are, the higher their intelligence, vocabulary, and math scores and the better their emergent literacy skills (Bierman, Torres, Domitrovich, Welsh, & Gest, 2009; Doctoroff, Greer, & Arnold, 2006). This means that, compared to other preschoolers, prosocial children know their letters better, understand that a book is read from left to right, recognize familiar words on signs (e.g., exit), and even write their own names better. The attributes that make a child *kindergarten ready* includes these emergent literacy skills, as well as prosocial behaviors. For example, in one study preschoolers who were respectful, cooperative, and caring (all prosocial behaviors) made greater gains in math after entering kindergarten (Galindo & Fuller, 2010). Once they are in kindergarten, prosocial children learn more, so that by the time they are in 3rd grade they have better reading skills and math test scores (Romano et al., 2010).

Remarkably, in a large study, low-income children who entered kindergarten at risk for academic failure were less likely to actually experience academic failure if they were prosocial. Their teachers completed a simple rating scale indicating whether each child engaged in prosocial behaviors such as cooperating with others without prompting, helping others, and understanding others' feelings. Children who were rated by their kindergarten teachers as more prosocial were less likely to ever be retained a grade or placed in special education throughout their schooling career, which sets them apart from their less prosocial, at-risk classmates (Jones, Greenberg, & Crowley, 2015). Furthermore, this study followed the children for 13 to 19 years and found that prosocial kindergarteners were less likely to be on public assistance, arrested, unemployed, or using drugs as young adults. The results were found beyond the effects of poverty, or family and neighborhood risk. Surprisingly, the children's level of aggression in kindergarten did not predict criminal activity in young adulthood; that is, *it was not the absence of aggression that mattered, but the presence of prosocial skills that mattered.*

The link between prosocial behavior and academic achievement does not end with kindergarten. Prosocial elementary students have higher reading, math, vocabulary, and IQ test scores (Adams, Snowling, Hennessy, & Kind, 1999; Miles & Stipek, 2006; Strayer & Roberts, 1989). One study found that

3rd graders who were more prosocial had higher achievement in 8th grade, beyond the effect of their initial achievement (Caprara, Barbaranelli, Pastorelli, Bandura, & Zimbardo, 2000).

❝Prosocial preschoolers have more school readiness skills. Prosocial 1st to 12th grade students have higher test scores and are less likely to be retained, even if they are at high risk for academic failure due to other factors.❞

I've heard secondary principals and superintendents say, "Yeah, that may be important in elementary school, but we're done with that kind of stuff in high school. The kids have got it down, or they're in my office!" This is misguided. As you learned in Chapter 1, on average, elementary students actually "have got it down" better than secondary students. Furthermore, those secondary students who are more prosocial than their classmates have higher GPAs and higher standardized test scores and are more invested in school (Carlo, Crockett, Wilinson, & Beal, 2011; Wentzel, 1993). Thus, prosocial students, from 1st to 12th grade, have higher achievement than students who are not prosocial (Bergin, 2014). The opposite is true for antisocial behavior. Students with behavior problems tend to have lower grades and test scores from 1st to 12th grade, although the link between antisocial behavior and low achievement is stronger in high school (e.g., Grimm, Steele, Mashburn, Burchinal, & Pianta, 2010; Trzesniewski, Moffitt, Caspi, Taylor, & Maughan, 2006; Xie et al., 2011).

❝Programs that increase prosocial behavior tend to increase grades and test scores as well.❞

A group of researchers reviewed and analyzed over 200 studies that evaluated programs designed to increase social-emotional skills (SEL) of students from kindergarten through high school. In their meta-analysis, they found that programs that successfully increased prosocial behavior also raised grades and test scores, *even when there was not an academic component to the program* (Durlak, Weissberg, Dymnicki, Taylor, & Schellinger, 2011). The rise was not enormous, but it was meaningful from an educational perspective. (If you are interested in details, the increases were about a third of a standard deviation. Because so many different variables influence a student's grades and test scores, a single variable seldom has a much larger effect size than this.) More importantly, it means that when you target improving non-cognitive skills, like prosocial behavior, you may get cognitive skills payoff as well. Prosocial behavior supports academic success.

Your students intuitively know that prosocial behavior and academic success go together. In the focus groups we conducted with 6th graders in which we asked them to nominate the most prosocial peer they knew, they would often describe these prosocial superstars as a "good student" or "has a high vocabulary" (Bergin et al., 2003). So we pushed them a little, asking, "Do you have to be a good student to be prosocial?" They all said, "No," it is possible to be prosocial but a poor student or mean but smart (you probably know someone who fits the bill). Yet, when we asked if the particular prosocial peer they were thinking of was a good student, they all said "Yes." In theory, they could separate academic success from being prosocial, but when they moved from the abstract to the concrete in their own schools, the prosocial students they knew were all more academically successful. An interesting study with both preschoolers and 9- to 10-year-olds similarly found that children subconsciously pair intelligence with niceness (Heyman, Gee, & Giles, 2003). The researchers told children stories about pretend characters who were either "mean and smart" or "nice and not so smart." When asked to recall the stories, children remembered the "nice" character as "smart." They unknowingly re-constructed memories so that the characters' intellectual ability matched their niceness or meanness. The children also said that if they had to make a choice, they would rather work with someone nice than someone mean but smart, which brings us to the next point.

Does Prosocial Behavior
Enhance Social Success at School?

Prosocial students tend to be happier than other students. This is partly because they are better able to maintain a state of inner calm (Miller, Kahle, & Hastings, 2015). When you behave kindly you are less affected by the daily stressors in your life (Raposa, Laws, & Ansell, 2015). When you anticipate feeling good about helping others, you are more likely to help, which then creates an upward spiral of positive feelings (Malti & Krettenauer, 2013).

Prosocial students may also be happier because they are liked better by their classmates and teachers. This is important because a strong *teacher-student relationship* predicts academic success and emotional well-being, which we'll talk about more in Chapter 5. Being liked by one's classmates is also important. Some students are liked by their classmates more than others. One of the ways that psychologists study this is to ask students which classmates from a class roster they would rather work or play with. This method is used from preschool to high school. Preschoolers who can't read may be asked to place pictures of their classmates into one of three boxes: like a lot, kind of like, and do not like (Denham, McKinley, Couchoud, & Holt, 1990). Older students may be asked to nominate the three classmates they like most; the nominations of all students are summed to create a score of how well-liked each student is. Psychologists also create *sociograms* or maps of the interactions in a classroom. On these maps, some children are isolates, some are connected to one or two other children, and some are at the hub of a buzzing network of classmates. Try mapping your own classroom; shorter lines indicate tight connections with lots of interactions between two students. Longer (or absent) lines indicate little to no interactions between two students. Can you identify the well-liked students from your sociogram?

Generally, the best predictor of whether a student is well-liked and socially connected in the classroom is prosocial behavior (Bandura, Barbaranelli, Caprara, & Pastorelli, 1996; LaFontana & Cillessen, 2002; Warden & Mackinnon, 2003). Classmates and teachers like students better who behave prosocially (Rodkin, Ryan, Jamison, & Wilson, 2013). Acts of kindness and integrity are vitally important because they enhance relationships and happiness in others.

Think about your students who are especially prosocial. They probably have good friends in your classroom. Research confirms that prosocial students are more likely to be *friended* at school, which is much more important than it might seem to you at first glance. Students who feel well-liked and have friends at school (compared to away from school) are more engaged in school and they have higher GPAs (Bellmore, 2011; Witkow & Fuligni, 2010). *It is particularly important to have friends in the classroom.* Even if they have friends in other classes, if students don't have a good friend in your class they will feel lonelier than friended students (Parker & Asher, 1993). Students are more engaged—enjoying and actively participating—in classrooms where they have friends, in contrast to students who feel friendless and socially uncomfortable (Thorkildsen, Reese, & Corsino, 2002). The level of engagement may explain why students learn more when they have friends in class. Students with classroom friends also make the transition to kindergarten and middle school more smoothly (Berndt, Hawkins, & Jiao, 1999; Wentzel, Barry, & Caldwell, 2004).

---

66 Prosocial students are happier, liked better by teachers and students, and have friends in class. Having classroom friends leads to greater engagement and learning."

It is a good policy to keep friends together from year to year as you create new class lists, and to place friends together when you are composing cooperative learning groups within your classroom as Mrs. Koztin did.[4] Often, teachers assume that pairing students with friends is a bad idea because they won't focus on their work. Actually, the opposite is true. Research finds that friend pairs get more work done, and do it at a higher cognitive level, then when non-friend students are paired (Hartup & Abecassis, 2002). Friends provide higher quality support and help to each other, work more cooperatively, and are happier working together (Strough, Berg, & Meegan, 2001). Try to give your students as much opportunity as possible to form good friendships. This may surprise you, but many students do not actually have much time in the school day to interact or form friendships, and some school policies encourage friendlessness, such as giving students too little time for social interaction during breaks or having rules forbidding talking to classmates at lunch.

Mrs. Koztin, in the opening vignette, uses cooperative learning groups in her classroom. Not all students benefit from working with classmates because they don't have adequate social skills to deal with disagreements, compliment and encourage others, take others' perspectives, and do their fair share. Students who behave prosocially will benefit more from cooperative learning. One study found that about 37% of elementary school students had adequate social skills to be productive in cooperative learning groups. Not surprisingly,

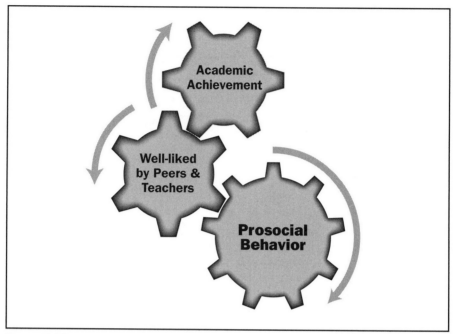

Figure 2.1 Prosocial Behavior Drives Both Being Liked and Academic Achievement, which also Drive Each Other

their classmates preferred to work with them and they were high achievers (Ladd et al., 2014). This book will give you the tools to help the remaining two thirds of students. Figure 2.1 depicts how prosocial behavior, social success, and academic achievement drive each other.

A Small Cautionary Note

As a teacher, you should be aware that there can be a negative side to too much prosocial behavior. Overly prosocial behavior can be a symptom of difficulties at home. For example, children can become too eager to please if they have a history of abuse or abandonment (Klimes-Dougan & Kistner, 1990). Some children also take on a parenting role and are over-the-top prosocial because parents are substance users, severely depressed, or emotionally dependent on them (Hay & Pawlby, 2003; Radke-Yarrow, Zahn-Waxler, Richardson, Susman, & Martinez, 1994). I have seen children who were caretakers of alcoholic mothers, or who monitored their mother's well-being throughout the school day because they feared for her safety due to a violent boyfriend. One teacher said,

> *One of my students lives in poverty because her mother is disabled. She takes care of her mother and younger siblings. Despite this staggering responsibility she earns really high grades, and seems to be doing well socially. Her ability to help others is amazing.*

Children who make substantive contributions to their households can fare well, and I hope that this student is genuinely doing well. However, such children may also be experiencing guilt, anxiety, or depression that they are hiding below the surface. One of my students, Barbara, was the youngest of five children. Her father left the family for a teenaged girlfriend when Barbara was a toddler. Her mother became an alcoholic, and as Barbara's older siblings left home, Barbara became the caretaker of her mother when she was drinking. Barbara was an exemplary student, active in choir and at her church, and eventually became a nurse. Her story is inspiring, but Barbara also was prone to major depression. It is common for children who fare well academically despite stressful homes to not fare as well emotionally. Such children merit careful watching and added support. Still, being overly prosocial may be a more adaptive coping strategy than becoming antisocial when in a difficult situation. If you have a student you suspect may be in this situation, consult your school's counselor to discuss how to support the student.

How Might Prosocial Behavior Lead to Greater School Success?

Ask people what makes a student successful in school. Most are likely to say "being smart." Yet, prosocial behavior may be a stronger determinant of school success than being smart. How does prosocial behavior affect achievement? There are at least four powerful mechanisms.

- First, prosocial students are liked better by their peers and teachers, which leads to increased achievement, as I discussed above and will cover more in Chapter 5.

- Second, prosocial students are happier, and they make their classmates happier. I'll discuss this more in Chapter 6 and explain how positive emotions enhance learning.

- Third, both prosocial behavior and academic achievement share an underlying attribute: self-control. Research shows that good self-control leads to prosocial behavior and self-control leads to the typical kinds of behaviors that make a student successful in a classroom (e.g., grit, sticking to a task until it is done, concentrating, setting and working toward long-term goals, and resisting distractions) (Normandeau & Guay, 1998).

- Fourth, because prosocial students are cooperative with others and obey classroom rules, they spend more time on learning tasks. They behave in ways that support learning such as taking turns, working smoothly on group tasks, helping and being helped. Research has clearly shown this for young children, but studies have not yet addressed this with older children (Bierman et al., 2009; Coolahan, Fantuzzo, Mendez, & McDermott, 2000; McClelland & Morrison, 2003).

❝Helping your students become more prosocial will help them have higher achievement, be better liked, and be less antisocial.❞

The last two mechanisms are interrelated. Preeminent researchers in the field have argued that the ability to control one's self in order to focus on learning is related to the ability to do learning work with others (Bierman et al., 2009; Wentzel, 2006).

This probably makes logical sense to you: Students who are more prosocial also learn more and are more successful in school than students who are less prosocial. School is a highly social environment, so social competence should contribute to success there. However, it might surprise you that students who have classmates who are more prosocial also learn more.

Classmates' Prosocial Behavior Matters, Too!

Regardless of their own prosocial aptitude, students learn more *if their classmates are prosocial* (Jia et al., 2009). That is, if you plopped the same student in two different classrooms, the student would likely have higher grades in the classroom that has more caring, friendly classmates. In a study of over 25,000 3rd to 6th graders, the children reported on their teacher's instructional practices (e.g., promotion of critical thinking, providing feedback, promotion of content knowledge) and the social climate of the classroom (e.g., whether classmates were friendly or bothered other students). *The social climate of the classroom more strongly predicted GPA than teachers' instructional practices* (Griffith, 2002).

In our study asking thousands of 4th to 12th graders to report how often their classmates were prosocial, we also asked them how engaged they were in their classroom. Students who reported having more prosocial classmates were significantly more engaged; they were more interested, deeply processing, and actively participating in the class (Z. Wang, Bergin, & Bergin, 2014). That is, their classmate's prosocial behavior predicted student's own engagement in class.

Let's revisit our question, "How does prosocial behavior affect achievement?" and add one more answer:

- Fifth, students learn more when they are surrounded by prosocial classmates because students feel greater motivation and social support for learning (Wentzel, 2006). Positive interaction with peers drives learning as they scaffold one another's thinking (kudos if you recall this from your college studies of Piaget and Vygotsky!).

In summary, the research suggests that you may increase the engagement of individual students and promote deeper learning in your classroom if you can raise the level of prosocial behavior overall. These effects occur for all students, but may be especially strong for at-risk students, thereby helping narrow the achievement gap. Most school districts grapple with the achievement gap; yours probably does, too. Let's take a brief look at how prosocial education contributes to narrowing the achievement gap.

Can Prosocial Behavior Narrow the Achievement Gap?

In the United States, low-income and some minority students consistently score lower on achievement tests, on average, than other students. This is known as the *achievement gap*. From kindergarten to high school, on average, students of Asian descent tend to have relatively high achievement and African American and Latino students tend to have relatively low achievement (Raudenbush, 2009). White students are in between. However, *the achievement gap is larger for socioeconomic status than it is for minority group membership* (Reardon, 2011, 2013). That is, students are more at risk for academic failure if their parents have low income and little education than if they belong to specific minority groups. The two factors often go together; Latino and Black students are disproportionately poor.

Closing the achievement gap has proven to be a complex challenge. It has been legislated against since the 1960s, yet it remains. Scientists have studied it extensively and many educational programs have been enacted to try to reduce it (e.g., Head Start, No Child Left Behind). Through these efforts we have learned many things about the achievement gap. We have learned that it emerges in preschool but is largest in high school. We have learned that the size of the U.S. achievement gap is moderate; some countries have larger and some have smaller gaps (Akiba, LeTendre, & Scribner, 2007). We have learned that the gap may be partly due to low-income and minority students having less *opportunity to learn* (OTL) at school.

One part of OTL is the *discipline gap*, which parallels the achievement gap. You will learn in Chapter 3 that from preschool through high school Black students, especially boys, tend to be more severely punished and are more likely to be suspended than White students, even for similar infractions (Bradshaw, Mitchell, O'Brennan, & Leaf, 2010; A. Gregory, Cornell, & Fan, 2011; Okonofua, Walton, & Eberhardt, 2016; U.S. Department of Health and Human Services, 2014). Suspensions and expulsions remove students from opportunity to learn at school, magnifying the achievement gap. This may partially explain why African American boys tend to have the lowest achievement on average. This may also help explain why students of color report feeling less cared for at school compared to White students.

You can make a difference. The research discussed throughout this book has often found that promoting prosocial behavior among your students *has stronger effects on your students who are at risk for low achievement* due to low income, minority status, or behavior problems. Key points from the research are:

1. **Improving prosocial behavior may narrow the achievement gap by reducing retention and special education placement for at-risk students.** Low-SES students who enter kindergarten at risk for academic failure are less likely to actually experience academic failure if they behave prosocially. They are less likely to be retained a grade or placed in special education throughout their schooling career, which sets them apart from similarly at-risk classmates who are less prosocial (Jones et al., 2015).

2. **Improving prosocial behavior may narrow the achievement gap more than focusing on reducing misbehavior in at-risk students.** Unfortunately, many schools tend to emphasize eliminating negative behaviors rather than promoting prosocial behaviors (Osher et al., 2016). This is slightly misguided, because promoting prosocial behaviors may be more fruitful. For example, in one study of 3rd and 4th graders, their positive behavior more strongly predicted academic achievement across the school year than their negative behavior did (Malecki & Elliot, 2002). On the flip side, in another study of low-income young children, a lack of prosocial behavior more strongly predicted poor school readiness skills than the presence of antisocial behavior (Bierman et al., 2009).

3. **Improving prosocial behavior in *classmates* may narrow the achievement gap for at-risk students.** Having prosocial classmates promotes achievement. Having prosocial classmates is especially important for at-risk students who are less likely

to develop behavior and emotional problems over the school year if they are in classrooms with more prosocial classmates. The opposite occurs—they tend to develop more problems—if at-risk students are in classrooms with fewer prosocial classmates (Hoglund & Leadbeater, 2004). Also, recall from above that in a large study of 3rd to 6th graders, the social climate of the classroom more strongly predicted GPA than teachers' instructional practices (Griffith, 2002). However, narrowing the achievement gap required having *both* good instructional practices and prosocial classmates. Neither alone closed the gap, but prosocial education was a necessary component.

4. **Improving prosocial behavior through positive teacher-student relationships may narrow the achievement gap for at-risk students.** In Chapter 5 you will learn that if you develop a positive relationship with students they will learn more in your classroom. This is especially powerful for students who have insecure relationships with their parents (Berkowitz, Moore, Astor, & Benbenishty, 2017; O'Connor & McCartney, 2007). This circumstance is disproportionately characteristic of at-risk students (Tarabulsy et al., 2005), presumably due to the stresses their families experience. The role of positive teacher-student relationships in raising student achievement has been documented for students at risk due to behavior problems, low income, minority status and low self-control (Berkowitz et al., 2017; M.-T. Wang, Brinkworth, & Eccles, 2013). At-risk students are more motivated to pay attention, follow class rules, and cooperate in the classroom when they feel cared for, which narrows the achievement gap (Matthews, Kizzie, Rowley, & Cortina, 2010).

In Chapter 1 you learned about a study that found high school students in classrooms where teachers focused on building positive relationships with them became more prosocial in that teacher's classroom. These were predominantly students at risk for academic failure, yet they were cooperative and engaged in the classrooms of teachers they felt cared for them and expected more of them. The same students misbehaved to the point they were suspended from other teachers' classrooms (A. Gregory & Ripski, 2008). Thus, how prosocial at-risk students are depends to some degree on what happens in your classroom, regardless of what happens in other classrooms.

5. **Improving prosocial behavior through bonding to school, not just to you, may narrow the achievement gap for at-risk students.** In Chapter 5 you will also learn that some of the practices described in this book can be implemented on a school-wide basis (Hamre, Hatfield, Pianta, & Jamil, 2014; Ottmar, Rimm-Kaufman, Larsen, & Berry, 2015). Doing so will promote school bonding, which is especially effective for at-risk students (G. Green, Rhodes, Hirsch, Suarez-Orozco, & Camic, 2008; Gruman, Harachi, Abbott, Catalano, & Fleming, 2008; M. Johnson, Crosnoe, & Elder, 2001; Osterman, 2000). At-risk students who feel bonding to their school tend to have higher achievement and are less likely to drop out or become delinquent (Dynarski et al., 2008; M.-T. Wang & Fredricks, 2014).

6. **Improving prosocial behavior through emotional support may narrow the achievement gap for at-risk students.** In Chapter 6 you will learn that creating an emotionally supportive classroom promotes prosocial behavior. This may be particularly effective for at-risk students (S. Johnson, Seidenfeld, Izard, & Kobak, 2013). That is, in classrooms with a positive climate, the negative relationship between low-income and achievement is weaker (Berkowitz et al., 2017). Low-income students who have adults in their lives who use the strategies explained in Chapter 6 tend to develop good emotion regulation despite living in poverty (Raver, 2004). This is crucial because good emotion regulation and feeling positive emotions increases learning, whereas feeling chronic negative emotions (e.g., anger, frustration, sadness, anxiety) interferes with learning.

Most children don't arrive at school perfectly prosocial (mine didn't). Yet some students tend to be less prosocial and have greater struggles with emotional competence because cascading problems beset them before they've had a chance to cope with preceding problems. Unfortunately, research shows that teachers tend to be harsher with these at-risk students rather than focusing on building their skills (Webster-Stratton & Reid, 2008). Instead, you can help your at-risk students develop the strong prosocial skills they need to navigate a world with discrimination and income inequality. You can create a safe, supportive classroom experience for all your students. This book gives you several research-based strategies and tools to make a difference for each student who enters your classroom, where they will find an oasis of kindness and cooperation. Stay tuned for Part 2, where you will learn how to do this.

FOR REFLECTION AND DISCUSSION

What are you currently doing to promote friendship development among your students? How do you select groups for group work? Is it based on friendships? Why or why not?

Which students did you nominate as the most prosocial students in your class from Chapter 1? Are these students "smart" and academically successful? What behaviors do these students engage in that makes them academically successful?

Think about the various classes you've had. Which one stands out as a prosocial class, where as a group they were prosocial toward each other? Was this an academically successful class? Did high-risk students fare better than expected in this class?

Is there an achievement gap at your school? Is there a discipline gap? If so, what is your school doing to try to close the gaps? Is it working? How might prosocial education contribute?

PART 2

WHAT SPECIFIC APPROACHES CREATE MORE PROSOCIAL CLASSROOMS?

In the previous section you learned what prosocial behavior is and how this important non-cognitive skill can increase your students' success in the classroom. In this section you will learn four tools for increasing prosocial behavior: effective discipline, practice (with reinforcement and modeling), positive teacher-student relationships, and building students' emotional competence.

Some of what you will learn in this section may be outside your comfort zone because it is not what is typically taught in professional development or what is handed down from experienced teachers to novice teachers. Your classroom may look a little different from classrooms that some teachers or administrators would label well-managed. Yet, research suggests that implementing these tools will lead to happier, better behaved, kinder—and therefore higher achieving—students. If a teacher, mentor, or administrator questions your use of these tools in your classroom, hand him or her a copy of this book!

Two Approaches:
Curriculum Add-On versus Interactional

There are two approaches you can take to increase prosocial behavior among your students. One is that you implement a program or curriculum that adds to and supplements your regular academic curriculum. The second is that you interact with your students in specific ways during your regular instruction. This book takes the latter approach. Any teacher in any subject, from preschool to high school, can immediately initiate these behaviors in their classrooms, with *no material cost and no addition to the curriculum.* You can incorporate these practices naturally into your ongoing practice. You will learn to promote prosocial behavior in your students in ways that are integrated into your regular curriculum that will transform the way you interact with students and students interact with each other.

If you want to use an add-on curriculum as well, there are some to choose from. In fact, it is quite common to approach non-cognitive skill development through formal programs that supplement the regular curriculum with activities such as story-based lessons, role-playing, or social skills training modules (Domitrovich et al., 2017). Most of these programs are designed to be *universal,* meaning they are provided to the entire school by regular classroom teachers. Others are *targeted,* meaning they are provided to specific students who need special help, typically in small groups that are conducted by a counselor. The U.S. Institute of Education Science together with the Centers for Disease Prevention and Control commissioned rigorous studies of seven commonly used universal programs to determine if they are effective or not. Generally they found that curriculum add-on programs have small or no effects (Social and Character Development Research Consortium, 2010; Vincent & Grove, 2012). In another review of 59 studies of add-on programs designed to increase positive social behavior, an overall small effect was found (Durlak et al., 2011). Even with a small effect, the benefits may be worth the costs. Researchers have estimated that for each $1 invested, $11 are saved in costs associated with misbehavior, such as absences, staff time to handle misbehavior, mental health and social services, alternative placements, and law enforcement (Belfield et al., 2015). If your school wants to adopt such a program, or is mandated to do so (e.g., by your school board or legislature) you can find programs designed for preschools to high schools at the *Collaborative for Academic, Social, and Emotional Learning* website. Check out the Department of Education's *What Works Clearinghouse*[5] website, and search under "student behavior," to see if there has been an evaluation indicating whether your selected program is effective or not. Notice whether it promotes positive behavior, rather than emphasizes reducing misbehavior as most SEL programs do (Domitrovich et al., 2017).

An example of a universal program that does have some positive effect is the Caring School Community (CSC) which has been recognized by the U.S. Department of Health and Human Services as an exemplary program. The CSC is designed for elementary schools and emphasizes building a sense of community across the school and increasing caring within the classroom. The school hosts family activities, assigns student buddies across grades, and has other community-building efforts. Research has found that when schools implement the CSC program successfully and become more caring places, students become more prosocial, particularly students in schools with many impoverished students. As I discussed in Chapter 2, a splendid side effect is that these programs tend to raise students' grades and test scores as well. So what do teachers do in the CSC? You will learn about a few of the things in Part 2 of this book: how to develop warm teacher-student relationships, use inductive discipline, and be authoritative (Solomon, Battistich, Watson, Schaps, & Lewis, 2000; What Works Clearinghouse, 2007). You will also learn how and why they are effective so that you can adapt the approaches to your own situation.

Discipline: Key to Teaching Empathy and Values

In an elementary classroom, a group of students are sitting on the carpet as the classroom morning meeting comes to an end. The students are dispersing to several learning stations. Ms. Bailey asks Jordan to join her and some other students at a table to work on reading in a small group. Jordan lays his head on the floor as he says, "No. I didn't bring my book. I hate reading." Ms. Bailey says, "I have an extra you can borrow today. Come join us." Jordan says, "No. I don't want to." Ms. Bailey, firmly but pleasantly, says, "You'll want to see what happens in the next chapter." Jordan, continuing to lie on the floor, says, "Nuh uh." Ms. Bailey, still firm but pleasant, smiles at Jordan and says, "I know you don't want to read right now, but you will need to learn how to read well. If you become a mechanic like your Daddy, you'll need to read manuals that tell you how to fix a car." Jordan sighs, and walks tiredly over to the table.

Discipline is a daily issue in most classrooms. In fact, in a national study 41% of teachers said that student misbehavior interfered with their ability to teach.[6] In this chapter you will learn how to turn misbehavior into an opportunity to teach self-control and prosocial behavior. Discipline is the leading chapter in Part 2 by design because *the type of discipline you use may be one of the most powerful ways you influence your students' prosocial behavior.* However, before we jump into a discussion of how to correct students' misbehavior in affirming ways, we need to first discuss hungry and sleepy students—which affects discipline.

How Do Hunger and Sleepiness Affect Students' Behavior?

Part of Jordan's misbehavior in the classroom was due to sleepiness. Hunger and sleep deprivation can make the most kindly people behave with resistance, sharpness, irritation, and meanness. When a toddler is behaving miserably, the first thing parents think is "It must be nap time" or "It must be lunch time." The same is true for older students (and even your colleagues and especially your principal).

During your college education you may have learned about Abraham Maslow's pyramid of human needs (Maslow, 1970). At the bottom of the pyramid are basic human physiological needs like water, food, and sleep (see Figure 3.1). Next come physical and psychological safety needs (e.g., security, stability). These are followed by social needs (e.g., affection, acceptance). Then comes respect and self-esteem needs. At the pinnacle is self-actualization, or fulfilling one's potential. The gist of Maslow's theory is that your students are motivated to meet the lowest-level need that is unmet before they are interested in higher-level needs. For example, students who feel unsafe because they are frightened by the bully in French class are not going to be focused on whether they are mastering French idioms. Maslow believed that students are inherently prosocial, and that unmet needs are the root cause of students' misbehavior. Hungry students are cranky. Sleepy students just want to put their head down, regardless of how scintillating your lesson might be. The upshot is that if your students' basic needs are met, they will behave better and learn more.[7]

Whether you agree with the details of Maslow's theory or not, most of us recognize that we are not our finest when our basic needs are not met because we are tired or hungry. Research confirms that conditions like heat, hunger and tiredness foster aggression and misbehavior in students (Anderson, 2001). When antisocial behavior is high and prosocial behavior is in short supply in your classroom, first determine if a snack is called for rather than (or in addition to) discipline. Also, pay attention to whether your students are well rested.

Sleep deprivation has reached epidemic proportions among children in

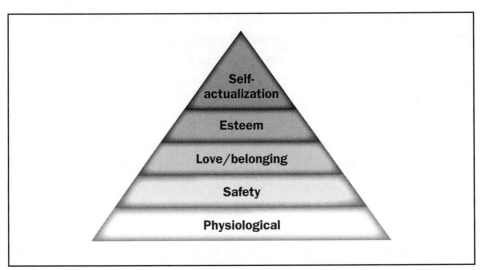

Figure 3.1 Maslow's Hierachy of Human Needs

the United States. This is true for students of all ages, but particularly for high school students. Roughly 85% of teenagers are sleep deprived (Dahl & Lewin, 2002; Owens & AAP Adolescent Sleep Working Group, 2014; Snell, Adam, & Duncan, 2007). How can you tell if your students are sleep deprived? The symptoms of sleep deprivation are low motivation, trouble concentrating, slow information processing, trouble remembering, minimal emotion control or movement control, making lots of mistakes, and restlessness, irritability, or impulsiveness (Bates, Viken, Alexander, Beyers, & Stockton, 2002; Fredriksen, Rhodes, Reddy, & Way, 2004). Because they share the same symptoms, sleep deprivation can be misdiagnosed as ADHD, depression, and emotional disorders, and students with these disorders can become worse if they are sleep deprived (El-Sheikh, Bub, Kelly, & Buckhalt, 2013; Short, Gradisar, Lack, & Wright, 2013).

❝ Before moving toward discipline, ask, 'Is my student hungry or sleepy?' as a simple fix for misbehavior.**❞**

How much sleep do your students need? A good rule of thumb to remember is *10 for 10.* That is, 10-year-olds need about 10 hours of sleep per night. Younger children need more, and older children need less. So 1st graders need about 11 hours and preschoolers need about 12 hours (this includes any nap time). One exception to this rule is that teenagers in a growth spurt need more sleep than a 10-year-old; growth is fueled by sleep. If you have students who have been adequately rested, but are suddenly sleepy even though they are getting the same amount of sleep, they may be in a growth spurt.

You may think that sleep is a pointless subject for teachers because there is little you can do about sleep deprivation. Actually, as an authority figure, you can influence your students' sleep behavior by convincing them or their parents of the importance of sleep (Bergin & Bergin, 2010). You can take a close look at your school's schedule: When do activities or classes start and when do after-school events end? You can give reasonable levels of homework that do not keep students up late. You can educate students and parents about good sleep hygiene, such as keeping a consistent bedtime seven days a week or avoiding screen viewing, large meals, caffeine, or heavy exercise before bedtime (Bergin & Bergin, 2010; Roehrs & Roth, 2008). You can notify parents when you see clear signs of sleepiness, such as Jordan's, in your classroom.

As a teacher you should be interested in your students' sleep because sleep deprivation diminishes students' emotional well-being and learning, in addition to increasing misbehavior. Sleep-deprived students are more likely to have lower grades or fail classes (Buckhalt, El-Sheikh, Keller, & Kelly, 2009; Kahn et al., 1989). Teens who stay up late and sleep in on weekends are more likely to earn lower grades, compared to those who keep a more consistent bed and wake routine between school days and weekends (Wolfson & Carskadon, 1998). Teens who stay up late to study have more academic problems the next day, such as lower quiz scores and trouble understanding class content (Gillen-O'Neel, Huynh, & Fuligni, 2013).

You might expect that this is just because sleepy students come from more chaotic homes without routines or parental supervision, so who knows if it is the sleep per se or something else that causes them to struggle in school? To answer this question, researchers got parents of 4th to 6th graders to agree to put their children to bed about a half hour earlier or later than usual for just three nights in a row (Sadeh, Gruber, & Raviv, 2003). Those who went to bed earlier had improved attention, memory, and other abilities that underlie standardized test scores—an effect size comparable to two years of development! In another study, toddlers were randomly assigned to miss a nap (I do not know how the researchers got their mothers to agree to this), and found that both the toddlers' emotions (more anxious, less happy) and problem-solving ability with puzzles were impaired (Berger, Miller, Seifer, Cares, & LeBourgeois, 2011). Sleep promotes learning and helps students remember more because memories are consolidated during sleep (Rasch & Born, 2008; Strickgold & Walker, 2004).

Nourishment also promotes learning because thinking and paying attention take energy. The brain is fueled by glucose and other nutrients that come from food. Experienced teachers have learned that snacks can improve students' ability to stay on task. Encourage your students to eat a high-protein breakfast every day (not just testing days), and to bring healthy snacks whenever they must go for more than a few hours without a lunch break.

The key message is to eliminate as much misbehavior as possible by ruling out hunger and sleepiness as root causes. Once you've accomplished this, there still will be plenty of opportunity to exercise your discipline skills. Students misbehave frequently, so most teachers will engage in discipline multiple times per day, although this will vary by age and attributes of the students. As you learned in Chapter 1, preschoolers are the most aggressive of any age. Thus, it won't surprise you that in one preschool, researchers observed 49 instances of misbehavior per 15 minutes (Arnold, McWilliams, & Arnold, 1998). Teachers in high school may not deal with misbehavior as frequently, but the misbehavior of teenagers can be more serious and challenging, so secondary teachers also need to have well-honed discipline skills. The principles of discipline you will learn in this chapter are appropriate for any age group.

What Are the Different Types of Discipline?

Before talking about approaches to discipline that influence prosocial behavior, we need a brief primer on different types of discipline. Some people use the term *discipline* writ large to mean anything that has to do with classroom management, and others use it just to mean meting out punishment to errant students. For the purposes of this discussion, discipline refers to an attempt to change students' misbehavior. Let's begin with the best form of discipline for most situations: induction.

What is Induction?

Induction is a fancy term for reasoning with a student during discipline. A more technical definition of induction is the process of giving a student a reason for obeying a directive or abiding by rules, and explaining to the student the consequences of not doing so. In parenting research, one of the most robust findings is that discipline is more effective when it is accompanied by a compelling justification (Maccoby, 1992). You can see why this might be. Giving students a reason for asking them to change their behavior gives them information about why a rule is important and what your values are, so they can begin to share in those values. It also makes the directive more legitimate. We are all more likely to comply with rules for which we see a good reason.

❝ Induction is a type of discipline where you give the student a reason for obeying the rule or stopping the misbehavior. One reason could be how the misbehavior made a 'victim' feel.**❞**

Victim-centered induction is a particular type of induction that focuses the attention of the misbehaving student on his or her victim. *It is particularly important for cultivating a prosocial orientation.* During victim-centered induction, you follow these steps:

1. Point out how the student's misbehavior affects others.

2. Ask the student to imagine being in the others' place.

3. Suggest concrete acts of reparation.

For example, "Eli, we do not push in line. How would you like it if John had pushed you? Show John what a good class friend you can be." It does not take lengthy "talking-it-out" episodes. It is not a therapy session. A couple of short, to-the-point statements are sufficient.

What Induction is Not: Forms of Discipline to Avoid

Psychological Control

This type of discipline appeals to the third level of Maslow's hierarchy—the need for belonging, affection, and affirmation—by threatening the fulfillment of those needs. Teachers who use this approach control the student by withholding approval. They do this by expressing disapproval, withdrawing affection, ignoring the student, implying the student is a *bad* person, conveying dislike, or making the student feel excessive guilt (Barber, Xia, Olsen, McNeely, & Bose, 2012; Q. Wang, Pomerantz, & Chen, 2007). For example, "Eli, we do not like you when you push like that" or "I might've known it would be you at the center of the pushing, Eli; you take this whole class down" or "Just leave my class; I've had it with you." This approach is also called *conditional regard* because the teacher may be warm toward students, but only as long as they do what the teacher wants (Roth, 2008). Of course, there is some disapproval inherent in any discipline encounter because you are communicating that you do not like what the student is doing in the moment. However, disapproval is minimal in induction, but it is the very heart of psychological control.

The following is an example of psychological control, combined with power assertion, at a middle school. Malik pushes Darnell, who shouts back at him. As Mr. Richard approaches them, Malik lies and says that Darnell did the pushing.

> *Mr. Richard says to Darnell, "I'm sure you started all this. You are always trying to start something! Get over to the table and lay your head down!" Darnell starts to say "That's not fair, I didn't . . . " but Mr. Richard cuts him off saying, "Get over there or else you are going to sit there the rest of the night. I do not want to see your face until I tell you to get up!"*

This type of discipline can be successful in getting students to behave properly in the moment, because students want your good regard. However, it inhibits students' development as a human being, and threatens their self-esteem. Not surprisingly, students develop anxiety, depression, low self-confidence, and increased misbehavior over time when disciplined in this way (Barber, Stolz, & Olsen, 2005; Rakow et al., 2011; Roth, 2008). One study found that students in classes where teachers use guilt-inducing discipline learn less, compared to students in classes where teachers use a more positive, redirecting discipline style (Viljaranta et al., 2015). Students themselves think induction is a more appropriate form of discipline and as they get older disapprove of the shaming techniques used by psychologically controlling adults (Helwig, To, Wang, Liu, & Yang, 2014). One caveat is that there are times when students must be removed from class because they are putting others' safety at risk. However, shaming and removing a student should not be the heart of a discipline encounter or the discipline of choice.

Power Assertion

In this type of discipline the adult relies on power, size, or resources to control the child. It most often involves withdrawing privileges ("You won't be allowed to sit by your friend now"), but can also involve physical power such as spanking or carrying a student away from the situation, or merely threatening to do one of these things. You can recognize it by an "or else" clause, which may be stated or just left implicit. For example, "Do not do that again, or else you will get a demerit" or "If you do that again, you will have to go to the time out chair" or "Once more, and you'll be suspended." Do you recognize it in Mr. Richard's discipline?

You have probably seen power assertion in action because it is common in schools. It can range from harsh to mild (e.g., being kept in from recess). Harsh forms are often called *zero-tolerance policies* in which students are threatened with in-school and out-of-school suspensions and expulsions, referrals to law enforcement, and even arrests. These punishments may have their place for serious misbehavior, but because they have been increasingly used to punish milder forms of misbehavior and are disproportionately applied to minority or low-income youth, they are coming under greater censure. From preschool through high school, Black students, especially boys, are more likely to be suspended than White students (A. Gregory et al., 2011; U.S. Department of Health and Human Services, 2014). Black students are also more likely to be referred for minor misbehavior (Bradshaw et al., 2010). Teachers tend to recommend more severe punishment for Black male students and report feeling more disturbed when they have a second infraction, compared to White male students (Okonofua et al., 2016). This widespread effect is known as the discipline gap as a follow-on from the achievement gap because it results in less opportunity to learn for Black students.

You have probably noticed that power assertion is not very effective over the long run because it does not support better behavior or prevent misbehavior. In fact, schools that emphasize power assertion tend to have overall low achievement, poor school climate, and more dropouts (Emmer, Sabornie, Evertson, & Weinstein, 2013; Noltemeyer, Marie, McLoughlin, & Vanderwood, 2015). Schools that are suspension-oriented tend to have low academic quality and are careless about school climate (Lamont et al., 2013). Suspensions and expulsions are particularly problematic because not only do they remove a student from academic learning time, but also they make students feel they are not part of the community, which may lead to dropping out. The U.S. Department of Education and U.S. Department of Justice have recognized this, and in 2011 launched a joint initiative to support schools in using discipline approaches that create positive learning environments and keep students in school (Restorative Practices Working Group, 2014).

Why is Power Assertion so Problematic?

A 3rd grade class is seated on the floor, listening to Ms. Bennett read a story for a few minutes before going to Music class. Olivia stands up without asking and walks over to the tissue box on the other side of the room. Ms. Bennett loudly says, "Olivia, sit down!" Olivia continues to walk to the tissues and grabs several, without looking at Ms. Bennett, who stands up and yells, "Olivia go to your table and sit down. You are not going to Music!" When Olivia reaches her table she sits down and says "I do not like that book anyway." She sits quietly with her head down. When the other students leave the room to go to Music, she looks up, then looks down at the floor and quietly says "Why can't I even go to Music? What's wrong with me?"

There are serious costs to using *power-assertive discipline* in the classroom even in mild forms like Ms. Bennett uses. First, it models antisocial behavior; students who are controlled by threats and punishment learn to mete out threats and punishments when they are thwarted. Discipline is where students learn values. From power-assertive adults they learn that when you are in a position of power it is acceptable to threaten and coerce others, and lash out when frustrated rather than cooperate and work as a team. Students who are controlled by power assertion become more aggressive and delinquent over time (Bender et al., 2007; Coie & Dodge, 1998).

Second, power assertion creates resentment in the student toward you, jeopardizing your relationship. It diminishes the possibility of cooperation, responsiveness, or reciprocity between the disciplinarian and the student, as it did for Olivia and her teacher. It generates defiance. It creates angry students, and anger interferes with learning. I visited a school where students had to stand against the wall during recess if they talked during lunch. The staff felt this was a reasonable punishment. Yet, when I asked how they would feel about working in a school where they had to stand against a wall in a public arena for talking to colleagues during lunch, they were appalled at the thought. You would not respect or cooperate with anyone who treated you like that.

Third, it raises the level of coercion that students come to expect. You've probably noticed that students quickly adapt to the level of coercion you use in a classroom. Some will not comply until you threaten punishments, if they have adapted to the use of punishment. As they become accustomed to power assertion and threats, they will expect threats before they will comply. They will ignore the mild threats, and expect more and more powerful "or else" clauses (C. Davis, Brady, Williams, & Hamilton, 1992; Patterson & Bank, 1989). As a result you end up escalating the levels of coercion, and you begin feeling more like a police officer than a teacher.

Fourth, students become less compliant over time. When your threats are powerful enough to motivate a student to change behavior, so that you get compliance in the moment, you are reinforced for using power assertion. However, what you may not see is that you are undermining the students' compliance over the long run (Erath, El-Sheikh, & Cummings, 2009; Gershoff, 2010). This is because they are not internalizing your values (Kochanska, Aksan, & Joy, 2007), as will be explained later in this chapter. Despite these serious costs, most classrooms I have observed have used some form of power assertion.

❝Power assertion has several serious costs, yet it is commonly used in classrooms.❞

Power assertion also can be reward oriented. You have probably used bribes to get your students' to obey you; most teachers (and parents) do so occasionally. Yet, you are still highlighting power and some of the costs listed above pertaining to punishment also pertain to using rewards. To understand this, we need to traipse into the territory of behaviorism. Power-assertive discipline and behaviorism may not be the same, but they have strong overlap as practiced in typical classrooms.

Is it Okay to Use "Consequences"? A Primer on Behaviorism

One of the grand theories of human development is *behaviorism*. The basic premise is that control of behavior is located outside the student, and that behavior is *learned* (or *conditioned*) depending on *consequences* in the environment.

Classical Conditioning

Many of the consequences in life are automatic, such as salivating when you smell chocolate chip cookies baking (just like Pavlov's salivating dogs who unwittingly helped him earn a Nobel prize). If you remember studying *classical conditioning* you will recognize this as an unconditioned response (i.e., not learned, involuntary, not under your control) to an unconditioned stimulus. Sometimes *unconditioned responses* can be learned to an otherwise neutral stimulus. For example, walking into a school building should not inherently trigger anxiety or anger in anyone; it is inherently a neutral stimulus. Yet, some students will learn to feel anxiety or anger when they walk into a school through classical conditioning because they have been repeatedly disciplined at school in a harsh way that arouses anxiety or anger. Students like Olivia or Darnell come to pair these emotions with the disciplinarian, which might generalize to school and other authority figures. This conditioned negative response to school is no longer under their voluntary control; the mere sight of school can elicit anger, shame, racing hearts, and sweaty palms. This is one mechanism for how power-assertive discipline may lead to defiant students, low morale at school, and dropping out.

Classical conditioning also works in a positive direction. Students who repeatedly have positive experiences will come to pair good feelings with being at school so that just walking through the school door will make them smile. (The same is true of teachers, so do your best to help your colleagues feel warmly welcomed in your building.) In addition, even when negative reactions have been paired with a neutral stimulus, this can be *unlearned*. That is, if students like Olivia or Darnell who have learned to dislike school because of harsh, power-assertive discipline later have positive experiences at school, their negative response to school can be extinguished.

We are all susceptible to classical conditioning, no matter our age. In fact, Pavlov's experiment has been repeated with human babies. For example, if you play a bell each time babies reach for a colorful stick, they will learn to reach out in the dark at the sound of a bell when there is no stick (Keen, 2011). However, teens and adults are more susceptible to classical conditioning than younger students, perhaps because they are more efficient at learning, so secondary teachers should be especially aware of what you are doing in your classroom and school to condition students' behavior (Hofmann, De Houwer, Perugini, Baeyens, & Crombez, 2010).

Operant Conditioning

---

66 Reinforcement is any consequence that increases the probability of a behavior. Punishment is any consequence that decreases the probability of a behavior."

Another branch of behaviorism is called *operant conditioning*. This differs from classical conditioning in that it focuses on voluntary behavior that is under students' control, such as doing their classwork or waiting their turn to speak. Voluntary behavior is learned through reinforcement or punishment. *Reinforcement* is a consequence that increases the probability of a behavior. In a classroom, *reinforcers* might be good grades, praise, gold cards for good behavior, promise of a class party, and so on. *Punishment* is a consequence that decreases the probability of behavior. Punishment might include *time out* in early childhood classrooms, threats of being kept in from recess in elementary classrooms, and bad grades, demerits for bad behavior, removal from the football team, and so on in secondary classrooms. Often the pinnacle of punishment in the classroom is to be sent to the principal's (or vice principal's) office. The principal has his or her own set of consequences that may range from a talking-to to parent conferences to suspension. Can you see the relationship to power-assertive discipline?

Reinforcement and punishment are defined by their outcomes. That is, if you intend something to reduce a students' misbehavior, such as threat of being sent to the principal's office, but the misbehavior does not decrease, then the threat is not actually working as a punishment. Listen to one 5th grade teacher:

> *In my school, when students are aggressive they get sent to the office, where they get a snack, take a nap, or play on an iPad. We know this isn't working, but we keep doing it because we don't know what else to do and we want to de-escalate the situation as quickly as possible.*

(Stay tuned. You'll learn a more productive approach to discipline below.)

In other words, the students are getting reinforced, not punished, for aggressive behavior. The same is true for reinforcement. If you intend for something to increase good behavior (e.g., promise of a class party), but good behavior does not increase, then the promised reward is not actually working as a reinforcer.

This approach is used to treat students with behavior disorders. When it is used deliberately by school psychologists or counselors it may be called *applied behavioral analysis*. They typically follow specific steps in which they observe what the reinforcers of specific student's misbehavior are, set goals for behavioral change, reinforce positive behavior change in small steps, and provide feedback. If you have a student in need of this degree of careful shaping of behavior, get the help of your school psychologist or counselor who have been trained to use behaviorism correctly.

Operant conditioning is applied constantly in classrooms to control students who do not have behavior disorders. In fact, it may be the dominant way of controlling students' behavior (Evertson, Emmer, & Worsham, 2000; Wolfgang, 1995). Many behavior management books you may read, and many programs your school may adopt, focus on operant conditioning techniques; it is important to understand the pros and cons you will learn about below. Even without formal programs, teachers often set up a program of rewards and punishments in their classroom which they may call consequences that they mete out when students misbehave.

Is it a good thing that operant conditioning is so widely implemented in schools? It depends. It definitely works when implemented well in the sense that behavior changes; you can deliberately shape your students' behavior regardless of their background experiences. That feels empowering and can result in a smoother running classroom. The following is a description of my own experience early in my career using operant conditioning:

In our "special" room, a few teachers taught basic phonics and reading skills to students, up to age 12, who had failed to learn to read in their regular classroom. We had students for one class period per day. Our goal was to have each child reading independently within 6 weeks. To achieve this difficult goal, we used heavy-handed behavior modification techniques. Three students sat on each side of a table, with a teacher at the head. We ignored all misbehavior completely so that it would not be reinforced in any way. Because these were students with a history of anger over prolonged failure at school, they misbehaved constantly when they first arrived in our room. We were even kicked under the table, so we wore shin guards. We positively reinforced each time a child even came close to appropriate behavior, such as telling us what sound a letter made, by giving them a plastic chip. Every 15 minutes they

> *could turn in their chips for a prize from our treasure chest. More chips bought cooler prizes. They could "trade-up" their prizes. It worked remarkably well. We met the goal for almost every child, sending them back into their classrooms with basic reading skills.*

However, there are more and less effective ways to use operant conditioning. It is often not implemented well in classrooms because it requires a degree of intent deliberateness that overtaxes busy teachers. Common mistakes are (1) not reinforcing behaviors that should be reinforced, (2) reinforcing the wrong behaviors, and (3) thinking that something is working as a reinforcement or punishment when in fact is it not (i.e., the target behavior is not increasing or decreasing). In one study researchers asked students and teachers to rank how reinforcing 17 items were (e.g., stickers, toys, candy), and found that the rankings were different. Things the teachers thought were highly reinforcing, the students did not rank highly (Resetar & Noell, 2008).

You might think that a fourth common mistake is being inconsistent with the reinforcement (it is easy to sometimes forget to reinforce a specific behavior). However, it is OK to be inconsistent. In fact, intermittent reinforcement is more effective in sustaining long-term behavior than continuous reinforcement, once the behavior is stabilized (you should use consistent, continuous reinforcement until it has stabilized). Yet, even when operant conditioning is implemented well, there are costs to using it.

What Are the Costs of Using Operant Conditioning?

Controlling student behavior through a program of rewards and punishments tends to devolve into power-assertive discipline, even if this was not the original intent, because of the many demands for teachers' attention. When operant conditioning is implemented as power-assertive discipline it has the same costs as power-assertive discipline. That is, it models antisocial behavior, it creates resentment and jeopardizes relationships, it raises the level of coercion students expect, students become less compliant over time, and they do not internalize values or standards for behavior. This is true even for the seemingly mild and widely endorsed form of punishment known as time out.

Time Out for Time Out

Time out is a punishment designed to decrease the probability of negative behavior. The child is removed from the normal environment to an environment without reinforcers. Some teachers put students in time out for trivial behavior issues. Like other forms of operant conditioning, it can work in terms of decreasing misbehavior (Morawska & Sanders, 2011). However, young children report that they feel lonely, rejected by their teachers, and scared (Readdick & Chapman, 2000). How sad! In other words, it has some of the same costs as other forms of power assertion. Like other punishments, it does not teach appropriate behavior.

If You Must Use Behaviorism,
then Focus on Rewards Rather than Punishment

Because of these weighty costs, many psychologists are opposed to the use of punishment, and instead argue that operant conditioning should focus on reinforcing positive behavior rather than punishing misbehavior. B. F. Skinner, arguably one of the most famous psychologists ever and a master of changing behavior, was among this group. He was staunchly opposed to punishment. This is partly because it is not as effective as reinforcement, since it is hard to predict the outcomes of punishment, and partly because it does not teach appropriate replacement behaviors.

Yet, even this apparently positive application of operant conditioning can have costs in the classroom. The energy that teachers must put into monitoring and disbursing rewards (and negotiating the effect on students who do not earn the rewards) can be overwhelming and take time away from other important duties. Rewards are hard to dispense equitably (students know that when only the so-called bad kids get rewards for good behavior, the system is really about controlling their behavior). Teachers often ignore or forget behavior that should be reinforced. Reward programs in a classroom can cause students to focus on the reward rather than what they are learning: "Do I get points for that?" Most importantly, while rewards may work in the short run, they may not generalize to other behaviors or result in internalization. In fact, use of rewards can have negative, yet subtle, effects on students' motivation and growth in self- control (Grolnick, Deci, & Ryan, 1997).

❝ Operant conditioning can be effective in changing
behavior, but it can have costs similar to power-assertive
discipline, even if you focus on rewards rather than
punishment.**❞**

Rewards Can Undermine Motivation:
The Over-Justification Effect

Students' motivation to behave well may actually be undermined when teachers dispense stickers, gold cards, or candy on a regular basis for good behavior. In a famous study, researchers found that after children were rewarded for
an activity, their motivation to engage in it was diminished (Lepper, Greene,
& Nisbett, 1973). This same effect has been found for children and adults in
many different situations (Lepper, Keavney, & Drake, 1996; Ryan & Deci, 1996).

Why might this happen? Students interpret their own behavior. If the
reward is highlighted, making the power of the reward dispenser especially
salient, then it is clear to students why they are complying and they attribute
their behavior to external reasons. "I am doing this to get the reward." That
is, the behavior is *over justified*. In contrast, if the power being wielded over
students is minimal, subtle, ambiguous, or unclear, then students are free to
attribute their behavior to internal reasons: "I am doing this because I choose
to." The behavior is *under justified*. Nevertheless, rewards do work in situations
where there is no intrinsic motivation to begin with, and when rewards are
subtle or unexpected. You'll learn how to use rewards appropriately in the
next chapter.

In summary, operant conditioning can be used to effectively change behavior. It works with students whose behavior is disruptive and out-of-control.
However, there are serious potential costs to using it. One way to reconcile
these two realities is to use behavior modification in the short term if behavior is out of control, but only until behavior has reached reasonable levels.
Then, use it intermittently over time, while gradually transitioning to use of
induction instead. For example, at one school teachers felt that the students'

behavior was so out of control that it was interfering with learning. The teachers implemented a program in which they gave students popscicle sticks for appropriate classroom behaviors. After students amassed enough sticks, they could turn them in for prizes. It took a few weeks for the behavior to reach an acceptable level, and then the staff quit giving out the popscicle sticks. They explained to the students why there would be no more popscicle sticks, celebrated with the students their improved behavior, and occasionally gave unexpected prizes for an especially good day or week while praising the students' good behavior.

You may be wondering what to do in a situation where one (or a few) students may need behavior modification, but other students in the same classroom do not. You can use reinforcement as a targeted rather than as a universal intervention in your classroom. That is, only one or two students in your class might get a star for good behaviors until their behavior is similar to the rest of the class. Counselors and special educators are trained in ways to manage targeted behavior modification, so get their help. Generally praise is a powerful enough reinforcer that you do not need tangible rewards, even for challenging students. You'll learn more about how to best use praise in the next chapter.

General Principles of Effective Discipline

The first step in understanding what constitutes effective discipline is to be clear about what the end goal of discipline is, so let's begin there.

What is Your Goal During Discipline?

Your goal during any discipline encounter might be either to just get compliance in this moment so that you can get on with the task at hand or to help your students internalize social norms for positive behavior and develop self-control (Deci, Vallerand, Pelletier, & Ryan, 1991). The goal of any adult's interaction with any child at any time ideally should be the latter, but in reality there are times when getting through the learning task you had planned for today seems more important. You do not want some students with behavior problems to detract from the learning of other students, and you want your students to spend as much learning time on task as possible. The good news is that induction is the best form of discipline for either goal. *Induction keeps your classroom running smoothly, while also helping your students develop self-control and prosocial behavior over the long term.* In contrast, if you use power-assertive discipline you might get compliance in the short term, but you actually undermine the development of self-control and internalization in students. Similarly, if you use psychological control, you undermine internalization because students feel externally controlled or compelled to behave out of desire for affection and fear of losing it, rather than because the behavior has become part of their own values and identity (Roth, 2008).

Psychologists distinguish between *situational compliance* (i.e., mere compliance in the moment) and *committed compliance* (i.e., internalization of the values of the disciplinarian). Students who have situational compliance might comply with a directive or classroom norm and appear cooperative when they are being supervised, but not when you look away or leave. They require your ongoing control. In contrast, students who have committed compliance, or who have internalized classroom norms, will comply even when no one is monitoring them (Kochanska, Aksan, & Koenig, 1995). Self-control and internalization of social norms develops out of committed, not situational, compliance.

"Students' compliance can be situational or committed. Self-control and internalization of values grow out of committed compliance.**"**

Have you ever wished your students had better self-control? Then take a hard look at your discipline approach. It is during *discipline encounters* that students' learn self-control, depending on how you approach discipline (Grusec & Goodnow, 1994). Discipline teaches students the boundaries of socially acceptable behavior and shapes their values (Grusec & Kuczynski, 1997). It provides them with rich information about their own and others' behavior. You want your students to adapt well to their social world and behave in ways that make others accept and like them, rather than act on inappropriate impulses unless an authority figure threatens them with consequences. How can you know whether a discipline encounter was effective or not? Ask yourself, "What did the student learn?" from the encounter. If it was prosocial behavior and self-control you are on the right track. Use discipline as an opportunity to teach new skills and more appropriate behaviors in a way that supports prosocial behavior. Discipline is a teaching moment.

Principles of Effective Discipline

There are just a few specific principles of effective discipline to keep in mind that will help you make good decisions about your discipline approach.

Principle 1: Get Compliance

Teachers who are lax in discipline tend to have even more misbehavior in their classrooms. You probably learned quickly that if you did not get compliance in the here-and-now, that it is even harder to get compliance in the next encounter. On the other hand, if students comply once, they are more likely to comply in the next encounter (and so are their ever-watching classmates). Compliance tends to beget compliance. This is because compliance creates a cooperative mindset and behavioral momentum (Lee, 2005; Williams & Forehand, 1984).

This is so well-recognized among therapists that one approach to treat behavior disorders is called *errorless compliance training*. In this approach, students are given directives that tend to result in high levels of compliance (e.g., "Give me a high five!") and then students are introduced to directives that there is a lower probability they will comply with until the students are compliant even with directives they formerly refused to comply with (C. Davis et al., 1992; Ducharme et al., 1994). There is no force or punishment for noncompliance, so that the students have the choice to obey. (This is to avoid the *over-justification effect*, which you may remember is that students attribute their behavior to external causes that over justify their behavior.) Parents are taught to express positive emotions during compliance training in order to foster cooperation from their children. This will sound familiar as you read through the next few pages because this form of behavior therapy draws upon principles of effective discipline.

Principle 2: Keep Power Minimal

All adult-child interactions have some power imbalance inherently. Thus, you could argue that all discipline is power-assertive to some extent. But discipline encounters differ in the degree to which power is emphasized. One researcher described five levels of power assertion: (1) unqualified power assertion where the child has no choice, (2) power assertion with some reason mixed in to support the adult's use of power, (3) power assertion with some acknowledgement of the child's perspective that is a little cushioning, (4) persuasion that gives the child choice whether to obey or not, and (5) mere suggestion such that the child does not experience any pressure to comply (Sigel, 1960). You can think of discipline like a physicist: There is a tension between two forces in any discipline encounter, the force to comply and the force to resist (Rollins & Thomas, 1979). Too much force has the negative effects of power assertion, but too little may not get the child to comply. A modest level of control, just enough to get compliance but without overdoing it, may be ideal (T. Smith, 1983).

Previously, you learned how the over-justification effect works in *reward situations*. It also works in discipline encounters. A discipline encounter creates negative emotions in a student, such as uneasiness, anxiety, or anger. The student interprets that negative arousal as either internal or external. Internal interpretations lead to committed compliance or internalization of values from the disciplinarian. "I feel bad because I interrupted my classmates' project." External interpretations lead to situational compliance. "I feel bad because the teacher is going to give me a demerit." This is because when the power of the disciplinarian is highlighted, there is very little dissonance between the student's compliant behavior and the student's original motive for the misbehavior. The student does not need to change attitudes to accommodate the new behavior. "I just did it so I wouldn't get in trouble." "I'm only doing it because I have to." The student interprets compliance as a result of force. The student wants to engage in the forbidden behavior as soon as your oversight is lifted. In contrast, when power is quite subtle, and it is not clear how to justify compliance, students have to adjust their attitude; "I did it because I'm a cooperative student." Power is weak, unclear, or insufficient to justify compliance, so students attribute compliant behavior to personal desires, dispositions, and internal motives. Students interpret their compliance as freely chosen.

This is pretty subtle, but it is powerful. In a classic experiment, researchers had an adult tell kindergarteners that if they played with a forbidden toy she would be "annoyed" (low threat) or she would be "angry" (high threat). Students in the high-threat condition later had a stronger desire to play with the toy compared to students in the low threat condition (Zanna, Lepper, & Abelson, 1973). Students are more likely to internalize your values after they've complied, if there are no strong threats (Lepper, 1983).

❝Shape students' interpretation of their compliance during discipline by using subtle, low levels of force and giving them a positive, internal interpretation of their compliance.❞

Rather than leave it to chance that students will generate an adaptive reason for their compliance, you might want to guide their thinking. *Give them positive reasons for their behavior:* "You did this because you care about your classmates." If plausible, students may adopt your reasoning, as well as a new standard to live up to and evaluate their future behavior against. Attributing their behavior to positive motives gives students a boost in adopting good values and appropriate classroom norms.

Principle 3: Keep the Encounter as Emotionally Positive as Possible

Emotions often run high during discipline encounters, but even in what might seem like mundane discipline encounters ("Lily, please stay in your seat!") the mood or tone of the moment affects compliance. Students in more positive moods are more compliant (Feldman & Klein, 2003). Even something as simple as adding a smile or praise of the student to your directives will increase the student's compliance (Lytton, 1980). For example, smile at Lily as you say "I'm glad to see that Maria enjoys your friendship, but please stay in your seat now." On the other hand, if students feel high anxiety in a discipline encounter, due to threats or negative emotions conveyed, they may (or may not) comply in the short term, but are less likely to comply with you in the long run (Carlsmith, Lepper, & Landauer, 1974). It is appropriate for students to feel some anxiety, remorse, guilt and other negative emotions when they have done wrong, but it should be induced in the context of a warm, supportive relationship in which the student feels safe and liked.

“ Students are more compliant when asked pleasantly in the context of a positive relationship that is characterized by reciprocity.**”**

In addition, the emotional tone of your relationship with the student will affect compliance. Committed compliance (rather than situational compliance) comes from a positive bond between teacher and student. The more positive your relationship, the more receptive the student will be to your directives.

Reciprocity is an important component of compliance. The more you are ready to accept students' attempt to influence you, the more students' will accept attempts from you to influence them (Kochanska, 1997; Maccoby & Martin, 1983). For example, students' may ask you to review material ("Can we go over the quiz?"), or to let them choose assignment topics ("Can I write about snapping turtles instead of toads?"). If learning objectives can still be met, accept students' attempts to influence you whenever possible, as this master teacher did with her high school students:

> *Ms. Gray's students said, "This is boring!" while learning the intricacies of grammar. She asked them if they could make it more interesting. They said "Yes," so Ms. Gray allowed them to split up into small groups to devise lessons on grammar that they then presented to the rest of the class. Their lessons involved graphic montages, rap songs, and skits, which were fun—and they aced the unit quiz!*

Reciprocity is particularly important for fearless, bold, strong-willed students who are not intimidated by power assertion. You've probably had students who, no matter what you threatened, responded with this attitude: "So? Go ahead and throw your biggest threat at me. Been there, done that. Survived it. I'm not threatened by it." Sound familiar? Fearless students are most powerfully affected by a positive relationship with the disciplinarian, and pleasant emotions from the disciplinarian in the moment. That is why fearless students may be very challenging in one teacher's classroom, yet not in another teacher's classroom; their reaction to discipline depends on the tone of the relationship with their teacher. I'll discuss how to set up positive relationships with challenging students in Chapter 5.

Principle 4: Allow Negotiation Whenever Possible

You may want to think of your classroom as a space where you are in control, but that would be self-deceptive. Your students have free will. No matter what level of force you apply, you can never fully make someone else do what you want. Students are free to choose whether to obey or not, and have other options for their behavior. The classroom is a negotiated space; neither you nor your students have total control.

A student can choose to respond to discipline in three distinct ways: *compliance*, *negotiation*, or *defiance*. These responses have very different outcomes for students. Compliance is defined as a positive response to a directive, some degree of acquiescence, or adherence to classroom norms even if a directive has not just been delivered (e.g., not interrupting others).

Noncompliance is pretty common in classrooms. In one study of early childhood and elementary classrooms, 23% of directives were not complied with, and 37% were only partially complied with (Atwater & Morris, 1988). As high as these numbers are, you may have days when they feel like serious underestimates. I have not seen a study on secondary classrooms, but I suspect results would be similar based on my observation of many classrooms. It is very common in secondary classrooms for students to be told not to bother the student next to them but they do anyway; or told to put their phone away, but they do not; or told to quickly get into their workgroup, but they saunter to do something else.

Some teachers may believe that unquestioning, prompt compliance to their directives is the ideal, but is it? You've probably read about Stanley Milgram's famous study of adults who obeyed the command to administer electric shocks to others, even when they screamed (Milgram, 1974). You really do not want to promote mindless obedience to authority figures regardless of the circumstances. Skillful resistance can be healthy for students. Some of the most competent and emotionally healthy students you have are probably not totally compliant, but neither are they defiant. Partial compliance may be acceptable or good enough.

❝Negotiation on the part of students during discipline is not the same as defiance, and can be adaptive for both student and teacher.❞

Asserting one's own wants or needs and negotiating with the teacher during a discipline encounter is not the same thing as defiance, and may indicate healthy social skills on the student's part. Students who say, "I do not want to do that, instead can we . . ." are more likely to have advanced social skills and fewer behavior problems. In a healthy teacher-student relationship, you are able to compromise between the need for compliance, and the student's need for autonomy. Healthy relationships involve give and take. Negotiation, not mindless compliance, indicates the student is able to balance autonomy with classroom norms in a socially acceptable way. I would worry about students who never resist directives. Overcompliance is characteristic of some abused children (Crittenden & DiLalla, 1988).

Defiance is another matter and does not bode well for students. Defiant students are more likely to have negative relationships with parents who use power-assertive discipline. Thus, be careful to distinguish adaptive noncompliance (pleasant negotiation) from maladaptive noncompliance (angry, unreasonable defiance).

How to Put all These Principles Together:
Persistent Persuasion

Teachers are clearly strongly tempted to use power-assertive discipline because most classrooms have some system in place to punish student misbehavior. Yet, research shows that if you want to produce long-term (committed) compliance, internalization of values, and self-control in students, you should avoid discipline that emphasizes power, and instead use induction. When students see their behavior as obviously controlled by an external agent (e.g., a teacher), they attribute their compliance to the threat of punishment rather than to their own internal motivation. One reason teachers use power assertion, despite its costs, is that they do not feel they have a good alternative. In this section, I'll provide that alternative.

You have learned the basic principles of effective discipline: Get compliance, keep power minimal, keep the tone positive, and allow negotiation whenever possible. How do you put this together? How do you ensure that you use enough power to get compliance without overdoing it? How do you keep the power subtle and ambiguous so students can attribute their compliance to their own choice, while you maintain a positive relationship? In particular, how do you do it with students in your classroom who have already adapted to heavy-handed power assertion from their parents or former teachers? This is especially common in low-income communities (Douglas, 2006; Erkman & Rohner, 2006; Evans, 2004; Tang, 2006). How do you get students to respond to discipline without threats?

One approach is to use *persistent persuasion* (a less orthodox term might be "gentle nagging"). Ms. Bailey used it in the opening vignette in this chapter. It involves *repeating induction until you get compliance* (Bergin & Bergin, 1999). That is, you continually repeat a command until the student complies, but without increasing the level of power or using coercion or threats. You deliver the command in a reasonable tone of voice, without increasing the level of hostility. You do not use an "or else" clause (either implicit or explicit). You can restate the command, perhaps slightly altering rationales for compliance each time you repeat, or making offers to help, or responding to the students' negotiation during these repeats. Keep the tone neutral to positive. Remind the student of previous compliance with a similar directive earlier (to create behavioral momentum). Do not quit until the student complies. When you get compliance, attribute the compliance to the child's good nature. The critical pieces are these: (1) There is no coercion; (2) There is no hostility, just firmness or friendliness; and (3) There is no quitting until compliance is achieved. Two examples follow:

In a kindergarten classroom, the group is transitioning from block play to a math activity. Andrew often wants to be the center of attention so he puts his blocks away in exaggerated slow motion, making grunting noises.

> **Ms. Simpson:** *Andrew, please put away your blocks quickly and quietly and join us.*
>
> **Andrew:** *(Continuing his slow-motion antics) It's fun.*
>
> **Ms. Simpson:** *Andrew, you can't make noise now because we are settling into our math activity.*
>
> **Andrew:** *I can because I am.*
>
> **Ms. Simpson:** *You are distracting your friends in the class from learning their math. Come here (motioning Andrew over).*
>
> **Andrew:** *(Ignores teacher)*
>
> **Ms. Simpson:** *Andrew, you need to come join in our lesson or you won't learn what you need to.*
>
> **Andrew:** *I want to stay here (sprawls on the floor).*
>
> **Ms. Simpson:** *I know you do. But you also want to become math-smart like your class friends. Do you remember yesterday, when you named ALL the numbers in our book? It feels good to become math-smart!*
>
> **Andrew:** *OooKayyyy.*
>
> **Ms. Simpson:** *That's right. You are a cooperative friend, Andrew.*

In a high school chemistry class, the students are in small groups finishing a lab that they began two days earlier. Sophia is playing on her iPad instead of doing the lab.

> **Mr. Allen:** *Sophia, please get started on your lab.*
>
> *Sophia rolls her eyes and looks away.*

> ***Mr. Allen:*** *(moving closer to Sophia) This lab is really cool, but you need to get your equipment to participate.*
>
> *Sophia just shrugs.*
>
> ***Mr. Allen:*** *Do you remember how your group was the first to get the correct model in our ion unit?*
>
> ***Sophia*** *(smiling): Yeah.*
>
> ***Mr. Allen:*** *You can do this. Get your equipment and your whiteboard. Mary, can you help her get started?*
>
> ***Sophia:*** *Okay. (moves toward Mary)*
>
> ***Mr. Allen:*** *Thanks, Sophia. You always make good contributions to your team.*

This approach satisfies all the principles of effective discipline. The tone is pleasant, there is no over-justification, so committed compliance and greater self-control are likely to develop. Power is subtle and ambiguous. Because you do not threaten, or highlight consequences, or get angry, the student is free to attribute compliance to personal desire rather than, "The teacher made me." The emotional state does not become overly negative, so you are not creating resentment or jeopardizing your relationship. You can preserve your caring relationships. You can even repair a strained relationship that has been damaged by former punishments, helping you back off any negativity, yet still get compliance so that you do not have to fear losing control in your classroom.

One of the great side effects of this approach is that it lowers your students' expectations for coercive discipline, whereas power-assertive discipline raises it. It lightens the atmosphere for the entire class, not just the target students. In contrast, power-assertive discipline creates a more negative classroom climate. Students are less likely to comply with a teacher they have witnessed being negative and punitive, even if they themselves were not the target of the punishment (Carlsmith et al., 1974).

Persistent persuasion also sets up a structure for negotiation. Teachers who allow students to negotiate may develop greater sensitivity and attunement to their students as they themselves learn to be better listeners. Remember that the goal of discipline is both to get compliance and also to move the child toward greater self-control and prosocial behavior. Persistent persuasion helps to do this.

Does Persistent Persuasion Take Too Much Time?

As you first learn to use it, persistent persuasion feels like it takes a lot of time. Yet, escalating conflicts with power assertion also takes time, but does not have the same payoffs. The beauty of the persistent persuasion form of induction is that it will take less and less time to get compliance as the school year progresses because students *are more likely to obey the second time with less effort and your students will become more self-controlled.* During persistent persuasion you model self-control, because this approach requires self-control.

Taking your time to obtain compliance can be beneficial because it gives the student time to regain self-control, and gives you more time to guide the student's appropriate behavior. You communicate clearly to the target student, and the rest of the class, what behavior is expected and you invite power sharing so that students can decide to adopt your agenda. It turns discipline into a teaching moment, not a punishment.

I've used this technique for many years and have taught it to teachers, principals, and counselors. I've taught counselors in group homes and severely behaviorally handicapped (SBH) classrooms to use it successfully. Usually educators respond with skepticism because they believe that consequences (that vital "or else" clause) must be attached to discipline to attain compliance. Yet, after trying it, teachers enthusiastically support this method because it puts them firmly in control of their classroom while also creating a pleasant classroom climate. Non-coercive discipline really does work. Persistent persuasion has a sound theoretical base and research support (Bergin & Bergin, 1999). It is an empowering approach for teachers who find they do not like themselves or their students during power-assertive discipline. An elementary teacher told me she liked herself better while using persistent persuasion. It was liberating to her; she felt in control, while doing something positive for her students. A high school teacher told how she changed her discipline approach to persistent persuasion:

I had several students with behavior problems in one of my classes. I was often frustrated because they needed constant attention to stay on task, and too little learning was occurring. I decided to use persistent persuasion. Every time the students were off-task, I would move near them and calmly restate the directive, in as positive a way as possible, until they complied. This happened often at first, and they acted like I was crazy, but they would comply. After several days, they would comply as soon as I moved near them because they figured out that I wasn't going to leave until they did what I asked. I have to admit that I am surprised, but it works! After a few months there has been a vast improvement in time-on-task, and we actually have good class discussions without off-task antics.

You may choose to use a different approach if you are not comfortable with persistent persuasion. However, make sure that it aligns with the principles of effective discipline discussed above.

Is Discipline Always Necessary?

Discipline is not always necessary. Many adults think that if you do not punish misbehavior, students are getting away with something. Yet, if a child harms another, and clearly feels guilty and tries to make reparation, the most effective approach may be to praise and acknowledge the reparation attempt.

Sometimes misbehavior is not because students do not want to behave, but rather because they lack a skill or are not sure what is expected of them. That is, they may not be able to follow the lesson, they may not know how to organize themselves or their work, or they may not have the right social skills. When this is the case, it is better to teach the missing skill than to discipline a student.

Ask "Why?" First

One way to determine whether discipline is necessary or not is to ask, "Why?" Before jumping into a discipline episode ask, "What is going on?" "Why did you do that?" Ask students what is motivating their misbehavior so that you can help them find a more productive solution.

A constructive approach to discipline for recurring misbehavior is called *collaborative and proactive solutions* (Greene, 2011). It involves three steps:

1. You express empathy for the errant student. "Help me understand . . . ." "Why did you do that?" You listen without criticism. You are simply trying to understand with an open heart and mind.

2. You express your concerns and how you think others might be affected (victim-centered induction comes in here).

3. You invite the errant student to come up with solutions that he or she can own and realistically enact. You might have to guide this a little to help the student think through outcomes of various solutions.

Like persistent persuasion, this approach helps you maintain a positive relationship while also finding genuine solutions to recurring misbehavior.

Be Intentional about Discipline

Students' prosocial behavior is influenced both by how they are disciplined and what they are disciplined for. You communicate core values to your students during discipline encounters based on what you become upset about. If you become upset about unkind or immoral behavior, you are communicating that these values are important. If you do not become upset about such behavior, but you do become upset about lining up properly, or horseplay in the classroom, you are communicating that compliance with social convention is more important than kindness or morality. Think about this situation in a school library.

> *Two students, Crystal and Junie, were arguing because both wanted the same book from the library. The teacher settled the dispute, with Junie getting the book. Crystal was angry and went to Junie to whisper "I'm gonna kill you." in her ear. When an observer told the teacher, she just brushed it off saying "Crystal is an only child and spoiled; she'll get over it."*

Junie is a compliant, prosocial child who did not deserve to be bullied like this. What values did the teacher communicate to Crystal, Junie, and all the other students who may have been aware of the behavior? Would you expect prosocial or aggressive behavior to increase in this classroom?

You have heard the phrase, "Choose your battles carefully." This teacher should have chosen to fight the battle to stop bullying. Other battles should be abandoned if they are not important, such as students keeping both feet on the ground while sitting at a desk. One master teacher who was just learning to use peristent persuasion reported that she realized that she didn't have a good rationale for asking a student to do what she wanted as she began to use perisistent persuasion, so she gave up the command. Using persistent persuasion helped her become more thoughtful about whether discipline was really necessary and become more judicious in her directives. As a result, her class became more cooperative and helpful.

Does Induction Discipline Promote Prosocial Behavior?

At the beginning of the chapter I said that the way you discipline your students may be the most powerful approach to increasing their prosocial behavior. Research on parenting robustly shows that parents who use induction are more likely to have children who are prosocial, from young children to adolescents (Kerr, Lopez, Olson, & Sameroff, 2004; Kochanska, Koenig, Barry, Kim, & Yoon, 2010; Krevans & Gibbs, 1996; Padilla-Walker, Carlo, Christensen, & Yorgason, 2012; Paulussen-Hoogeboom, Stams, Hermanns, & Peetsma, 2007). In one of my studies, I found this to be true even with toddlers who are not yet talking (Bergin, 1987). That is, I found that mothers who would reason with their 2-year-old during a discipline encounter had children who were more compliant and prosocial.

One of my doctoral students set out to see if prosocial behavior could be increased in early childhood classrooms just by increasing teachers' use of induction. She conducted an experiment in which she trained teachers to use induction when students misbehaved. The training was fairly simple; she explained to the teachers what induction is and how to use it (just as I've explained in this chapter), and then she visited each teacher once a week for a few weeks to discuss specific episodes in which the teacher used induction (something you could do with colleagues). After a mere seven weeks, the students in those teachers' classes increased in prosocial behavior a whopping 140% (Ramaswamy & Bergin, 2009). Conduct your own experiment in your classroom, and see whether your students increase in prosocial behavior as you emphasize induction more.

Why Does Induction Promote Prosocial Behavior?

There are several reasons that induction increases prosocial behavior in students. The first two reasons I've already discussed. First, in contrast to other forms of discipline, induction is more likely to lead a student to internalize your values. Second, induction promotes self-control, rather than other-control, in students. As a result, students disciplined with induction are more likely to obey rules even when no authority figure is standing over them (Bergin & Bergin, 1999).

A third reason is that induction gives students information they need to guide future behavior in similar situations. As adults we sometimes expect that students know why they should not be doing something, but they do not always. In contrast, just saying "No!" or "Stop that!" or "I'm going to have to move your seat" does not give students information to guide their future behavior. A benefit of using induction in a group setting is that every student within earshot learns the same information as the target student.

Fourth, induction communicates *caring* and respect for students because you are bothering to take the time to reason with them. You are modeling prosocial behavior in the discipline encounter. As you communicate respect, you generate reciprocal respect and give your discipline more legitimacy in students' minds. Recall that in my study I found that toddlers become more prosocial when their mothers use induction rather than other forms of discipline. How is it possible that reasoning with toddlers would lead to greater prosocial behavior before they have the language skills to fully understand what you are talking about? I suspect the reason is that they feel respected and cared for when their parents use such discipline, which motivates them to imitate their parents.

Fifth, induction gives you space to shape students' moral disposition during discipline encounters. It allows you to communicate that you assume the best possible motive, rather than the worst possible motivate, of the misbehaving student: "Eli, I know you didn't mean to bother John." It gives you space to listen to and develop empathy for the student's perspective. It gives you space to make a quick comment of attribution: "Eli, you are a caring classmate!" when students make reparation. These kinds of statements communicate to students that you believe in their best possible selves. These are brief, simple statements that can be powerful in shaping a moral identity in students. Students try hard to live up to their teachers' expectations about their goodness.

I want to close this chapter with a vitally important message: *Victim-oriented induction is particularly powerful in promoting prosocial behavior because it helps students come to value others' well-being.* It shifts their focus from self to other, which is what prosocial behavior is all about. Furthermore, when you suggest to students how to make reparation when they have harmed another you are helping them practice prosocial behavior and learn to manage guilt in productive ways. In contrast, power assertion and psychological control turn students' attention to the self because these discipline approaches arouse resentment and anxiety.

NOTE ABOUT AGGRESSIVE STUDENTS

One high school teacher said she doesn't think there is any profession that has to deal with more aggression than a secondary teacher in an urban setting, except police officers. Her students have criminal records and some have been involved in robberies, stealing cars, breaking and entering homes, and even killing a store owner. Yet, aggression is not limited to secondary students. Although the aggression of older students can be more serious because it reaches criminal levels, aggression can begin very young. In fact, another preschool teacher reported that her students tell her "shut the f--- up" and "go to h---." In addition, aggression is not limited to urban settings. Many students in small towns live with grandparents because their parents are incarcerated for domestic violence and drug abuse. I've worked for over 15 years with impoverished, substance-abusing families and know the myriad of challenges children in such families face. How can you help such students?

You've learned that one of the most powerful ways you increase your students' prosocial behavior is to use effective discipline. Similarly, one of the most powerful ways you reduce your students' aggression is to use effective discipline. In fact, research on effective therapy for students with serious behavior problems emphasizes training parents to use positive, effective discipline, which has the added benefit of reducing parents' stress levels (Kazdin, 1993; Reid, 1993).

The principles you have learned in this chapter are different from some famous anti-bullying programs that are quite controlling and emphasize sanctions for misbehavior (Olweus, 1993). That is, they are power assertive. Such anti-bullying programs have not been terribly successful (Merrell, Guelderner, Ross, & Isava, 2008; D. Smith, Schneider, Smith, & Ananiadou, 2004). However, a study of several hundred junior high students found that when teachers used practices that help students internalize prosocial values, the students came to value being more considerate towards classmates and there was *less bullying* (Roth, Kanat-Maymon, & Bibi, 2011). Figure 3.2 shows the outcomes (and their effect sizes) in this study.

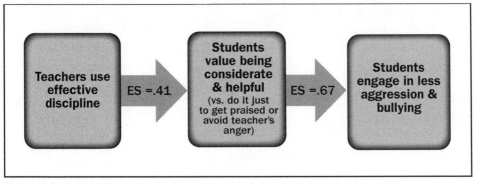

Figure 3.2 Student Outcomes Linked to Teacher's Discipline Approach

What did the teachers do in this study? They listened to students' perspectives, minimized power assertiveness, and gave students reasons for their directives. Teachers explained to students why it is important to be considerate to each other and how a lack of consideration hurts others. In other words, they used induction, especially victim-centered induction.

FOR REFLECTION AND DISCUSSION

Do I look for issues of hunger or sleep, or skill deficit, before I assume my student does not want to obey? Think of a specific time when this was the case. How did you handle the situation? What, if anything, would you do differently now?

Think of the last two discipline encounters you were involved in.

- What was your goal? What was the student's goal?
- Did the situation comply with the principles of effective discipline (i.e., did you get compliance, was power minimal, was the tone positive, did you accept negotiation)? Why or why not?
- At the end of the discipline encounter, did the student learn to be more prosocial and more self-controlled?

Are you using operant conditioning effectively in your classroom?

What is the size of the discipline gap in your school? What can you (and your Peer Learning Community or department) do to help narrow this gap?

CHAPTER 4

Practice, Modeling, and Reinforcement Build Prosocial Habits

In Mrs. Haynie's 3rd grade classroom, students are working on math. If they finish their required math work, they can do "challenge" problems. One student shouts to another, "Kyle, Kyle, we got them all right on the first try!" Kyle promptly looks up from his work and says, "Good job!" Throughout the day, Mrs. Haynie encourages her students to express appreciation for and praise one another. She tells them to give their neighbor a high-five when they answer math problems correctly.

In a middle school classroom, Mr. Oberbeck has his students clap anytime a classmate presents a book report to the class, or state in chorus, "Thank you, Abby."

Both of these teachers were giving their students opportunities to practice an important prosocial behavior; encouraging others. You'll learn about the role of *practice* in building prosocial habits in this chapter. You'll also learn about the role of *modeling* and *exhorting* in building students' prosocial habits. Finally, you'll learn about the role of *praise*, with particular emphasis on when praise is helpful or harmful.

Does Practice Increase Prosocial Behavior?

Much of our daily behavior is driven by habits that seem to operate on autopilot, without conscious mental effort. These habits are the result of many, many repetitions of specific behaviors that eventually form our identity and character, as in this adage:

> *"Watch your thoughts for they become words. Watch your words for they become actions. Watch your actions for they become habits. Watch your habits, for they become your character." (Quote ascribed to Margaret Thatcher, Frank Outlaw, and various other people)*

You intuitively know this because you put a lot of effort into training students to develop prosocial behaviors such as "Say thank you," "Wait your turn," and "Help your neighbor," in the hope that these will become well-ingrained habits. Operating from habit is good, if those habits are prosocial.

One mantra of psychology is, "The best predictor of future behavior is past behavior." Experiments have confirmed this because when students are given the opportunity to behave prosocially once, they are more likely to do it again (Chernyak & Kushnir, 2013). Thus, your students are likely to become more prosocial over time if you give them opportunity to practice prosocial behavior (Mussen & Eisenberg, 2001). In one of my studies, I found this to be true of toddlers (Bergin, 1987). That is, the more their parents gave them opportunity to practice prosocial behavior (e.g., letting them "help" load the dishwasher) the more prosocial the children became. You might think this makes sense for toddlers who are just learning social behaviors, but what about teenagers? Actually, adolescence is a window of opportunity for developing prosocial habits and scripts because teenagers are highly motivated by social and emotional events that accompany prosocial behavior, such as being welcomed into a group, being admired, and establishing a positive image.

There are several ways you can give your students opportunity to practice prosocial behavior. One is to promote students' praising and encouraging one another as a natural part of ongoing classroom activities, as both Mrs. Haynie and Mr. Oberbeck did. Another approach is taken by a grassroots movement called the "Great Kindness Challenge." Students are given a checklist of simple, kind acts they can do at school. They are encouraged to try to complete them all in a week. The goal is to help students practice kindness, increase consciousness of prosocial behavior, and create a happier school atmosphere. I'll discuss a few other approaches next.

Give Your Students Opportunities to Work Together

You can give your students *opportunity* to work together by the way you design seating in your classroom. Seating arrangements determine whether students are able to interact and cooperate during class. Students come to like others they sit near (proximity fosters friendships) and students who are seated at the center of the room come to be liked better (Neal, Neal, & Cappella, 2014; van den Berg & Cillessen, 2015). In fact, placing a rejected student next to a well-liked student typically results in the rejected student becoming better liked over the next few months. So be deliberate about your seating arrangements from the perspective of promoting prosocial behavior.

You can also give your students opportunities to work together by assigning group projects. Group work can help students learn cooperation and establish good peer relationships; in addition, they learn content, become better critical thinkers, feel more motivated, and develop communication skills (Friedlaender, Burns, Lewis-Charp, Cook-Harvey, & Darling-Hammond, 2014; Igel, 2015; Roseth, Johnson, & Johnson, 2008). Students report liking one another better during cooperative learning (Gillies, 2003). However, group work can be orchestrated on a continuum from quite poorly to very well. You've probably had great experiences and pitiful experiences with it. There is considerable research on how to tip the scale to the "great" side. Briefly, key guidelines are (Emmer & Gerwels, 2002; Fuchs et al., 2000; Kuhn, 2015; Watkins & Wentzel, 2008):

1. Hold both individuals and groups accountable.

2. Actively monitor the groups and make sure each student has a role.

3. Use groups of two to five students for optimal collaboration and discussion.

4. Use tasks that are open-ended or loosely-structured.

5. Train students to *explain the answer to each other* rather than just state the correct answer.

This last guideline is important. In one study of 9- to 13-year-olds, high-achieving prosocial girls were trained to be good group-work partners; specifically they were trained to validate and elaborate on their partners' comments (instead of just saying, "No, that's not right"), to give positive feedback, and to talk aloud while they were problem-solving. Then they were paired in group work with boys who had a history of behavior problems during group work—the boys had ADHD, were domineering, and irritated peers. The boys' behavior changed as they learned to actively listen and cooperate with these trained prosocial partners (Watkins & Wentzel, 2008).

You cannot just assume that your students already have the skills to collaborate effectively. Roughly one third of elementary students have sufficient skills, but the rest may not (Ladd et al., 2014). Not surprisingly, classmates prefer to work with the students who already have these skills. Thus, many students will need your support to manage conflict, behave prosocially (e.g., compliment and encourage others), control their emotions, and see others' perspectives so that they can be productive during group work, which, in turn, will help them become even more prosocial. Group work then becomes an upwardly spiraling process for enhancing students' prosocial behavior. As you promote more prosocial behavior in general in your class, that will translate into more effective group work, which will translate into more prosocial behavior.

Help Your Students Feel Responsible for Each Other and Accept Offers of Help

You may have noticed that your students do not help each other if someone else is available to help, but if they are the only ones present, they typically respond promptly to help others (Plötner, Over, Carpenter, & Tomasello, 2015). This is partly because teachers inadvertently train students not to be helpful.

Teachers do this either by responding so swiftly that classmates cannot do anything but watch or by criticizing students for going to the aid of another without permission, as happened in this classroom:

> *In an elementary classroom, the students were working in centers when the teacher asked Zachary to clean off the dry erase board. One of the students, Cooper, overheard and jumped up to help. The teacher said "It's not your turn to be the teacher's helper. Zachary is my helper this week. If you try to take his job, I will have to put you in the Safe Seat."*

I have seen teachers tell students, "Doug can pick up his own pencils. I do not want everyone out of their seats helping" even if these same teachers have a list of classroom rules posted on the wall that includes "Help others." In one study, researchers asked students why they do not always help classmates. The students said they are not supposed to do anything when adults are available to help (Caplan & Hay, 1989).

You can counter these kinds of experiences by telling your students that they are responsible for helping one another in your classroom, and by accepting their offers of help (and praising them in the process). A secondary teacher said he is going to stop ignoring "teachable moments" when he could help students be more prosocial toward each other. An elementary teacher decided to build this into her daily routine. She said she used to begin each morning with a class meeting in which students told something about themselves—a self-focused activity. Now she has them talk about someone else, and what they can do to help each other out. A middle-school teacher said:

> *When I taught 1st grade, if someone dropped pencils, lots of classmates would quickly jump in to help pick them up. I could ask for volunteers to help me clean up and almost all would scurry to be the best helper. But in my 6th grade class, if I*

> *ask the same thing, only one or two students will help, and if someone drops pencils, usually no one helps. I realized that I was responsible. I had trained my students to inhibit their impulses to help. I would tell them that it was my job to take care of things. I thought I was doing them a favor because so many of my students have difficult home lives where they take care of themselves or their siblings. But now I realize I was depriving them of the opportunity to be prosocial at school and create a caring classroom.*

You can also give students' opportunity to practice prosocial behavior by assigning them chores that benefit others in the classroom or school. For example, in a 3rd grade classroom the students were practicing typing on a computer keyboard. One student helped everyone use the hand sanitizer, two others checked classmate's posture and gave them helpful feedback, another was the door holder as the class passed through the door, another was the official "reporter" who was to tell the homeroom teacher what they had done in the computer class. For another example, a high school teacher had her students quickly clean up the classroom at the end of class each day. Initially, students groaned about it, but before long they began to do it of their own accord. You can also assign students to be *shoulder partners* who help and check each other's work. Of course there have to be some limits. One middle school science teacher told her students, "Help your neighbor if your conversation is about sources of heat. If it is about Oreos or something else, I will ask you not to talk to your neighbor."

You can also provide opportunities to serve others through a structured program in your school, such as reading buddies, tutoring other students within the school, or programs for the community, such as cleanups and food drives. When structured opportunities for prosocial behavior involve the community, it is referred to as *service learning*.

Provide Service Learning

Community service projects are more common in secondary than elementary schools, where about half of students do some kind of volunteer service (Hart, Donnelly, Youniss, & Atkins, 2007). The students who do more volunteer work in the community tend to also be the ones who are more prosocial in their classrooms. They also tend to have higher GPAs, be religious, and be more sociable compared to other students. Research shows that students' participation in community service predicts many positive outcomes, such as greater self-esteem, responsibility, acceptance of others, school bonding, moral reasoning, commitment to the community and less delinquency (Hart et al., 2007; van Goethem, van Hoof, Orobio de Castro, Van Aken, & Hart, 2014).

Which causes which? That is, does being *good* students cause them to engage in more community service, or does engaging in community service cause students to be good? It is not entirely clear, but based on the latter assumption many high schools and organizations, like the National Honor Society, require students to participate in community service. Does forcing students to serve their communities have the same benefits as voluntary service? Research suggests it might under some conditions, but not always. That is, forcing students into community service sometimes backfires, creating greater disengagement from school, but sometimes it is beneficial for students (Hart et al., 2007; Planty, Bozick, & Regnier, 2006; Wilson, 2012). Community service is beneficial, whether voluntary or mandatory, when it is a high-quality experience.

What constitutes a *high-quality experience*? It has as many of these seven attributes as possible (van Goethem et al., 2014; Youniss, McLellan, Su, & Yates, 1999):

1. Meets the real needs of the receivers

2. Is not anonymous, but rather students get to interact with the receivers

3. Is ongoing rather than a single-exposure experience

4. Stretches students' skills with real responsibilities

5. Presents choices for which activities students will participate in

6. Provides opportunity for students to develop relationships

with workers at the service site and to work as part of a group, rather than alone

7. Provides opportunity to debrief and discuss the experience as a group

Students need opportunity to practice being prosocial toward others and to feel responsible for the well-being of classmates and others in their community. Nel Noddings, a former math teacher, middle school principal, and my professor at Stanford, wrote a wonderful book called *Caring*, in which she argues that students should be given the opportunity to practice caring for each other at school (Noddings, 1992). Research supports her view: Prosocial behavior will become a habit if students are given the opportunity to practice their prosocial behavior repeatedly. Practice coupled with seeing models of prosocial behavior may be especially effective (Rushton, 1982), so let's discuss the role of models next.

Do Models Increase Prosocial Behavior?

In Chapter 3, you learned about behaviorism. According to strict behaviorism your behavior is shaped entirely by reinforcement. Yet, in his famous Bobo doll experiments[8] Albert Bandura found that children learn from watching other people get reinforced for behavior, without getting reinforced themselves. He called this vicarious reinforcement. Bandura developed a *social-cognitive theory* that was an outgrowth and rebuttal to strict behaviorism of the B. F. Skinner variety. He pointed out that thoughts drive much of behavior, thoughts such as beliefs about your ability to be prosocial and your values. A key influence on those thoughts are other people who serve as models of behavior.

Your students learn from the models around them, whether they are real people or fictional characters in movies and books. You can increase your students' prosocial behavior by drawing their attention to the prosocial behavior of others: "Raul, that was thoughtful of you to sharpen your team's pencils." When they see firsthand, or hear of, others' prosocial behavior it will motivate them to follow the models' example (Schnall, Roper, & Fessler, 2010). They will also follow your lead if you model kind, polite behavior as a caring teacher. The effect of modeling is greater when the teacher has an especially warm relationship with the student (Yarrow, Scott, & Waxler, 1973). Warmth increases students' motivation to imitate you.

“Point out models of prosocial behavior, especially models that are similar to your students”

It may be particularly effective to point out the prosocial behavior of other students. This is because models are more potent when they are similar to one's self, and when there are multiple models. For example, in a study of diverse middle schools, students who reported their classmates as engaging in more prosocial behaviors (e.g., standing up for others, helping others, resolving fights) were more prosocial themselves (Spivak, White, Juvonen, & Graham, 2015). In another study, elementary students who interacted more with prosocial peers in their classroom become more helpful and cooperative across the school year (Molano, Jones, & Willett, 2014). They also increased academic achievement! Thus, students who see classmates model prosocial behavior are more likely to behave prosocially.

Social cognitive theory has an explanation for this. When prosocial models are similar to themselves, your students will develop greater self-efficacy for behaving prosocially. Self-efficacy is a belief that you can accomplish a behavior yourself; it is a judgment about your own competence that powerfully affects your behavior. If you have high self-efficacy for prosocial behavior (e.g., feel you can successfully help someone) you will engage in more of it. *Multiple models* are more effective than a single model because they increase the likelihood that students will see at least someone similar to themselves. For example, if a new student entered Mr. Oberbeck's class in the opening vignette, he might feel too insecure to clap for or thank classmates for their presentations, but once he sees several other students do it, he is more likely to engage in the prosocial behavior as well, and become more encouraging or affirming of others in general.

Can You Exhort Students into Kindness?

In Chapter 3, you learned that induction is powerful in promoting prosocial behavior. Induction is form of reasoning with students during discipline in which you explain why directives or rules should be obeyed, which gives them information about your values so that they can begin to share in those values. Does it follow that exhorting students to behave more prosocially is also powerful in promoting prosocial behavior? It depends.

Adults exhort students to behave prosocially in many forums: at school, at church, in sports, and at home. Teachers often do this through posters on the wall that espouse prosocial behavior, or they post classroom rules about being kind and polite. Or they have didactic lessons that focus on the values of sharing, helping, cooperating, respecting, waiting turns, and so forth. Experimental studies have found that when students are prodded, encouraged, or commanded to help, they do not necessarily increase in helpfulness. However, *exhortation that is combined with modeling and empathy training is effective* (Eisenberg-berg & Geisheker, 1979; Grusec, 1982; Warneken & Tomasello, 2012). Table 4.1 provides an example to help you understand this. Again, the differences in these statements are subtle but powerful. Exhortation provides information about what behavior is appropriate and inappropriate. Empathy-focused exhortation provides the same information, but also gives the student a reason for being prosocial and focuses the student on the feelings of the recipient. Can you see the relationship to victim-centered induction from Chapter 3? If you exhort your students to behave prosocially, be sure to combine the exhortation with *empathy training* and *prosocial modeling* to maximize its effectiveness.

Table 4.1 Empathy Training and Exhortation Examples

Empathy Training	(a) It would make him happy if you shared. (b) He'd be so sad if you didn't share.
Exhortation	Sharing is the right thing to do.
Exhortation + Empathy Training	Sharing is the right thing to do because it makes him happy.

Another way that you communicate prosocial values is by what you choose to discipline students about. You tend to get angry and expend effort to correct misbehavior that violates core values, whereas you get less emotional and put less effort into correcting misbehavior that does not violate core values. Recall in Chapter 1 the father who took time off work to go to his son's school to discipline the boy for lying to his teacher about taking home a note. That was a powerful lesson from the father about the value of honesty. The boy is not likely to easily forget that lesson, but he could easily forget hours of exhortations about honesty.

As a teacher you similarly communicate your values during discipline encounters. Recall from Chapter 3 the example of the two girls who wanted the same book from the library. Crystal threatened Junie after the teacher gave the book to Junie. The teacher brushed off Crystal's bullying, doing nothing about it. What value did the teacher communicate? That bullying is "no big deal" to her. In contrast, imagine that the teacher got after Crystal for stepping out of line on the way back to the classroom. The teacher would be communicating that staying in line is more important than treating others with kindness. Students process these messages deeply. Crystal already knows that bullying is okay in this teacher's classroom. Ironically, I suspect that if you asked this teacher what she valued, she would say she values kindness and abhors bullying. Yet, her disciplining behavior sends the opposite message to her students. You communicate your values to students everyday by demonstrating which behaviors you are willing to take the time to support or eliminate.

❝ When exhortations are combined with empathy training by an adult who espouses and acts on prosocial behavior, they are more effective in promoting prosocial behavior.**❞**

Become Aware of the Values You Communicate

You may not even be fully aware of your values. One exercise that makes this clear is to answer the question, "What behavior would you do *anything* you could to prevent your child from doing?" When I ask this in my university classes, most answers are dropping out of school, drugs, murder, theft, and unwanted pregnancy. But some people respond with more mundane behaviors, such as telling lies or bullying others. You can turn this question around and ask, "What behaviors are you willing to expend great effort to get your child to engage in?" Would it be expressing gratitude, helping a neighbor, or telling the truth?

Try another exercise. If you had to choose whether your own child was kind or smart, which would you choose? (No cheating by saying you want both. Forcing a choice helps you clarify values.) In one study, parents of 5th graders were asked to select which of the following values were the three most important to them.

1. Respecting one's parents

2. Having a good sense of humor

3. Putting work before play

4. Following rules and regulations

5. Having confidence in oneself

6. Attending church regularly

7. Showing consideration of other people's feelings

8. Going out of one's way to help other people

9. Trying one's best in everything one does

Which three would you rank as most important? Students were more likely to stand up for others and to be careful not to hurt other's feelings if their parents ranked prosocial behavior (numbers 7 and 8) as most important (M. Hoffman, 1975).

Your principal's values matter too. Students who are in schools where principals value prosocial behavior are more likely to value prosocial behavior as well.[9] How might principals' values influence students' values? Research suggests that it may be through school climate. That is, principals who value benevolence toward others tend to foster a supportive school climate. Over time, students in those schools come to value benevolence and behave in a more supportive way toward others. The effect is small, but meaningful (Berson & Oreg, 2016). This suggests that students' values are malleable, so be thoughtful about what values you convey.

Practice What You Preach by Showing that You Care

Adults can espouse *prosocial values* but then behave in a way that contradicts those values, such as using harsh discipline. In these situations, students typically reject the adults' values. My research and that of others have found that parents who hold prosocial values and are warm have children who are more prosocial than their peers (Bergin, 1987). Students are more motivated to accept their parents' values when they have a positive, secure relationship with their parents. The combination of holding prosocial values while also behaving in a kind way toward the child is more powerful than doing either in isolation. Research suggests the same is true for teachers. Just as with modeling, exhorting is more effective in the context of a warm teacher-student relationship, in which you graciously support students' offers of help. When students feel that their teacher cares about them, they behave more prosocially. What makes students feel cared for? That is the subject of the next chapter.

In summary, your students can develop prosocial habits through practice, by witnessing models, and by having others around them espouse prosocial values in word and deed. Another powerful tool you can use to help your students develop prosocial habits is reinforcement. In Chapter 3, you learned about behaviorism, one of the grand theories of human development. The basic premise is that as students come to pair reinforcement or punishment with a specific behavior, they will increase or decrease the behavior. This raises the question of whether you should use reinforcement in your classroom to increase prosocial behavior. Let's see what the research says.

Should You Reinforce Prosocial Behavior?

Behaviorism does work—on rats, pigeons, dogs, and even spouses. Behavior that is reinforced is repeated. Thus, you might assume that rewarding students for engaging in prosocial behavior would increase it. Research suggests it does. On the other hand, as you learned in Chapter 3, there is a cost to heavy-handed behavior modification or power-assertive control of students, thanks in part to the over-justification effect. Thus, you might also assume that rewarding students for engaging in prosocial behavior would decrease it. Research suggests it does. This seeming paradox occurs because effects are different for tangible versus social reinforcers.

Avoid Tangible Rewards

An elementary school had a school-wide program designed to support more positive behavior. One student, Trisha, was a highly social 4th grader who talked to her classmates during lessons. Her teacher had been unable to get her to stop, so she implemented behaviorism. She gave Trisha a "Daily Progress Report" and throughout the day would give Trisha points for "good behavior." After accumulating daily points, Trisha would earn a small reward (e.g., a pencil or snack). This worked for a short time. Then, Trisha's daily points dropped off, and she began whispering to her classmates. When asked why she wasn't continuing to earn her rewards, Trisha shrugged and said she wanted a better reward. So the teacher offered her movie tickets. Eventually, this reward also was no longer attractive enough. (adapted from Crone, Hawken, & Horner, 2015)

Trisha's story highlights some of the problems with giving students tangible rewards in order to shape their behavior. Despite these problems, some teachers try to increase students' prosocial behavior by giving them tangible rewards, such as stickers, prizes, or gold cards. This seems like a reasonable thing to do, except that in Chapter 3 you learned that tangible rewards can *undermine* behavior that students are already somewhat motivated to engage in.[10] This is true of prosocial behavior (A. Martin & Olson, 2015) although material rewards may work in the short-run. Students are more likely to be prosocial when they are rewarded for doing so in the moment. However, they are *less* likely to engage in prosocial behavior in the *long run* if they are rewarded (Eisenberg, VanSchyndel, & Spinrad, 2016). For example, in one study when 3rd graders were given tangible rewards for tutoring 1st graders, they were less willing to tutor later, and their tutoring was more tense and hostile (Szynal-Brown & Morgan, 1983). Similarly, in another study, some 6- to 12-year-olds who helped others were given a small toy for helping, and others were not. Those who had been rewarded were less likely to help when given another opportunity to be helpful (Fabes, Fultz, Eisenberg, May-Plumlee, & Christopher, 1989). Interestingly, the negative effect of rewards was strongest for students whose parents frequently used rewards to control their children's behavior. Research has found similar results for adolescents (Carlo et al., 2016). In summary, giving students tangible rewards for prosocial behavior can decrease their helpfulness over time.

Is the situation different for young students? That is, do they need rewards in order to learn to behave prosocially? Research suggests that sometimes tangible rewards (e.g., a gold star) can increase prosocial behavior among young children in the short run, but reduces it over the long run (Fabes et al., 1989; Honig & Pollack, 1990). Recall from Chapter 1 that babies enter the world with a disposition to be benevolent toward others. Toddlers are quite willing to share and to help others with no promise of reward and even at some personal cost, such as having to leave an attractive toy and climb over obstacles (Hay, Caplan, Castle, & Stimson, 1991; Warneken & Tomasello, 2008). Measures of their pupils, which become dilated when they see others in need, suggest that they are physiologically aroused, and that arousal subsides when they have helped others, or they see someone else has helped the other (Hepach, Vaish, Grossmann, & Tomasello, 2016). Young children are not simply motivated by social interaction, or getting credit for helping, or reward, but by the desire to see that others are helped (Hepach, 2017). However, when toddlers are given tangible rewards for helping, they tend to help *less* later, compared to toddlers who are not rewarded, just like older students. For example, in one study, 20-month-olds saw a strange adult drop a pen or paper and try, unsuccessfully, to reach for it. Almost all (78%) toddlers spontaneously helped. The adult (an actor) reacted in one of three ways: (1) gave a toy to the child (reward), (2) praised the child ("Thank you, Peter, that's really nice!") or (3) gave no response. Later, when help was needed again, toddlers who received either praise or no response continued to help at a high rate, but those who received a reward were only half as likely to be helpful. Similarly, in another study, 3-year-olds were either rewarded (given an eraser), praised, or given no response for sharing marbles and stickers. Those who received rewards were later less prosocial (Ulber, Hamann, & Tomasello, 2016). In these studies, rewards undermined prosocial behavior. These were quick, experimental demonstrations of the effect of reward in a laboratory setting. Imagine what the cumulative effect might be if students are rewarded regularly over long periods of time for good behavior. You might see an even greater drop in prosocial behavior. Perhaps you have seen this cumulative effect in your school.

" Use of tangible rewards may undermine students' intrinsic motivation to behave prosocially, including very young children. This may be due to the over-justification effect."

Why would rewards undermine motivation to behave prosocially? Your students can behave prosocially either because kind acts are inherently rewarding (e.g., you feel good when you make others' happy), or for some external purpose (e.g., getting a good behavior point on the class chart). If their prosocial behavior is freely chosen, students interpret their behavior as "I shared, so I must be the kind of person who likes to share" (Chernyak & Kushnir, 2013). If an external purpose is obvious and emphasized, then students may attribute their motive for behaving prosocially to the external purpose (an outside force) as opposed to wanting to help others (an internal force). The external purpose supplants the original intrinsic motivation, and then when the reward is withdrawn the prosocial behavior stops. This is the over-justification effect in a nutshell. Giving students a reward creates a new extrinsic motivation to behave prosocially, causing the internal motive to be prosocial to fade. Your students are not necessarily conscious of this effect, nor does it require the high-level abstract reasoning of older children; the effect occurs for toddlers.

In addition to the over-justification effect, some researchers also believe that tangible rewards may undermine other motives to behave prosocially, such as the motive to maintain a happy mood (behaving prosocially makes you feel happier), or to derive satisfaction from making someone else feel happy, or to cement a relationship with the recipient (A. Martin & Olson, 2015). Whether this is correct or not, at the very least research indicates that *rewards are not necessary to get typical students to behave in a prosocial way towards others*. Students' prosocial behavior is motivated by something other than tangible rewards. A key takeaway is that it is better to facilitate the natural intrinsic motivation students have to be prosocial. If you use superfluous material rewards they may have harmful effects on prosocial behavior, undermining your students' motivation and feelings of autonomy (Ulber et al., 2016).

Praise Prosocial Behavior

In contrast to tangible rewards, praise—a social reward—usually increases prosocial behavior. Why? Praise is subtle. It does not have to be a big deal; a nod, smile, or thumbs-up is enough. This subtlety minimizes the power or coercive component of your interaction with students, leaving the students free to attribute their good behavior to their own volition. Many parents, but not all, thank and praise their children for helping, so many parents seem to know this intuitively (A. Dahl, 2015; Recchia, Wainryb, Bourne, & Pasupathi, 2014). Adolescents whose parents do this tend to be more prosocial (Carlo et al., 2016). You might assume that teachers praise students a great deal, but studies have found that praise is not actually used often or efficiently in most classrooms (Hardman & Smith, 2003). It is easy to get caught up in trying to contain misbehavior rather than praising good behavior (Maag, 2001).

❝ Avoid tangible rewards, but occasionally use social rewards like praise, a nod, or a smile of affirmation.❞

In Chapter 3, I introduced you to a study by one of my former doctoral students who found that when teachers were trained to use induction, their students dramatically increased in prosocial behavior (Ramaswamy & Bergin, 2009). She also trained some of the teachers to use social reinforcement, such as praise, a smile, or a pat on the back. Using the same techniques to teach social reinforcement as she used to teach induction—explaining what it is, giving some examples, and then visiting the teachers a few times to discuss how specific episodes went—she found after just 7 weeks that prosocial behavior almost doubled (i.e., increased 87%) in the classrooms of teachers who were trained to use social reinforcement. This increase was not as large as in the classrooms of teachers who learned to use induction (i.e., increased 144%), but it was a significant increase.

One cautionary note from this study is that teachers who tried to use both induction and reinforcement at the same time had the smallest increase in prosocial behavior among their students (although there was an increase over the comparison group). That is, when they tried two new approaches simultaneously, they were unable to do either with power. This suggests that you might want to focus on improving just one practice at a time so that you master it before implementing an additional practice. Start slowly and work your way toward mastery.

Good Praise versus Bad Praise

While many studies find that praise increases prosocial behavior, not *all* studies find this (e.g., Warneken & Tomasello, 2008), although they all find that it is more effective than tangible rewards in the long run. This may be partly because the effect of praise depends on the circumstances (Henderlong & Lepper, 2002). If a student is behaving prosocially solely to get praise, praise could be as undermining to long-term behavior as tangible rewards. So how do you find the right balance, without going overboard with praise? Recall from Chapter 3 that intermittently (i.e., inconsistent, occasional) reinforcing students is better for promoting behavior over the long run than reinforcing students every time. Thus, a smattering rather than an onslaught of praise for prosocial behavior may be ideal.

The effect of praise also depends on who delivers it. *Praise is especially powerful when it comes from an adult the student respects and has a positive relationship with* (Mussen & Eisenberg, 2001). You'll learn how to improve relationships with students in Chapter 5 so that your praise is maximally effective. *Praise is also powerful when it comes from peers.* Many people mistakenly think of peer pressure as bad, yet peer pressure is often positive. Students encourage one another to be prosocial. When students get a thumbs-up from their peers for sharing or helping others, they become even more prosocial (van Hoorn, van Dijk, Meuwese, Rieffe, & Crone, 2016). Most of the prosocial behavior your students enact will be small, obscure things that you may not even be aware of that occur in the course of ongoing classroom activities (e.g., a student sharpening a pencil for a classmate). Often, peers are the only ones who witness each other's prosocial behavior. Furthermore, whether a behavior is prosocial or not depends on the circumstances in ways that only peers may be aware of. For example, a 6th grader told of a girl who frequently brought candy to share with classmates. You might think this is prosocial, but he said it was not prosocial because she was doing it just to make classmates like her (Bergin et al., 2003). A smile can be prosocial or not depending on the circumstances (e.g., a smirk vs. a moment of affirmation). The fact that many prosocial behaviors are small, obscure, and depend on the circumstances may explain why your students are likely to be more effective at reinforcing each other than you are, so encourage them to praise each other's prosocial behavior. Table 4.2 gives you a quick overview of when praise is motivating versus deflating (Henderlong & Lepper, 2002).

Table 4.2 Characteristics of Good and Bad Praise

Good Praise (Enhances intrinsic motivation)	Bad Praise (Undermines motivation)
Comes from respected adults or peers	Comes from someone who is not trusted
Conveys information about competence (e.g., "You did that well")	Conveys information about social comparison (e.g., "You are better than the rest of the class")
Specific (e.g., "You were a good helper to Joey")	Not specific (e.g., "Good job")
Credible, realistic, sincere (little children seldom question your sincerity, but teens do)	Not credible (e.g., the students know they didn't try) or is over the top (e.g., "I've never seen such patience before!!")
Following a good job	Following a poor or mediocre job (students assume this means the teacher had low expectations)
Feels freely given	Feels controlling or evaluative, or makes students feel self-conscious
Follows behavior for which students had a choice	Follows behavior for which students were coerced
Conveys information about having achieved a standard or performance expectation (e.g., "I am pleased that you made sure everyone had a turn")	Does not convey information (e.g., "You are such an angel")

Clearly, you should use praise judiciously. However, despite some drawbacks to inappropriate praise, overall I like praise as a tool for increasing prosocial behavior for several reasons. Praise improves the climate of a classroom, fosters good moods, and builds relationships. Praise communicates important information, such as about students' competence (e.g., "You can be helpful"), and what is expected of students or behavioral standards (e.g., "Helping each other is the right thing to do") without being overly controlling. Praise can provide the push needed for students with little intrinsic motivation to be helpful, or who hesitate to help because they are shy. Praise also presents the opportunity to engage in two kinds of training: (1) empathy training and (2) identity training.

Empathy training occurs in at least three contexts. First, when you use exhortation such as in Table 4.1 above (e.g., "Sharing is the right thing to do because it makes him happy"). Second, when you use the victim-centered induction you learned about in Chapter 3. Victim-centered induction refers to pointing out to students how their misbehavior affected the victim: "Look at how sad Anna is; you hurt her feelings!" This trains students to focus on others' feelings and perspectives. This is a type of empathy training in the context of a discipline encounter. Third, when you praise a student following an act of kindness. You can use praise to point out to students how their prosocial behavior affected the recipient. "Look how Anna is smiling. Your help made her feel good!" Students who experience all three types of empathy training (during exhortation, discipline, and following prosocial acts) will learn that how they make others feel is an important standard to guide their behavior. Let's turn next to identity training.

Should You Praise the Act or Praise the Student?

You can shape your students' *self-identity* through praise. Students are quite vulnerable to believing what respected adults tell them about themselves—for good or ill. When they are told they are worthless, stupid, or troublemakers they will come to believe it and live up to that belief. (This is one reason that the psychologically controlling discipline you read about in Chapter 3 is so damaging.) In contrast, when they are told they are moral, compassionate, and helpful they will come to believe it and live up to that belief. You may feel like this is a heavy responsibility, but it is one that is unavoidable because it is inherent in the teacher-student relationship. It is also one of the joys of teaching because it means you can make a difference in shaping the identity of students toward a more *positive self-identity*.

A teacher once casually said to an 11th grade girl, "You know, you're pretty good at this math stuff. You ought to think about majoring in math in college." This girl had no math-related self-identity at that time, and yet this one casual comment shifted her future and she is a mathematician today. You probably have your own stories like this suggesting how susceptible students' identities are to shaping by their teachers. (If you do not have your own stories, read the book, *The Ones We Remember*, edited by Frank Pajares and Tim Urdan, which is a lovely tribute to teachers.)

How does this pertain to prosocial behavior? Praising students for their prosocial behavior will help them come to self-identify as moral, compassionate, helpful persons. However, it is most effective when the *praise is about the student rather than about the behavior*, as in, "You are a kind person," rather than, "That was a kind thing to do." This might seem too subtle to have an effect, but research shows that such subtle differences are powerful. For example, in one study 4- and 5-year-olds were told "You could be a helper" rather than "You could help" (Bryan, Master, & Walton, 2014). The children were later given a chance to help with some age-appropriate tasks, such as picking up blocks, opening a bin for someone whose hands were full, putting away toys, and picking up crayons that had spilled. Those who were told they could "be" a helper were more likely to actually be more helpful. In another study, elementary students received praise for prosocial behavior that was either *person-focused* or *act-focused*, as Table 4.3 shows.

Table 4.3 Person-Focused or Act-Focused Praise

Person-Focused	Act-Focused
▪ "You are the kind of person who likes to help others whenever you can. Yes, you are a very nice and helpful person."	▪ "It was good that you gave some of your marbles to those poor students. Yes, that was a nice and helpful thing to do."
▪ "You know, you certainly are a nice person. I bet you're someone who is helpful whenever possible."	▪ "You know, that certainly was a nice thing to do. It was good that you helped me with my work here today."

Students who received either type of praise behaved more prosocially afterwards compared to students who received no praise (Grusec & Redler, 1980). However, students who received the person-focused praise were more likely to behave prosocially in a variety of different kinds of situations and enacted different kinds of prosocial behavior, which means it generalized to new situations, compared to the act-focused praise. Students as young as 5 years old already differ from one another in terms of how much they self-identify as a prosocial person or not (Thompson, 2012). But it is never too late to influence students' self-identity. In the elementary study, even 5th graders, whom you might assume have a fixed notion of themselves, were influenced by person-focused praise (Grusec & Redler, 1980).

Person-focused praise changes students' self-identity or how they perceive themselves, which in turn affects how they behave. Students who feel that being prosocial is core to their self-identity are more likely to expect to feel good after behaving in prosocial ways, and so they are more honest, compassionate, and helpful (Dinh & Lord, 2013; Hardy, Walker, Olsen, Woodbury, & Hickman, 2014). This is true even of very young students. For example, in one study 5-year-olds who self-identified as honest (e.g., they would tell someone right away rather than trying to hide something they broke) were more prosocial in their classrooms two years later (Kochanska et al., 2010). One middle school teacher said:

I am lucky to teach in a school where most of our students are prosocial. However, one student is aversive and annoying on a daily basis. He enjoys drawing negative attention to himself. His teachers and classmates find him hard to tolerate and no one wants to work with him on projects. Some teachers think he has conduct disorder, but he hasn't been diagnosed yet. After reading your book, I decided to give him opportunities to practice kindness. I began to accept his offers to help clean the science lab. He does not do a "good" job in that his cleaning isn't really up to par, but I thank and praise him for what he does well, especially in front of the other students. I've also quit responding to his annoying antics. As I am reinforcing the

> *prosocial and ignoring the antisocial behavior, I've seen a turn-*
> *around. He has begun conversing with me about our shared*
> *interest—photography. He even showed me the results of a*
> *"shoot" he did yesterday. I feel like we are beginning to have a*
> *good relationship, and his classmates are beginning to see him*
> *in a different light.*

" Praise the child, not the act. This is unique to prosocial behavior. Do not apply this principle to the realm of misbehavior or academic achievement."

One important note of caution about this is that you do not want to use person-focused criticism in response to negative behavior. Unlike praise, *criticism should be about the behavior, not the student*, as in "That was a bad thing to do" rather than "You are a bad person." The same is true for academic achievement. Praise should be about the academic behavior, not the student. As Carol Dweck and others have repeatedly found in research, when you attribute students' academic success to "working hard" rather than "being smart," you create a *growth mindset*. That is, you train students to believe that ability is changeable and can be developed. Such growth mindsets lead to persistence in the face of failure or obstacles, greater motivation, and higher achievement (Paunesku et al., 2015; Yeager & Dweck, 2012). Remarkably, it has this effect even on toddlers (Gunderson et al., 2013). Figure 4.1 summarizes these principles.

There is a whole field of psychology known as "attribution theory" that provides the foundation for understanding how this works. The basic notion is that you and your students have a natural tendency to explain behavior, meaning you attribute behavior to some cause. The attribution you make for your behavior today will influence your behavior tomorrow (Weiner, 1985). You want your students to attribute their prosocial behavior to internal, stable causes ("I am a good person who wants to help others") rather than external, temporary causes ("I helped because the teacher made me"). At the same time, you want your students to attribute academic achievement

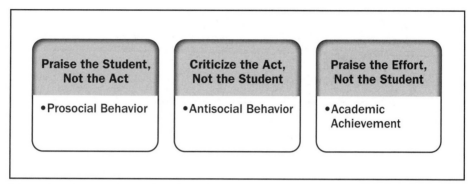

Figure 4.1 Research-based Conditions for Praise

to effort ("I worked hard on that assignment") rather than internal, stable causes ("I'm smart").

In summary, avoid giving students tangible rewards, but do praise them for engaging in prosocial behavior. When praising students for prosocial behavior, praise the student, rather than the act, to help them develop a self-identity as a prosocial person. However, do not over-generalize this process to either negative behavior or academic achievement.

As Figure 4.2 illustrates, when you combine praise focused on the student for behaving prosocially, in combination with models and opportunities to practice prosocial behavior, and exhortation about why it is important to help others, you will build prosocial habits in your students. Research has shown that a combination of these practices is more likely to result in students holding prosocial values and acting with compassion and justice (Eisenberg, Wolchik, Goldberg, & Engle, 1992; Hardy, Carlo, & Roesch, 2010; M. Hoffman, 1975).

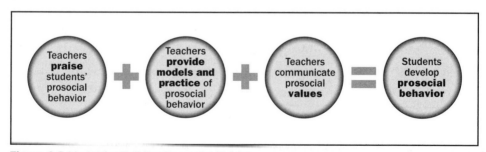

Figure 4.2 Model for Building Prosocial Habits

NOTE ABOUT AGGRESSIVE STUDENTS

There are multiple influences pushing on your students at all times, including models of aggressive behavior. These aggressive models may be other students in your classroom. If some of your students are aggressive, other students may become more aggressive over time (Molano et al., 2014). To prevent this from happening, you want your aggressive students to experience a saturation of prosocial classmates who can be positive models and help them replace aggressive behavior with prosocial behaviors. Part of creating this kind of classroom involves being careful to reinforce positive, not negative behavior. Aggressive students are reinforced when they get what they want through aggression. Instead, find ways to reinforce prosocial behaviors among aggressive students. That is, catch them being good, and praise them for it so that you begin to shape more positive behaviors. Many therapies for students with serious conduct disorder focus on providing opportunities to practice prosocial behavior followed by praise. This helps aggressive students begin to change their self-identity from "bad kid" to "good kid" and teaches them replacement behavior. In one intervention, school bullies are given meaningful jobs in the school that help others (e.g., setting up laptops, door greeter, tutoring younger students) in partnership with a highly prosocial peer (i.e., a model), and peers are encouraged to praise them for their helpfulness (Ellis, Volk, Gonzalez, & Embry, 2015). "Praise notes" are posted in the classroom or hallway or announced through the PA system. In others words, the intervention follows the principles you learned in this chapter about giving students opportunity to practice prosocial behavior in meaningful ways and being praised for it.

FOR REFLECTION AND DISCUSSION

Think about the last few times a student behaved prosocially in your classroom. What was your response? Did you ignore it, praise the student or the act, or use tangible rewards? Think about the last few times a student misbehaved in your classroom. What did you reinforce and how?

When was the last time you pointed out a prosocial model to your students? In your lesson planning, can you incorporate prosocial models? Think about a recent or upcoming lesson plan. What can you change to include prosocial models?

Do you make your students feel responsible for others' well-being in the class?

Do you accept offers of help even when it is inconvenient for you? Do you provide opportunities for your students to practice being prosocial?

When service opportunities are provided, are they meaningful, and is there time for group reflection?

CHAPTER 5

Positive Teacher-Student Relationships

Mrs. Wilton stands by the door as her 3rd grade students leave for recess so that she can say something positive to each student, and dole out hugs to those who want them.

Although it is lunch time, Mr. Crites' biology-chemistry classroom is buzzing with students. They like to "hang out" in his room while they eat their lunches. Mr. Crites talks with students about their lives: "How did your dad's surgery go?" "Are you ready for the track meet tomorrow or are you going to let Lincoln High beat us?" "I heard you got a job at the Custard Cup; I'll bring my family there this weekend!"

Both of these teachers have *secure attachment* with many of their students. Do you know what that means and why it matters for your students? Let's explore these questions and identify some tools you need to establish secure relationships with your students.

What is Attachment?

If you have ever tried to pick up a 1-year-old who is not yours, you have experienced the dynamics of attachment. The toddler will push away from you and lunge for the parent. Even after the toddler is safe in the parent's arms, the toddler will eye you with grave caution and cling tightly to the parent. This is the first manifestation of one of the most powerful forces in a child's development—the parent-child attachment.

You may remember from your study of child development how important it is for children at all ages to have a secure attachment to their parents. However, you may not be aware that children can have attachment-like relationships with teachers also (Bergin & Bergin, 2009). In fact, attachment, both to parents and to teachers, lays the foundation for your students' success from preschool through high school. Good teachers do not merely dispense knowledge; they also develop relationships with students, like Mrs. Wilton and Mr. Crites. Before we delve into how the teacher-student relationship affects prosocial behavior in your classroom, let's briefly review what attachment is, why it matters, and how it relates to your classroom.

Attachment is officially defined as "a deep, enduring emotional bond between people" (Ainsworth, 1973). Everyone has attachments, including you and all your students. You usually are attached to more than one person, but only to a select group of people. Attachment tends to occur in hierarchies, with a single preferred *attachment figure* at the top (e.g., mom or dad), and secondary figures (e.g., grandparents, siblings, teachers) farther down the hierarchy. Typically, your strongest attachments are to your parents and spouse. Children from troubled families where parents are drug users, abusive, mentally ill, or transient in their lives may attach to others instead. Although everyone has attachments, they are not all healthy, positive relationships. I'll discuss differences in quality of attachment later.

It makes sense that attachment matters for infants and toddlers, but what about older students? Actually, attachment is a lifelong issue because the need to be cherished and affirmed, and to trust those around you is a persisting need. You might not think of attachment as an issue for adolescents because most 15-year-olds will not wrap themselves around a mother's leg as she leaves them at school (in fact, they often pretend they do not even know she's there). Yet, feeling secure that their attachment figures will be available to them, no matter what, is the bedrock of healthy personality development in adolescence. Adolescents do not cling to their attachment figures, but they do touch base with them in subtle ways—like drifting into the room they are in for a few minutes for no particular reason. Some people mistakenly believe that adolescents shift attachment to peers, but actually parents continue to be at the top of most teenagers' attachment hierarchies (Markiewicz, Lawford, Doyle, & Haggart, 2006). In a crisis, they seek out their attachment figures. As an adult, you do the same. Think about the last time you had a crisis. Who were the first few people you turned to?

You need to understand these basics because attachment serves a very important function that promotes learning in your classroom. The function of attachment is to liberate children by helping them feel safe to explore the world while having a safe haven—a supportive attachment figure—to retreat to when they feel threatened, tired, ill, frustrated, or unhappy (Bowlby, 1969). The attachment figure's presence is soothing and restoring. A way to think about this is that attachment allows children to balance wariness and caution, which keep them safe, with curiosity and exploration, which allow them to learn and develop skills (see Figure 5.1). The application to the classroom is obvious. *Students are more likely to take learning risks in an environment where they feel safe, valued, and supported.*

Figure 5.1: Attachment Allows Students to Balance Safety and Exploration

How do Teacher-Student Relationships Vary?

The need to attach is so universal and strong that abused children will attach to abusive parents. However, the *quality* of attachment is not universal. In fact, it varies dramatically depending on how parents and teachers treat children. An ideal, or "secure," attachment has specific characteristics (Ainsworth, 1979; Behrens, Hesse, & Main, 2007; Beijersbergen, Bakermans-Kranenburg, van IJzendoorn, & Juffer, 2008; McElwain, Holland, Engle, & Ogolsky, 2014). Children who are secure with an attachment figure (AF) will:

- Invite the AF to join in an activity or move near the AF.

- Explore more when the AF is present.

- Prefer the AF to others, greeting the AF with genuine pleasure, conversing pleasantly, and showing positive emotions.

- Feel safe to express negative emotions, but do so with civility. (For example, you can feel anger discussing a hot topic or conflict with one another in a secure attachment relationship, but any anger or distress are readily resolved.)

In contrast, insecure children will ignore, turn away from, or avoid the AF. They may avoid difficult topics or suppress emotions because they do not feel safe enough to express them. Or, they may manipulate the AF with whining, tantrums, or babyishness. They may often appear angry, fearful, immature, hyperactive, and unsettled. They may have trouble recovering from distress. As they grow into adolescents and adults they may dismiss the importance of relationships, or have superficial relationships. In romantic relationships they may be needy or prematurely close, with frequent breakups (Bernier & Meins, 2008; Crowell et al., 2002; Hesse, 1999; Hodges, Finnegan, & Perry, 1999; Stevenson-Hinde & Verschueren, 2002).

Your students can have secure or insecure relationships with you as their teacher, just as they do with their parents. How do you know if you have a secure relationship? In secure relationships, students move toward teachers, are genuinely glad to see them, share their work readily, and express affection, as they did with Mrs. Wilton and Mr. Crites. In insecure relationships, students move away from the teacher. Or, they may demand attention, overly seek help, and be possessive, dependent, and needy, but resist classroom routines (Howes & Ritchie, 1999; Pianta, Nimetz, & Bennett, 1997). Teacher-student relationships are often characterized as having three basic dimensions (Pianta, 2001):

- Closeness (e.g., *I share an affectionate, warm relationship with this student*).

- Conflict (e.g., *This student and I always seem to be struggling with each other*).

- Overdependence (e.g., *This student asks for my help when it really isn't needed*).

Secure relationships would be high in closeness and low in conflict or overdependence. Insecure relationships may be high in either conflict or overdependence, or both. I once heard a world-renowned attachment researcher say that when he saw a teacher "want to stuff a student in the trash can," he assumed the student had insecure attachment because insecure students draw exasperation from teachers. Hyperbole aside, most teachers know to what he is referring. Later in this chapter, you will learn the tools to establish positive relationships with challenging students.

---

66 Teacher-student relationships can be characterized by three dimensions: closeness, conflict, and overdependence. You can use these survey items to reflect on your relationship with specific students.**"**

Teacher-student relationships vary enormously, even in the same classroom. You may have a student whom you feel very close to and another with whom you have difficulty relating. One way researchers assess the quality of teacher-student relationships is to ask teachers and students to rate items such as those in the paragraph above, and the following items:

1. When I'm with my teacher, I feel mad. (Reverse scored)

2. The teacher is fair with me.

3. When I'm with my teacher, I feel good.

4. The rules in my classroom are clear.

5. My teacher thinks what I say is important.

6. When I'm with my teacher, I feel happy.

7. My teacher cares about how I do in school.

8. My teacher likes to be with me.

9. My teacher has plenty of time for me.

Young children may be asked to respond to a shorter, simpler version such as (Lisonbee, Mize, Payne, & Granger, 2008):

10. Does [teacher's name] smile at you?

11. Do you like [teacher's name]?

You can use these items as a tool to reflect on your relationship with each of your students. Try responding to each item from the perspective of a student using a scale of *not at all true, not very true, sort of true,* and *very true.* You may want to focus on students who seem invisible to you, or whom you find especially challenging.

If you teach young children, it is easier for you to develop relationships that are true attachment relationships because you spend substantial time daily with students. However, in upper grades the structure of school does not always allow attachment-like relationships to develop; you have too many students whom you may only be with for a few hours a week for just one or two semesters. This may be why research finds that teacher-student relationships tend to be less close and less warm as students progress from 1st grade through middle school, followed by a leveling-off in high school (Hughes, Wu, Kwok, Villarreal, & Honson, 2012). But even in elementary school, a sizable portion—about one quarter—may not have a strong relationship with their teacher (O'Connor, Dearing, & Collins, 2011; Spilt, Hughes, Wu, & Kwok, 2012).

This means there is room for improvement in teacher-student relationships at all grade levels, but if you are a secondary teacher, you may need to put extra effort into establishing positive relationships. Later in this chapter, you will learn how to do this at all grade levels, but first let's focus on why the quality of the relationships you have with your students matters.

Why Do Teacher-Student Relationships Matter?

You want your students to have healthy personalities and emotional well-being. Attachment is the foundation of both, which in turn influences their academic achievement and prosocial behavior in your classroom.

Academic Achievement

The research linking attachment to achievement is impressive and robust. Students from preschoolers to high schoolers who have secure attachment to their parents have higher language arts and mathematics test scores, higher grades, greater curiosity, and greater language skills (Aviezer, Sagi, Resnick, & Gini, 2002; Bus & van IJzendoorn, 1997; Diener, Isabella, Behunin, & Wong, 2007; Granot & Mayseless, 2001; Weinfield, Sroufe, Egeland, & Carlson, 1999). Similarly, students who have positive relationships with their teachers have higher test scores and GPAs, and are also less likely to be retained or referred for special education (Curby, Rimm-Kaufman, & Ponitz, 2009; Jia et al., 2009; Leyva et al., 2015; O'Connor & McCartney, 2007; Roorda, Koomen, Spilt, & Oort, 2011). The following three studies are just examples from the research showing that teacher-student relationships predict academic achievement:

- Study 1: Elementary students who had positive relationships with their teachers in 1st grade were more engaged and worked harder in 2nd grade, and earned higher test scores in 3rd grade (Hughes, Luo, Kwok, & Loyd, 2008).

- Study 2: Adolescents who responded positively to the items listed above, meaning they had good relationships with teachers, had higher engagement in school, higher grades in language arts and mathematics, and higher test scores in mathematics (Murray, 2009). The first four items were particularly strong predictors, so check them out.

- Study 3: High school students learned more when their teachers became more sensitive and supportive of them (Allen, Pianta, Gregory, Mikami, & Lun, 2011).

You are probably wondering whether this is merely correlational. Your experience tells you that it is easier to form positive teacher-student relationships with good students. Perhaps it is the higher achievement of these students in the first place that causes the link between positive relationships and higher grades and test scores. However, the students in Study 2 were not selected for being good students. In addition, Study 3 was an experiment in which teachers were randomly assigned, or not, to an intervention. Over the course of a year, the intervention teachers attended a couple of workshops and received coaching in relationship building, as well as instructional practices. Students of the intervention teachers, regardless of whether they were good students to begin with, increased in learning compared to students of the other teachers. Together, these studies point to the notion that if you improve teacher-student relationships, your students are likely to learn more.

❝ Positive teacher-student relationships predict higher grades and test scores. The effect is large for all students, but particularly for boys and at-risk students. ❞

The *effect size* (an index of the power of a research finding) of teacher-student relationships on tests and grades is large (Cornelius-White, 2007; Mashburn et al., 2008). I put effect sizes on a continuum from "Ho hum, shrug worthy" to "Sit up and pay attention!" The effect size of teacher-student relationships fits in the "Pay attention" category. To put it in perspective, the effect size is larger than class-size effects, and which curriculum or instructional approach you use. This means that positive teacher-student relationships may be one of the more powerful aspects of effective teaching. The effect size of positive teacher-student relationships on academic achievement is stronger for boys than for girls, yet boys report feeling less close and having more conflict with teachers than girls (Spilt et al., 2012). The effect size may also be stronger for students with low self-control, who tend to fare better over time if they have a positive teacher-student relationship (M.-T. Wang et al., 2013). This suggests that you may want to give extra attention to developing positive relationships with boys and with your students with low self-control.

Why might relationships with teachers increase students' test scores and grades? There are several reasons documented by research, and you may be able to think of others.

- First, students are more engaged and motivated to work harder for teachers they have a positive relationship with. Students have higher confidence in their ability to do the work in the class, and have greater interest and enjoyment, and they value the learning activities. This motivation, in turn, results in greater learning (Hughes et al., 2012; Spilt et al., 2012; Wentzel, Muenks, McNeish, & Russell, 2017).

- Second, secure students are better able to work independently (Sroufe, Fox, & Pancake, 1983; Weinfield et al., 1999). Remember that clinginess and overdependence are typical of insecure teacher-student relationships.

- Third, feeling secure in relationships helps students control their emotions better, which allows them to take on difficult challenges and stay calm in the face of frustration or discouragement (Braungart-Reiker, Garwood, Powers, & Wang, 2001; Sroufe, 1996).

- Fourth, insecure students live with chronic stress and anxiety (e.g., Kerns & Brumariu, 2014). This chronic stress leads to health and sleep problems, which can interfere with learning (Bernier, Matte-Gagné, Bélanger, & Whipple, 2014; Maunder & Hunter, 2001). This chronic stress also leads to anxiety disorders and depression (Madigan, Atkinson, Laurin, & Benoit, 2013).

In Chapter 6 you'll learn how anxiety and depression interfere with learning. It is hard to pay attention when you are anxious. This may explain why *insecurely attached children tend to manifest ADHD symptoms whether they are diagnosed with ADHD or not.* While there are many pathways to ADHD, my colleagues in attachment research have estimated that 40% to 80% of ADHD diagnoses have their foundation in *insecure attachment.* In contrast, secure students feel less stress and are more likely to have long attention spans and better ability to control their thinking (e.g., Bernier, Matte-Gagné, & Bouvette-Turcot, 2014; Clarke, Ungerer, Chahoud, Johnson, & Stiefel, 2002; Goldwyn, Stanley, Smith, & Green, 2000; Moss & St-Laurent, 2001). Keep in mind the balance metaphor above; secure attachment gives your students feelings of safety from which to take on challenging tasks.

Prosocial Behavior

The quality of students' attachment predicts their prosocial behavior. Research on parent-child attachment has found that children who are securely attached are more prosocial within the family and with peers (Bohlin, Hagekull, & Rydell, 2000; Davidov & Grusec, 2006; Eberly & Montemayor, 1998; Houltberg, Morris, Cui, Henry, & Criss, 2016; Van Ryzin et al., 2015). Both their teachers and their classmates view them as more socially competent, whether they are preschoolers or high school students (e.g., Allen, Porter, McFarland, McElhaney, & Marsh, 2007; DeMulder, Denham, Schmidt, & Mitchell, 2000; Doyle, Lawford, & Markiewicz, 2009; Englund, Kuo, Puig, & Collins, 2011; McElwain, Booth-LaForce, Lansford, Wu, & Dyer, 2008). In contrast, both teachers and classmates view students with insecure parent-child attachment more negatively, describing them as more mean, dishonest, disruptive, angry, aggressive, anxious, or withdrawn (e.g., Fearon, Bakermans-Kranenburg, van Ijzendoorn, Lapsley, & Roisman, 2010; Madigan, Brumariu, Villani, Atkinson, & Lyons-Ruth, 2016).

❝ There is more prosocial behavior and less aggression in classrooms where teachers develop positive relationships with students.❞

The same effect occurs for teacher-student relationships. Research has found that students who have positive, warm relationships with teachers are more prosocial (Bergin & Bergin, 2009; Howes & Ritchie, 1999; Kienbaum, 2001; Mitchell-Copeland, Denham, & DeMulder, 1997). They tend to have more empathy, compassion, and harmonious interactions with others. They are more cooperative and compliant with teachers' directives. This does not mean that they are mindlessly obedient, or will never challenge your directives, but overall they will tend to be more cooperative with your reasonable demands (Laible, Panfile, & Makariev, 2008). Students who have positive, warm relationships with teachers are also less likely to have behavior problems such as aggression, drug use, and early sexual activity (e.g, O'Connor et al., 2011; Stipek & Miles, 2008; M.-T. Wang & Fredricks, 2014).

Your relationship with each student can make a difference. In fact, according to a large national study in elementary school, the effect you have on your students' social skills is likely to be greater than your effect on their academic achievement (Jennings & DiPrete, 2010). This same study found that *when teachers promoted their students' social skills, the students' academic achievement improved.* That's an exciting two-for-one deal you should not pass up! You do not have to choose between supporting social or academic skills, but can do both at once. The study also found that some teachers were better than others at promoting their students' social skills. The better teachers were those who had higher levels of education—so kudos for reading this book!

❝ Students draw behavior from you that confirms their internal models of adults as caring or not. With patience and perseverance, you can disconfirm negative models. ❞

Why do secure parent-child and teacher-student relationships influence prosocial behavior? When students' own emotional needs are met, they are better able to meet others' needs. In addition, students learn positive social and emotional skills in healthy relationships with parents and teachers that they then apply to other social settings, such as with classmates. Furthermore, students develop internal models of themselves and others based on whether they have secure ("I am worthy of love and others are trustworthy and caring") or insecure ("I am not worthy of love and no one is going to look out for me") attachments. These internal models determine how they will approach new classmates and teachers (McElwain et al., 2014). These models are fairly stable after age 3 years, unconscious, and resistant (but not impossible) to change. Your students will behave in ways that confirm their internal models of adults by drawing either caring or hostile behavior from teachers, so that their internal models become self-fulfilling prophecies. Nevertheless, despite your students' risk factors and their past relationship histories, you can develop a positive relationship with them. Let's turn to how to do that next.

How Do You Develop a Positive Teacher-Student Relationship?

You have probably found that some students are more difficult to relate to, just as some babies are more difficult for parents to bond with. Yet, the grand dame of attachment research, Mary Ainsworth (1979), argued that parent-child attachments are primarily driven by the parents' behavior. Research has robustly supported her view. Even the most difficult infants become securely attached and less difficult over time with sensitive parenting (Bokhorst et al., 2003; Pauli-Pott, Haverkock, Pott, & Beckmann, 2007). So what are those parent behaviors?

Thousands of studies have found that the key parent behaviors resulting in secure attachment with their children are sensitive responsiveness and showing interest in and enjoyment of the child. Sensitive, responsive parents respond promptly and contingently to the child's needs. Some researchers have described watching them as akin to watching a well-choreographed dance of attunement between parent and child. The parent might respond with reassurance when the child is anxious, or with delight when the child has just succeeded at something difficult. The parent supports the child's exploration of the world by scaffolding the child to just the right degree (e.g., providing a little help with tasks just beyond the child's zone of proximal development), adapting the task, giving the child choices, allowing the child to set the pace, and encouraging the child (Ainsworth, 1979; Bernier, Matte-Gagné, Bélanger, et al., 2014; van IJzendoorn et al., 2007; Verhage et al., 2016). In contrast, parents of insecure children are either unresponsive to them or inconsistent, or they intrude on the child's activities with their own agenda. They may be psychologically unavailable or neglectful. They are often angry or irritated with their children (Leerkes, Parade, & Gudmundson, 2011; Scher & Mayseless, 2000; Stevenson-Hinde & Verschueren, 2002). When such negative parents are trained to be more sensitive and responsive, their children become more secure (Bakermans-Kranenburg, van IJzendoorn, & Juffer, 2003).

Can you see how the same kinds of behaviors are relevant to your teaching? Research (Bergin & Bergin, 2009) suggests you are likely to have a secure, warm, positive relationship with your students if you behave in the ways I outline next. Researchers have asked students what makes them feel cared for by their teachers (Jeffrey, Auger, & Pepperell, 2013; Wentzel, 1997). I have added what students said in the boxes below.

1. Be sensitive, meaning you perceive their interests and needs, have warm, positive interactions, and respond to their frustrations or distress. Greet students by name, praise good effort and positive behavior, and send home positive notes about students.

Students Said *to Do* This	Students Said *Not to Do* This
Talk to students, pay attention to them, listen, ask questions, talk about their problems, and be a friend	Yell, ignore, interrupt, forget students' names, or do not bother to ask when something is clearly amiss

2. Be responsive, meaning you give your students choices when possible, respect their agendas, and give them some control over learning tasks. Students feel closer to teachers who do this. When you cannot give them a choice or control, give them a good rationale for what you are asking them to do.

Students Said *to Do* This	Students Said *Not to Do* This
Compliment and encourage students and praise their good work	Insult, embarrass, pick on or hurt students' feelings

(Note that even students who are not the target of teachers' misbehavior dislike teachers who pick on other students.)

3. Be thoughtful about discipline. As you learned in Chapter 3, power-assertive discipline harms relationships, whereas induction promotes respect for the disciplinarian and motivates students to internalize your values.

Students Said *to Do* This	Students Said *Not to Do* This
Tell the truth, keep promises, respect and trust students	Threaten students or send them to the office

4. Be well prepared for lessons and push your students to higher achievement.

Students Said *to Do* This	Students Said *Not to Do* This
Make special effort to teach well and make class interesting, help each student learn, ask if students need help, call on and make sure each student understands	Be boring, get off task, continue to teach when it is clear students are not paying attention, and do not try to help, answer questions, nor explain things

The first three behaviors are not surprising because they are part of being caring toward anybody, not just teachers toward students. However, the last behavior might surprise you a little. Teachers tend to think of caring and teaching as separate roles. Students have a different view. To students, *teaching well is integral to being a caring teacher* (Jeffrey et al., 2013). That is, being well-prepared for class and checking to make sure each student understands the lesson shows that you care about students' achievement. Consider this math class:

Jazmine enters Mr. Cohen's 9th grade math class 10 minutes late. Mr. Cohen is in the middle of a lesson, but pauses very briefly to say, "Jazmine, take off your hoodie, you know the rules, and open your book to page 311. Inez, please help her find where we are." Then, he continues where he left off, walking the students through calculations. Mr. Cohen makes it clear the students are there to learn math, and he pushes them hard with no down time. He calls on every student by name at least 3 times during the lesson. He seldom praises, but when he does praise a student, they sit up taller as though it really means something to them.

I observed Mr. Cohen with a team of principals and superintendents. Most of them felt he was too cold with the students. One said, "He's certainly not the teddy bear type." Yet, all acknowledged that the students appeared motivated to please him. Mr. Cohen was not exhibiting all four behaviors listed above, but he was demanding and very well prepared for lessons, which was received by his students as caring.

How to Establish a Good Relationship with a Difficult Student

You know from experience that some students are harder to establish a good relationship with than others. Yet, even with challenging students, there are several things you can do that will help you develop a positive student-teacher relationship.

Understand Your Students' Attachment History

Some of your students are coming to you with internal models that they are unlovable and that no one can be trusted to care for them when they most need it. In self-defense, they put up barriers to keep others at bay, and dare you to care for them.

Students who have these defenses are reacting to their own history of attachment, either with their parents or with former teachers with whom they have had insecure relationships. This history influences the kind of relationship they will develop with you because they are likely to draw negativity from you (DeMulder et al., 2000). They may be defiant, which makes you angry. Alternatively, they may be immature, dependent, and needy, which causes you to baby them, but irritates you at the same time. They are likely to develop a conflicted relationship with you. These students have a double whammy of poor relationships with key adults at home and at school. In contrast, your students who have secure parent-child relationships are likely to draw warmth and sensitivity from you (Pianta, Mashburn, Downer, Hamre, & Justice, 2008). As I mentioned above, their internal models of themselves and others become self-fulfilling prophecies because they behave in ways that confirm those models. It is hard to develop a positive relationship with a student who dares you to care.

Further complicating the situation, you bring your own attachment history to the mix. The way you perceive your students is a reflection of your own parent-child attachment (James, 2012). If you have an insecure attachment history, it is even more challenging to develop warm, positive relationships with difficult students.

Still, it is possible to develop positive teacher-student relationships with insecure students. If you behave in the ways described in the section above, you can change your insecure students' internal models that adults are hostile, rejecting, unresponsive, or untrustworthy. This is hard to do and requires perseverance because insecure students will push back to get you to react in ways that confirm their internal models. In fact, sometimes students behave worse when you first are caring toward them, as though they are trying to get you to yell at them, until they are finally convinced that you sincerely care for them and won't give up on them. Simply understanding this will help because it fosters compassion in you, which will sustain you through the patience it takes to develop a more positive relationship with challenging students. For especially difficult students, it helps to find someone to support you through the process. I've known teachers to form Alcoholics Anonymous–style meetings or adopt a "sponsor" to help them maintain consistent caring toward students who are pushing back hard, until the student finally becomes accepting of the positive relationship. This can take several months. One teacher said:

> I have experienced this, and it is so hard and frustrating. I wish I had known earlier that the change isn't always gradual. You have to keep going even if it doesn't seem like it is doing any good, because sometimes (maybe most of the time?), it is like a switch being flipped. I had some difficult students where one day they just decided to be different and there doesn't seem to be an explanation for why that day. It wasn't one thing I did or one thing that happened, but it was the culmination of many things.

When students who have insecure attachment to their parents develop a positive relationship with you, they will learn more in your classroom (O'Connor & McCartney, 2007). A bonus for you is that when you develop a positive relationship with your insecure students, you will be happier as a teacher (Klassen, Perry, & Frenzel, 2012).

This may be particularly important if you teach in a school where students are different from you. A challenge in contemporary U.S. schools is that the majority of teachers are White and middle class, while many students are not (U.S. Department of Education, 2016). Thus, many teacher-student relationships have to overcome cultural mismatch based on class and ethnicity, as well as possible differences in attachment histories. This mismatch challenge may partly explain why students of color report feeling less cared for at school compared to White students. Nevertheless, your behavior can help close the *caring gap*. For example, in one study, Black high school students were engaged and cooperative in some White teachers' classrooms, but were suspended from other teachers' classroom. What was the key difference? Some teachers focused on building positive relationships with them (A. Gregory & Ripski, 2008). "Students want to know how much you care before they consider how much you know" (Freiberg, Huzinec, & Templeton, 2009, p. 66).

Use Banking Time

In addition to persevering in the behaviors listed above, there are specific interventions you can use to establish positive relationships with challenging students. Robert Pianta (1999), a former counselor and dean of education at the University of Virginia, developed an intervention for early childhood settings called *banking time* because as a teacher you "save up" positive experiences in relationship "capital" that can later be "drawn upon." For 5 to 15 minutes each day you give the student your undivided attention and convey interest in the student, and follow the student's lead in whatever activity the student chooses. This can be done during gym, free-choice time, center time, lunch, recess, or small-group instruction. (Note to parents: If you feel you are developing a negative relationship with any of your children, try this same approach. After just a few days, you will find that your relationship has become more positive again.)

This may seem unrealistic in secondary settings where there just isn't time for this kind of one-on-one interaction. Clearly, it is easier to establish positive relationships with younger children who stay in your classroom most or all of the day than in secondary schools where 150 students may pass through your classroom each day. However, I've seen secondary teachers achieve the same results in different ways. Mr. Szyperski, a middle school teacher, set aside 30 minutes after school almost every day to phone a portion of his students' parents. He would tell them what he liked about having their child in his class. As you can imagine, he was a beloved teacher. He was also quite demanding, but his students worked hard to please him. Mr. McCord, a high school teacher, would phone students who were absent to tell them they were missed. He would do this from the classroom so that classmates could chime in. Mr. Mali, in his book, *What Teachers Make: In Praise of the Greatest Job in the World*, shares his own version of this. Mr. Mali had a 7th grader, Caleb, who challenged him on an item on a geometry quiz that, Mr. Mali admitted, was poorly written. Mr. Mali told Caleb that he could prove his point for homework, and then followed up with a phone call to Caleb's mother:

> *It was not the first time one of his teachers had ever called home—I got the sense that she was used to fielding such calls—but it was the first time anyone had ever told her anything good. I wanted her to know that the intellectual curiosity and vivacity that her son had displayed in class reminded me why I chose to teach in the first place. I told her that I loved my job because of kids like Caleb. The quality of silence on the other end of the phone told me that she was crying. By reaching out to her that night I had created an ally.* (Mali, 2012, p. 36)

These secondary teachers developed their version of banking time with students to convey that each student mattered in their classrooms.

Focus More on the Positive than the Negative

Seemingly minor interactions shape relationships. In one study, 53 elementary teachers were observed for just 5 minutes at the beginning of the school year (Reinke, Herman, & Newcomer, 2016). The number of reprimands versus praise each student received during that 5 minutes was recorded. As you can imagine, some students got more negative feedback than positive compliments. Remarkably, this brief observation predicted students' behavior several months later, at the end of the school year. Students who received more negative feedback during that 5 minutes increased in problems with behavior, concentration, and out-of-control emotions. Teachers were unwittingly *reinforcing negative behaviors.* In contrast, students who received more positive compliments increased in prosocial behavior over the course of the school year.

The purpose of the 5-minute observations was to help teachers notice their behavior toward students that they may not even be aware of. You can do the same thing in your classroom. Just ask a colleague to step into your class and count the number of reprimands versus statements of praise for 5 minutes for each of the students you feel you are struggling to develop a positive relationship with. You may find it eye-opening. Of course, reprimands will happen because they are likely to be challenging students. However, take a close look at the ratio of positive to negative feedback. There is no magic number that indicates a healthy versus an unhealthy relationship, but the researchers suggest you think about a ratio of perhaps 3 to 5 statements of praise to one reprimand. Ms. Callahan, a master teacher, is remarkably adept at this, although she teaches many challenging students. She stands at the door to greet every student that enters her class. She finds something positive to say about at least a few (different) students before beginning class each day. Not surprisingly, her department has won awards for closing the achievement gap (see Chapter 2). Another high school mentor teacher said:

> *We had a senior transfer into our program. His file indicated that he had been diagnosed with ODD as a young child. We conferenced about him before he arrived. Two of his teachers decided they would not tolerate misbehavior from him, so they*

> *started off using harsh discipline. He responded in kind. He was defiant and either ignored them or was aggressive. He didn't do well academically; all his interaction with the two teachers was about behavior, not the lesson at hand. Another teacher, in contrast, was more nurturing, tried engaging him, and focused on his strengths. He was very helpful in her classroom and always on task. He also would come to my office to volunteer to help me with things like filing, or ask what I needed help with. You wouldn't know he was the same kid. I learned that teachers have the power to build kinder kids by building relationships and avoiding power assertion.*

Promote School Bonding

If you teach in a school with many students at risk for relationship problems, you can implement the same practices discussed above on a school-wide basis (Hamre et al., 2014; Ottmar et al., 2015). This will promote students' relationships with the school as a whole. Students who bond to their school are attached to teachers and others, they like school, and they participate in school activities (Hallinan, 2008). They have higher achievement and are less likely to drop out or become delinquent (Dynarski et al., 2008; M.-T. Wang & Fredricks, 2014). School bonding is especially important for students at risk due to poverty, frequent moving, or immigrant status, or being an ethnic minority at the school (G. Green et al., 2008; Gruman et al., 2008; M. Johnson et al., 2001; Osterman, 2000).

Unfortunately, like teacher-student relationships, *school bonding* diminishes in middle school. As students transition from elementary to middle school they tend to feel less bonding and less interest in school; they participate less in extracurricular activities, and earn lower grades (Juvonen, 2007; Skinner, Furrer, Marchand, & Kindermann, 2008). Raging hormones are the popular scapegoat for this, but research suggests hormonal changes are not the culprit. Rather, the structure of schools may be. When students move into middle school, they are more tightly controlled and given fewer choices than the year before when they were in elementary school. Not surprisingly, students in middle school report that their relationships with teachers are less positive.

How do you know if your students feel bonded to school? Table 5.1 has items that are commonly used to measure school bonding (Appleton, Christenson, Kim, & Reschly, 2006). Think about how your students might answer these questions.

Table 5.1 Items Used to Measure School Bonding

My Teachers	My Peers
1. Overall, adults at my school treat students fairly. 2. Adults at my school listen to the students. 3. At my school, teachers care about students. 4. My teachers are there for me when I need them. 5. The school rules are fair. 6. Overall, my teachers are open and honest with me. 7. I enjoy talking to the teachers here. 8. I feel safe at school. 9. Most teachers at my school are interested in me as a person, not just as a student.	1. Other students here like me the way I am. 2. I enjoy talking to the students here. 3. Students here respect what I have to say. 4. I have some friends at school.

If your students' responses to these items may not be as rosy as you would like, what can you do to increase school bonding? The most important thing is to establish warm teacher-student relationships. Relationships with other adults also help. An elementary school nurse said:

> *Seven-year-old Diamond arrives at my office complaining of a bruise on her hip about the size of a quarter. Diamond does not smile at all, and her head droops in sadness. The bruise is minor, and clearly an excuse to visit me. Diamond tells me she*

> *does not have any friends at school, her sister died a year ago and now her mother and her mother's boyfriend are getting married (which she seems particularly sad about). I listen compassionately, give her a hug, and then send her back to class.*
>
> *Then 11-year-old Samuel arrives looking very malnourished. He is a frequent visitor. He is a diabetic who does not comply with his medical regime and has no support from home. He thinks his blood sugar is low. I confirm that it is low. "Do you have your snacks?" He says that he does not, so I find some juice and crackers. He takes the juice and then begins talking about his home life.*
>
> *Later in the day Diamond returns, saying the bruise still hurts. She wants another hug. Both of these students, and several others during the day, come to my office to connect with me to fulfill their attachment and emotional needs. Although some have clear medical needs, others amplify their symptoms in order to connect with a caring adult.*

The greater the number of positive relationships students have (e.g., with teachers, nurses, coaches, counselors, lunchroom staff, janitors, librarians), the more likely they are to bond to the school.

Warm *student-student relationships* are also important. Students are more prosocial when they believe their classmates care for one another. That is, they are more likely to themselves become more inclusive, cooperative, and friendly, and to feel more bonded to school (Solomon et al., 2000). This prosocial behavior, in turn, leads to warmer student-student relationships, which becomes a beautiful upward spiral of a happy school.

The combination of caring classmates and caring teachers may be especially powerful in promoting academic achievement (Wentzel et al., 2017). Figure 5.2 shows how this combination works. Students who feel their classmates care for them come to believe they can master the work in the class (i.e., self-efficacy). Students who feel their teachers care for them have greater interest and enjoyment of the learning activities. As students come to feel they are a valued member of the group, they work harder, focus on mastering the material, and learn more.

Relationships take time to establish, especially attachment-like relationships which can take several months to establish. Thus, it helps to keep students, teachers, coaches, or counselors together long enough to form relationships, such as for repeated years. It also helps to keep schools small (Felner, Seitsinger, Brand, Burns, & Bolton, 2007). If this is not characteristic of your school, you can advocate for structural changes. If such changes are not feasible, then you can create small learning communities within the school and provide a variety of extracurricular activities so that all students can find a niche within the school.

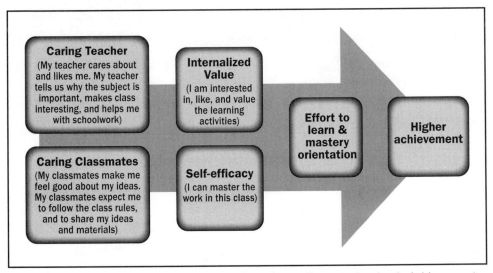

Figure 5.2 How Caring Teachers and Caring Classmates Promote Academic Achievement

Combine Discipline with Warmth
in the Teacher-Student Relationship

In Chapter 3, you learned that it is important to discipline students when they are unkind to others in order to promote prosocial behavior, yet in this chapter you've learned that it is important that you are warm and supportive of students. Some teachers may mistakenly believe these are incompatible goals, believing that if you are lax with discipline students will like you better. This is not true. Demanding that students behave appropriately, and being warm, accepting, and responsive are actually unrelated dimensions. You can be any combination of high or low in each. Psychologists typically use a 2x2 table to explain four different combinations of these dimensions. I like 2x2 tables for making complicated concepts easy to grasp. Real relationships are little more complicated and don't necessarily cleanly fit such tables, but Table 5.2 conveys the basic idea.

Table 5.2 Combinations of Discipline and Warmth

		Demanding of Appropriate Behavior	
		High	Low
Warm, Accepting, Responsive	High	Authoritative	Lax, Permissive
	Low	Authoritarian	Indifferent, Neglectful

You undoubtedly learned about these combinations, referred to as parenting styles, in your college years. Which of these styles is ideal? *Authoritative* parents are highly demanding of their children (e.g., regular bedtimes, say please and thank you, chores must be done), but are also warm, accepting, responsive and respectful of their children's perspectives (Maccoby & Martin, 1983). While they are *the most controlling and demanding* of their children, they control and demand in a positive, supportive way (Grolnick & Pomerantz, 2009). They provide guidance, firmness, structure, and discipline using induction. They provide choice and they support autonomy in their children as much as possible (Grolnick, 2003; Steinberg & Silk, 2002).

Both warmth and demandingness in parenting are vital to children's well-being. In addition, the two dimensions interact, meaning that how warm parents are alters the effectiveness of their discipline. Discipline is more effective in the context of a warm relationship. Authoritative parents, who are warm but demanding and use inductive discipline, are the most likely to have children who are prosocial (Baumrind, 1971; M. Hoffman, 1975; M. Hoffman & Saltzstein, 1967). Children of authoritative parents also have higher self-control and academic competence, emotional health, and social skills than other children

(Baumrind, 1973; Fletcher, Darling, Steinberg, & Dornbusch, 1995; Fletcher, Walls, Cook, Madison, & Bridges, 2008; Padilla-Walker et al., 2012; Qin, Pomerantz, & Wang, 2009; Spera, 2005; Steinberg, Blatt-Eisengart, & Cauffman, 2006; Steinberg, Dornbusch, & Brown, 1992).

Teachers have similar styles of teaching. You can probably readily identify colleagues who fit into one of these four styles. Some teachers (indifferent) have low expectations for students and no classroom rules. Students do what they want and slack in these classes. Other teachers (permissive) are warm, kind-hearted, and want to be liked by their students so they make no demands. Students do not obey the few feeble attempts at discipline. Still other teachers (authoritarian) have very strict rules with no flexibility, and students obey out of fear of punishment. Finally, the teachers who are most effective (authoritative) have high expectations but are perceived by students as fair in discipline and grading. These teachers have total control over their classrooms but in ways that students are not aware of, and have warm relationships with the students (Wentzel, 2002). Students are obedient for authoritative teachers because they see them as having legitimate authority. High school students described such teachers:

> - *Well, actually, it is not that he enforces his rules cause he do not have to because all the students respect him . . . if he ask the class, you know, be quiet so that we could get our class discussion started, they automatically be quiet.*
> - *When she talk to you with seriousness, she mean it, but then she also have a smile like "I'm on your side." I mean, "I feel where you're coming from but I'm still your teacher." (A. Gregory & Weinstein, 2008, pp. 469–470)*

These students were more engaged in class for authoritative teachers. They felt that the teachers cared for them and expected more of them, yet the same students were "behavior problems" in other teachers' classes. The authoritative teachers were equally likely to be male or female, and Black, White, or other ethnicities; they could be just like you.

Schools can also be characterized as authoritative or not. Some schools have caring climates, but also clear rules that are fairly and consistently enforced. When schools are authoritative there is more positive behavior among students and there are fewer behavior problems (A. Gregory et al., 2011; A. Gregory et al., 2010). Schools can have two different kinds of culture (D. Hoffman, 2009): (a) blame misbehavior on the context (e.g., "How can we create a greater sense of community so that this student wants to cooperate more?"), or (b) blame the student (e.g., "How can we get this student to cooperate more?"). Which is your school like? How might your strategies differ depending on which mindset you had?

In summary, you have learned why *positive teacher-student relationships* are important and how they help students become more prosocial, as well as more academically successful, in your classroom. However, not all teacher-student relationships have this effect, because they are not warm or close. You were introduced to some survey items assessing teacher-student relationships that can help you analyze your relationship with specific students. You have learned the tools you need to establish a caring relationship with students, including especially challenging students, and promote their bonding to school. Let's do a quick review of those tools:

1. Be sensitive (pay attention to students' interests and needs, have warm, positive interactions, and respond to their frustrations or distress).

2. Be responsive (give students choices and control when possible, respect their agendas)

3. Demand appropriate classroom behavior, while also being warm (i.e., be authoritative). Laxness in discipline is not required for a positive teacher-student relationship. Use inductive discipline, rather than power assertion.

4. Be well prepared for lessons and push your students to higher achievement.

5. Behave prosocially toward students (compliment and encourage them; be honest with them). Use the 5-minute check to see

if you are mostly praising or reprimanding specific students. Focus more on the positive than the negative.

6. Try to understand your students' and your own attachment history. For those with insecure attachment, disconfirm their internal models of others as untrustworthy and uncaring, and themselves as unlovable. This takes perseverance, so consider getting support from colleagues.

7. Enact specific interventions to build relationships with challenging students. This could include using the banking time method, telling your students or their parents what you like about them, or simply standing at the door as students enter your classroom and saying something positive to them.

8. Encourage your school to adopt a structure that allows relationship building, including with adults other than teachers, so that all students feel they belong (i.e., bond) to the school community.

As you use these tools, you will enjoy teaching more. One reason that teacher-student relationships affect learning and prosocial behavior is that they help students cope with emotions that might cause problems. In the next, final, chapter you will learn additional tools to promote a healthy emotional climate in your classroom.

NOTE ABOUT AGGRESSIVE STUDENTS

Some of your students may enter your classroom having become quite aggressive. Research shows that despite their penchant toward aggression, such students will become more prosocial, participate in class more, and like school more if you can establish a warm, close relationship with them (Brendgen et al., 2012; Meehan, Hughes, & Cavell, 2003; O'Connor et al., 2011; Thomas, Bierman, & Powers, 2011).

They will also become less disruptive and aggressive over time. Many studies have found that teachers who have positive relationships with students tend to have about one-third fewer behavior problems over the school year (Marzano, Marzano, & Pickering, 2003). The same is true at the school level. That is, authoritative schools where discipline is consistent and teachers are caring have fewer bullies and victims compared to other schools.

The effect of positive teacher-student relationships on aggressive students occurs even in classrooms with several aggressive students. That is, if teachers are sensitive, responsive, warm and supportive, the students will become less aggressive (Thomas et al., 2011). For example, in a study of 5th and 6th graders, when teachers were more sensitive and positive toward certain disruptive students, the students became less disruptive over time, *even if they had disruptive friends in the class* (Shin & Ryan, 2017). This is a "Sit up and pay attention" result, because usually the opposite happens, meaning that when there are several aggressive students in a classroom, their classmates become more aggressive over time (Werner & Hill, 2010).

It is difficult to establish a positive relationship with aggressive students. It is especially difficult if you have several highly aggressive students in your classroom. Yet it is possible. In this chapter, you learned tools for establishing positive relationships with challenging students.

FOR REFLECTION AND DISCUSSION

Would most students in your class say they feel cared for? Would they feel that way about the school as a whole?

How would you describe your relationship with each student in your classes? Can you identify those with whom you need to improve your relationship? Choose one or two students and write down some specific ways you plan to improve your relationship.

Think of a couple of students whom you find challenging. How do you think your own attachment history might be affecting your expectations of your students and your sensitivity toward them? How might your students' attachments to their parents be affecting your relationship?

How would you rate yourself on each of the positive teacher behaviors in this chapter? Which do you feel you would like to improve on? Choose one and make an improvement plan.

Which of the teaching styles in this chapter best characterizes your teaching style? Are you more controlling or lax? Are you more accepting or responsive toward your students or cold and distant? What changes do you think you should make?

CHAPTER 6

Emotionally Upbeat Classrooms

Jerome is typically a boisterous, outgoing jokester in class. He likes to banter with his teacher, Mr. Pauling. But today, Jerome enters the class looking sad, with his head down. He sits at his desk slumping, stares blindly ahead, and taps his foot without realizing it. Mr. Pauling gets the students set up in work groups, and then approaches Jerome. In a whispered conversation he learns that Jerome's uncle, Ray, is in the hospital and may not survive. Mr. Pauling knows that Jerome has a single mother and that Uncle Ray is Jerome's father figure. Mr. Pauling pats Jerome on the shoulder, and says he is sorry. He also says that Jerome is a strong young man with lots of support and will pull through this. He tells Jerome to take his time getting his emotions under control, and then join his work group. Later, Mr. Pauling notices Jerome still sitting at his desk alone, wiping tears away. Mr. Pauling tells Jerome to go to the office where he can call someone to take him to the hospital to visit Uncle Ray.

All students are happy sometimes and sad or angry sometimes. An emotionally healthy life involves both positive and negative emotions, but with a balance clearly tipping in the positive direction. Some researchers have suggested that to flourish we should experience a ratio of three positive to one negative emotion (Fredrickson & Losada, 2005). This is not a magic ratio, and it has been questioned by other researchers. Nevertheless, in general we want our students to feel more interest, joy, and excitement than to feel negatively.

This is the case for Jerome, who is typically a happy student. However, today his sadness is swamping his ability to learn and participate in class.

You will have noticed that some of your students are chronically angry, anxious, or sad. In this chapter you will learn how both temporary and chronic negative emotions affect your students' academic achievement and their prosocial behavior. You will also learn what you can do to help your students become emotionally healthy while creating an upbeat classroom climate.

How Do Emotions Affect Academic Achievement and Prosocial Behavior?

Have you ever tried to define the word *emotion*? It is harder than you might think. Psychologists define it as a reaction to an important event (you do not feel emotion in response to events that are not important to you), that has three components: (1) physiological changes, like flushed cheeks or sweaty palms, (2) readiness to act, like fleeing in fear, and (3) appraisal of the event. This last component, appraisal, is important to understand because you will learn later how to use it to help your students cope with negative emotions. The way you appraise an event affects your emotion. For example, imagine you have a student who is defiant with you. You might respond with anger if you appraise (i.e., judge) his behavior as intended to demean you. Your heart will race, your eyebrows furrow (the classic anger physiology), and your body will ready for counterattack. However, in the last chapter you learned that insecure students will be defiant and dare you to care because of defenses they erect through a history of being rejected by their parents or other attachment figures. Understanding this might change your appraisal of the student's defiance, causing you to respond with compassion instead. Your behavior toward the student will be very different depending on whether you feel anger or compassion.

Similarly, your students' behavior will vary depending on the emotions they feel. In your classroom, those emotions affect both their academic achievement and their prosocial behavior. In your teacher preparation program you probably learned much more about how to promote the cognitive development of your students than how to promote their emotional development, because that is the emphasis of most teacher education programs. However, the emphasis is a little wrongheaded in that emotions may be more powerful in shaping behavior and learning. Emotions provide the energy and motivation for complex behavior needed to be successful in the classroom. Emotions are sometimes necessary to connect thoughts (e.g., "I know she needs help and I should help") with actual behavior (e.g., "I help"). Emotions are built into the human species because they promote our success. Let's turn to how they influence learning next.

" Emotions involve physiological changes and thought processes, such as how you appraise an event. Changing your appraisal can change your emotion."

Happy Students Learn More

Emotions are always present and influencing our thoughts. They influence our attention because we pay attention to things that are emotionally significant (Huntsinger, 2013). They also influence our memories because we remember emotionally strong experiences in greater detail (Kensinger, 2007). What is one of your earliest school-based memories? It is likely to be connected to strong positive or negative feelings. Generally, positive emotions promote and negative emotions interfere with the kind of academic learning that you want your students to engage in during class, because they affect attention, concentration, and motivation.

Positive Emotions Promote Learning

Students who are interested, happy, or excited learn more. They are also more creative and productive on classroom tasks, projects, or problem-solving activities (Nadler, Rabi, & Minda, 2010; Valiente, Swanson, & Eisenberg, 2012). Interest is a key classroom emotion because it leads students to focus attention and pursue a learning goal (Gable & Harmon-Jones, 2008). This is why capturing students' interest at the beginning of a lesson with engaging questions (e.g., is coral a rock, plant, or animal?) or relevance to their lives (e.g., how does your computer connect to the internet?) makes them pay attention. Students put more effort into learning topics they enjoy or are interested in.

Happiness also drives classroom learning because it makes students want to participate in activities, be open to new ideas, and be more creative. Research suggests this is because mild positive emotions open our minds and broaden our thoughts (Fredrickson, 2001; Huntsinger, 2013). Happiness increases dopamine, which is a chemical that transmits signals in a part of the brain where working memory and creativity occur (Ashby, Isen, & Turken, 1999). In general, mild happiness, rather than exuberant excitement and joy, is ideal for focusing attention and speeding up information processing (Rose, Futterweit, & Jankowski, 1999). When students are overjoyed, it can be hard to focus (e.g., when they are preparing for a big party), but if a task is important to them, even over-the-top excitement does not really interfere with learning (Liu & Wang, 2014).

Negative Emotions Interfere with Learning

When you are distressed, do you have a hard time concentrating? Most people do, including your students. Jerome clearly did. *Negative emotions*, like sadness, anxiety, and anger interfere with learning. This is because the brain processes involved in controlling reasoning and problem-solving during classroom tasks, paying attention, or remembering, are the same as those used in trying to contain our negative emotions (Brock, Rimm-Kaufman, Nathanson, & Grimm, 2009; Compton et al., 2008). There is only so much processing space. When it is consumed by anxiety, anger, or sadness there is less left to think with. This is why using harsh discipline with students can derail learning. The students' minds are so consumed with processing the anger they feel that they cannot concentrate on the lesson. This happened to Shawn:

> *Shawn enters his 3rd grade classroom a little late; he was kept after in a previous class for misbehavior. He is angry, and immediately knocks some books from the shelf as he walks past. Mrs. Snow tells him to calm down and get out his markers for an activity. Shawn gets them out and throws them on the ground, and rips up the worksheet Mrs. Snow gave him. He shouts, "I hate this school and I don't want to do this stupid thing!" Mrs. Snow tells him to pick it up or he will have to go back to the previous class for time out. Shawn begins crying*

hot tears of anger as he picks up the markers in a dramatically slow way. Although Shawn sits at his desk, he spends the rest of the lesson smoldering about how unfair his teachers are, how they all hate him, and how he'll show them! He cannot pay attention to the lesson and does not learn anything.

Negative emotions that consume most of a student's processing space are also at play in test anxiety and math phobia. Anxiety swamps thought processes so that anxious students can appear dumber than they are. Some of your students live with chronic anxiety: Will there be enough food to eat tomorrow? Will my dad come home drunk again? Will my sister get well? Will my mom find a job? Will my dad go ballistic if I fail this test? Will my parents reject me if I do not get into Harvard?

For this reason, some researchers find that *teaching your students to regulate their emotions better may be more important that teaching them to reason better if you want to raise their academic achievement* (Ursache, Blair, & Raver, 2012; Valiente, Lemery-Chalfant, & Swanson, 2010). You do not have to make a choice; you can readily do both. Later in this chapter, you'll learn how to help your students regulate their emotions better.

> **❝**Positive emotions open your students' minds and broaden their thought, helping them learn more and be creative. Negative emotions make it hard for your students to pay attention or learn.**❞**

Do not worry about every little negative emotion. It is not only okay, it is part of a healthy emotional life to occasionally experience negative emotions. In fact, a little anxiety can motivate your students to better prepare for a test. A little sadness can help them concentrate better on detailed tasks. A little sadness can also make them less gullible, less prone to think stereotypically of others, more polite and generous, and possibly able to remember more (Forgas, 2013; Sussman, Heller, Miller, & Mohanty, 2013). Negative emotions primarily interfere with learning when they are excessive, chronic, and lead to ruminating. (This characterizes Shawn's emotions; he gets overly angry, is in trouble at least weekly, and cannot stop stewing about how mean his teachers are.) Nevertheless, the research suggests you want your students to experience positive emotions more than negative, so that they learn more. Also, so that they will be more prosocial, our next topic.

Happy Students Are More Prosocial

Students who consistently experience more positive emotions, such as joy, gratitude, and affection, are more prosocial. In Chapter 1, I described a study in which we asked 6th graders to describe the most prosocial student they knew. One of the most frequently mentioned attributes of these prosocial exemplars was their persistent happiness. Their peers described them as "always perky and never sad" or "always laughing and smiling" (Bergin et al., 2003). In another study, I found that parents and teachers similarly described the most prosocial preschoolers they knew as consistently happy, upbeat children (Bergin et al., 1995). Finally, in yet another study, I found that global ratings of toddlers' general level of happiness correlated strongly with how prosocial those children were (Bergin, 1987). Happy toddlers were more compassionate, amiable with peers, and showed more remorse after misbehaving. Other researchers have also found that students who express a lot of happiness in the classroom behave more prosocially toward others (Denham et al., 1990). In addition, students with prosocial reputations seldom are emotionally negative (Eisenberg et al., 1996). Together this research suggests that happy students tend to be prosocial exemplars.

Why might this be? One reason is that happy, cheerful students promote an upbeat mood in others. They spread happiness through emotional contagion and through having pleasant interactions with others. Happiness greases the wheels of social interaction. Helping others feel more upbeat is in itself a prosocial act. Chapter 1 lists 16 behaviors typical of prosocial students, many of which involve emotions. According to that list, prosocial students:

1. Contain their own negative emotions (e.g., avoid fights by ignoring taunting, and do not get mad or sulk when they make mistakes).

2. Avoid hurting others' feelings (e.g., apologize, laugh at corny

jokes, include others, play even if they do not want to, do not brag, do not make fun of others, and do not yell).

3. Help their peers contain negative emotions (e.g., defend peers who are being teased, calm peers who are fighting, and listen to and cheer up sad peers).

4. Help peers feel good (e.g., compliment other's performance, encourage them to try again, psyche teammates up, and joke around).

These prosocial students put a lot of effort into helping others feel happier. Promoting others' happiness is a defining feature of your prosocial students.

" Positive emotions cause your students to behave more prosocially, and prosocial students help those around them feel happier."

Another reason that happy students tend to be prosocial exemplars is that a person's mood in the moment influences whether that person chooses to behave prosocially. Have you found that when you are especially happy you are more likely to hold the door open for others, compliment others, or help in a number of ways? Many experiments have found that when you give people the opportunity to behave prosocially (e.g., donate to charity or help someone with a tedious task) they are more likely to do it if you first induce a positive mood in them (Batson, Coke, Chard, Smith, & Taliaferro, 1979; Feshbach & Feshbach, 1982; Gueguen & De Gail, 2003; Isen & Levin, 1972; Manucia, Baumann, & Cialdini, 1984; Moore, Underwood, & Rosenhan, 1973). It is remarkably easy to induce positive moods; you can ask people to reminisce about a happy memory, show a happy video, read a happy story, play happy music, do a fun activity, or just smile at them.

Why does an upbeat mood lead to more prosocial behavior? Perhaps because it energizes people to take action. Perhaps because it motivates people to try to hold on to that positive mood, and behaving prosocially feels rewarding and makes them even happier (Batson & Powell, 2003; E. W. Dunn, Aknin, & Norton, 2008; Wegener & Petty, 1994). Even toddlers are happier when given a chance to give a reward to a puppet than to receive a reward themselves (Aknin, Hamlin, & Dunn, 2012). Prosocial behavior is motivated by many things, including wanting to feel good about oneself and enjoying seeing others happy (Eisenberg et al., 2016). The old adage "'Tis better to give than to receive" may be wired into human biology. Thus, happy students behave prosocially, and behaving more prosocially makes students happier. They are on an upward spiral of positive emotions!

What is Emotional Competence?

Before you learn the tools to help your students become more emotionally competent, you need to understand that emotional competence has two components. First, it refers to students' ability to accurately read and understand others' emotions. Emotionally competent students can tell when a classmate is upset, or angry, or happy. Second, it refers to students' ability to recognize and control their own emotions. Emotionally competent students can dampen their anger when needed, cope with frustration or disappointment, and be happy without being overly boisterous. Some people instead use the term "emotional intelligence" (EQ), popularized by a best-selling book (Goleman, 1995). Technically, EQ is a subset of emotional competence. It refers to the ability to guide thinking and to think intelligently about emotions. In this chapter I'll use the more comprehensive term *emotional competence* to refer to the broader ability to read others' emotions and to regulate one's own emotions.

Reading Others' Emotions

Emotions are contagious. You may not realize it, but you unintentionally mimic other's emotions, which causes you to share in their emotions. For example, when someone is laughing with delight, you often cannot help but smile or laugh along. Similarly, sadness can be caught from others. Emotional contagion is built into our brains through what are called "mirror neurons." These neurons respond the same whether you do an action or you see someone else do the action (e.g., whether you laugh or you see someone else laugh; Iacoboni, 2009). Infants' brains respond to others' emotions just as adult brains do (Leppanen, Moulson, Vogel-Farley, & Nelson, 2007). In fact, infants are able to imitate your emotions within days of birth. Try smiling vivaciously at a new-born; you will find the baby mimics your smile (Becker & Srinivasan, 2014). Emotional contagion helps you understand others and strengthens relationships. Despite mirror neurons, some students struggle to read others' emotions accurately. Later in this chapter, you will learn how to help such students.

The ability to read others' emotions accurately can lead you to feel concern for someone else's feelings (i.e., sympathy) or to feel along with someone (i.e., empathic distress), or to feel so distressed yourself that you focus only on your own discomfort (i.e., personal distress). Sympathy and empathic distress motivate you to help others in distress and lead to deeper friendships (R. Smith & Rose, 2011). In contrast, personal distress motivates you to avoid others in distress (Losoya & Eisenberg, 2000).

Regulating One's Own Emotions

Emotion regulation involves changing the intensity and duration of your emotions so that they do not interfere with important goals. For example, you have to dampen anxiety in order to score well on an exam, or stoke righteous indignation in order to stand up to a bully (Gross, 2015). Sometimes you have to fake your emotions, such as smiling as you say, "Aren't we glad the principal is visiting our class today!"

Coping Strategies

You regulate your emotions by using coping strategies. Psychologists divide coping strategies into two kinds: problem-focused and emotion-focused. That is, you either focus on trying to change the situation and solve the problem that caused the emotion or you focus on trying to change your emotions. For example, imagine that you feel test anxiety. You can either study harder (e.g., problem-focused) or use relaxation techniques (e.g., emotion-focused). Which kind is better? It depends on the situation. If you can change the situation, then problem-focused might be better. However, if you have no control over the situation, then emotion-focused might be better.

Your students use a variety of coping strategies. Some that have been identified in research are listed in Table 6.1. As you can see, the strategies vary in how constructive they are. The least constructive include acting out with aggression or using drugs to numb emotions.

> " Reappraisal is a particularly useful coping strategy. It involves changing the way you think about an emotionally charged situation. "

Reappraisal is an emotion-focused coping strategy that is often one of the best choices when you cannot change the situation. Recall from above that one core component of an emotion is your appraisal of the event. How you interpret an event affects your feelings. For example, you might be disappointed that you did not get a position you applied for, but you tell yourself that staying where you are will allow you to work with a wonderful set of colleagues, or it might mean you will have more free time. For another example, if you are Shawn's teacher you might be angry about his destructive behavior and defiance toward you, but you tell yourself that his parents are divorcing and Shawn just does not know what to do with his fear and sadness about it. Such reappraisal can change your anger to compassion. Reappraisal can be powerful.

Table 6.1 Coping Strategies Commonly Used by Students

Less Constructive	More Constructive
Do nothing	Avoid the situation or leave; just walk away
Aggress: to resolve the problem (e.g., kick a classmate whose pen you want)	Talk: to friends, teachers, or parents; pray
Aggress: to release pent-up feelings (e.g., kick a chair)	Distract yourself or try not to think about the problem
Use substances to escape the emotions (e.g., alcohol, drugs, comfort foods)	Exercise: for low-arousal emotions like sadness
Cry: to release pent-up feelings	Relax: for high-arousal emotions like anger or anxiety
Cry: to elicit help from others	Seek help: from friends, teachers, or parents
Ruminate: rehash and dwell on negative thoughts	Take constructive action: to improve the situation
	Reappraise: try to think about the situation in a positive way, or change your goal

Compiled from Gross (2015); Seiffge-Krenke, Aunola & Nurmi (2009); Zimmer-Gembeck & Skinner (2008).

Faking Emotions (Emotional Dissemblance)

You have experienced times when you either carefully did not express any emotion (e.g., kept a "poker" face), or you expressed an emotion that was different from what you felt (e.g., "Thanks for the slippers; they're just what I wanted for my birthday!" and "I'm doing much better since the divorce, but thanks for asking!"). This emotional dissemblance is an important skill because it allows you and your students to successfully navigate your social worlds. Every culture has rules about how and when it is okay to express emotions, rules your students must learn if they want to have friends or hold a job, among other things. It also allows them to protect others' feelings, which is a prosocial act. For example, a 6-year-old smiled as he told his toddler brother that his scribbling was "really good!" Then he whispered, "It's not good, but I just want him to be happy." Of course this skill, like most, can also be used inappropriately. For example, it makes it possible for students to lie and look perfectly innocent when they are guilty of a misbehavior (e.g., "I didn't do anything wrong. He started the fight, not me.")

Both Aspects of Emotional Competence
Affect Prosocial Behavior

Both reading others' emotions and regulating your own emotions predict prosocial behavior (Eisenberg et al., 2006). Students who regulate their emotions well tend to feel more positive than negative emotions, such as happiness, gratitude, and affection. As you learned above, happier students are more prosocial. They are warmer toward others, make activities fun, are enthusiastic about class activities, attract others, and keep interactions running smoothly. They can fake their emotions in order to protect others' feelings, and they can contain anger so that they do not behave aggressively (Bartlett & DeSteno, 2006; Denham et al., 2003). Not surprisingly, both their classmates and their teachers like them better than others (McDowell, O'Neil, & Parke, 2000; Penela, Walker, Degnan, Fox, & Henderson, 2015; Rydell, Berlin, & Bohlin, 2003). Thus, students who can control their own emotions are more prosocial than other students (Fabes, Eisenberg, et al., 1999). In contrast, students who struggle with emotion regulation, becoming easily upset or over-reacting, tend to be less prosocial (Carlo, Crockett, Wolff, & Beal, 2012).

Students who read others' emotions well are also more prosocial (Denham et al., 1995; Wentzel, Filisetti, & Looney, 2007). They are more cooperative and liked by classmates because they easily establish positive relationships with others (Fabes, Eisenberg, Hanish, & Spinrad, 2001; Izard et al., 2001). In contrast, students who cannot read others' emotions tend to be less liked, are aggressive, and have behavior problems (Arsenio, Cooperman, & Lover, 2000; Coie & Dodge, 1998). They often cannot tell when others are irritated with them, or when they have taken a joke too far.

❝Students who regulate their emotions well tend to be more prosocial, happier, well-liked, and have higher achievement.❞

Students who read others' emotions may feel greater empathy and compassion. Most people assume that prosocial behavior (e.g., helping, sharing, comforting, cooperation) is primarily motivated by sympathy. This is partially correct. Research does find that students who are more sympathetic are more prosocial (Flournoy et al., 2016; Malti et al., 2016; Miller, Nuselovici, & Hastings, 2016). When they see someone in distress, prosocial students have a change in heart rate that indicates pausing to pay attention or orient toward the other; then their heart rate recovers, which is thought to motivate them to help the distressed other (Miller et al., 2016).

Yet, research does not consistently find that sympathy triggers prosocial behavior (Decety & Cowell, 2014; Paulus, 2014). You have probably felt a sympathetic urge to help someone, but did not. Your students have had similar experiences. Recognizing that someone is feeling distressed doesn't mean they'll help (Imuta, Henry, Slaughter, Selcuk, & Ruffman, 2016). Why might this be? There are forces that prevent students from behaving prosocially even when they feel empathic. These include self-interest, believing that it is not their responsibility to take care of others (see Chapter 4), and being overwhelmed by emotion themselves. This last reason might be a little surprising, but students who are unable to regulate their own emotions may become overwhelmed by personal distress themselves when they see others in distress, which renders them less likely to help the others (Denham et al., 2003; Eisenberg et al., 1997; Flournoy et al., 2016; Miller et al., 2016). This is one reason why some people avoid attending funerals. Thus, when it comes to prosocial behavior both aspects of emotional competence—reading others' emotions and regulating one's own emotions—are linked.

"Students who read others' emotions tend to be more cooperative and well-liked, although greater empathy does not always lead to prosocial behavior."

Importantly for teachers, *helping your students become more emotionally competent also increases their academic achievement.* As you learned above, negative emotions can interfere with learning. Students who are able to keep their emotions well-regulated tend to have higher achievement, beyond any effects of IQ (Ursache et al., 2012). Their negative emotions do not swamp their ability to pay attention or be engaged in class. Furthermore, *when schools enact programs to promote students' emotional well-being, the students' grades and test scores rise* (Durlak et al., 2011). Later in this chapter, you'll learn how to do this. But first, let's explore recognizing how well your students are doing emotionally.

Do Your Students Have Age-Appropriate Emotional Competence?

Two students may respond quite differently to the same emotionally charged situation. One might have a more intense response than another and take longer to recover, as this example shows:

Two kindergarten girls got on the wrong bus home from their first day at school. In a perfect storm of malfunctions (the bus radio and phone did not work, the school office was empty by the time the driver found a phone, and neither girl knew her address) the girls were almost two hours late getting home. The girls' parents were frantic; the neighborhood and police had been mobilized to find them. When they finally arrived home one girl got off the bus beaming with excitement. "Mommy, we had an adventure!" She promptly forgot the incident. The other girl got off the bus sobbing, was fearful to get on the bus the next day, and talked about the incident for months afterwards.

However, keep in mind that students with poor emotion regulation do not always have too much emotion; sometimes they have too little emotion. For example, children who are abused sometimes have blunted emotions which allow them to cope when they cannot escape the abuser but results in stunted development of emotion regulation. (They also sometimes have intense anger and explosiveness.) If abused children are taught emotion regulation skills, they are likely to fare better and not develop emotional disorders (Kim-Spoon, Cicchetti, & Rogosch, 2013).

Typical children become more emotionally competent with age, up to late elementary school when they plateau. Let's review what research says about what you can expect at different grade levels.

Preschoolers

What kind of skill in reading others' emotions and regulating their own emotions do preschoolers have? Let's explore what you can expect in a typical early childhood classroom.

Reading Others' Emotions

You learned that newborns can mimic others' emotions. Does this mean they understand what emotions mean? That's not clear until they turn almost a year old, when they begin to use "social referencing," which refers to looking at others to see how they should respond to novel situations. For example, imagine a dog approaches and the infant is uncertain whether to be frightened or excited. Typical infants will look to the parent's face. If the parent expresses fear, the infant will respond with distress. If the parent looks happy, the infant may approach the dog. This social referencing suggests that infants and toddlers can read and take meaning from others' emotions.

Preschoolers use social referencing a lot, although not as much as toddlers, because much of their world is still novel to them. For example, they may not laugh at a joke until they've looked at someone else to see if it is funny.

Or, if everyone around them is laughing they'll laugh, too, even if they do not know what's so funny.

Social referencing and emotional contagion help children learn to pair words with specific emotions. As early as age 2 years, some children use two basic emotion words: happy and sad. By age 4 years, they can distinguish angry, sad, disgusted, and fearful faces, and they know which emotions people feel in common situations, such as feeling happy if you get a gift (Bamford & Lagattuta, 2012; Lindquist, Satpute, & Gendron, 2015; Widen, 2013).

Preschoolers (and early elementary students) are poor judges of guilt. Piaget tested children's ability to judge guilt by telling them a story of Mary and John. Mary tried to help by carrying 8 dishes. She dropped and broke them all. John didn't want to eat his vegetables so he threw his plate on the floor and broke it. Who is naughtier? Young children believe Mary is naughtier because she did more damage. They do not take intention into account when judging guilt. Children in 2nd grade and older believe John is naughtier because he intended mischief.

Preschoolers' inability to fully judge intention and guilt leaves them vulnerable to feeling guilt for things that are not their fault. Children clearly feel guilt by age 3 years, because they seek to repair damage they may have caused, such as knocking over a special block tower someone else built (Vaish, Carpenter, & Tomasello, 2016). Guilt is an important, useful emotion. It helps students adhere to the norms of a group, and motivates them to repair any harm they have done. However, in excess, or when felt inappropriately, guilt can lead to emotional disorders. If you teach young children, you need to be aware of this, and relieve them of guilt for events that are not their fault.

Regulating One's Own Emotions

Very young children have some basic emotion regulation skills. For example, they sometimes are able to distract themselves when they feel sad, or look away when they are overly excited. Their lips may tremble when left with a babysitter, but they manage to hold back tears. However, preschoolers more often use the less-constructive coping strategies listed in Table 6.1 above, such as crying or acting out in anger, compared to older children (Dennis & Kelemen, 2009). This may be why 3-year-olds are the most aggressive of any age group (Underwood, 2002; Vlachou et al., 2011). They often need your help to regulate their emotions in the form of hugs, rocking, and soothing to calm down when upset. Between ages 3 and 5 years, preschoolers become better at doing this on their own. As a result, they are less frequently angry or sad, and crying diminishes (Lipscomb et al., 2011). They develop this ability primarily as they have experience with sensitive caretakers who soothe them, but they also develop this ability during pretend play. Have you noticed that during play young children will often practice expressing and containing emotions, such as pretending to have an angry mock fight, or spanking a doll, and then cheerfully get over it? They are practicing escalating and then containing their emotions.

Preschoolers can fake their emotions to a limited extent. They are better at exaggerating rather than squelching emotions. For example, if someone is watching, they may wail as though in great pain when they fall down but are not really hurt. They won't bother if there is no audience. They typically fail the "disappointing gift" test. This is a test of their ability to fake being happy when they are not. Sneaky scientists promise children a gift. When the child opens it, it is very disappointing (e.g., a baby rattle). Social etiquette requires that they smile and say "Thank you." By age 10 years, most children can do this; at ages 6 to 8 years, they manage to contain their negative emotions, but "leak" their unhappiness by twirling hair, or biting their lips. Preschoolers typically cry and pout. To carry the test further, scientists may ask the child to "trick" an adult into thinking they got a really cool gift. For example, a cool gift (e.g., toy car or bracelet) is in one box, but a dud (e.g., broken pencil) is in the other. The child's task is to convince a strange adult, who does not know what is in each box, that the dud box actually has the cool gift. If they are successful, they get to keep the cool gift, but if not, the adult gets it. To be successful they have to inhibit their reaction to the dud, and put on a convincing fake smile. First graders (generally, at ages 6 or 7 years) can typically do this (and enjoy it), but not 4-year-olds (Kromm, Färber, & Holodynski, 2015).

Are Tantrums Normal?

Tantrums emerge at 16 months, crest around 20 months, and then abate so that by age 2 years, the worst is over. Most (80%) preschoolers still might have a tantrum occasionally (e.g., monthly), but daily or weekly tantrums are abnormal, and they should disappear altogether by age 5 years (Wakschlag et al., 2012). However, you should be aware that tantrums that are long, involve aggression, come out of thin air, are directed at adults other than the parents, and are followed by intense shame or guilt are not normal. These extreme tantrums may indicate the preschooler has an emotional disorder and needs professional help (Cole, Luby, & Sullivan, 2008; Wakschlag et al., 2012).

How should you handle a typical tantrum? Tantrums are episodes of intense sadness, with peaks of anger, during which children might yell, hit, kick, cry, and throw themselves on the floor (J. Green, Whitney, & Potegal, 2011). The best approach is to wait until the peak of anger is over (unless the child is in danger). If you try to soothe or reason with the child during the anger phase, you will prolong the tantrum. When sadness is left, then comfort the child. Sad children seek comfort.

Elementary Students

What kind of skill in reading others' emotions and regulating their own emotions do elementary students have? Let's explore what you can expect in a typical elementary classroom.

Reading Others' Emotions

Elementary students make remarkable strides in their ability to talk about emotions. They learn to accurately use complex emotion labels (e.g., embarrassed, jealous, miserable). This improved emotion vocabulary helps them understand their own and others' emotions better. They also learn that the way you think about something can cause an emotion as much as the situation itself (Bamford & Lagattuta, 2012). Finally, they also learn that you can have multiple emotions in the same situation (e.g., I'm sad I lost the contest, but I'm glad I made the first cut), which younger children do not understand.

Regulating One's Own Emotions

Elementary students also become better at controlling their emotions, although even at this age they are better at controlling their emotions when in the presence of an attachment figure (Blandon, Calkins, Keane, & O'Brien, 2008; Gee et al., 2014). Typical elementary students can pass the disappointing gift test. Their use of the coping strategies from Table 6.1 changes in these ways (Saarni, 1999):

1. Less need to rely on others to help them manage distress.

2. More coping strategies in their tool kit. About age 5 years students first begin to use reappraisal, or changing the way they think about the situation to help them cope better, and then become increasingly skilled at it (E. Davis, Levine, Lench, & Quas, 2010).

3. Better able to judge which strategy in their tool kit to use in a particular situation, such as whether to try to change the situation and solve the problem (i.e., problem-focused) or try to change their emotions (i.e., emotion-focused).

4. Come to use emotion-focused strategies more.

By age 10 years, typical children should have adult-like ability to regulate their emotions. First graders are fairly transparent, but by the end of elementary school students can usually conceal their emotions. *However, they can have experiences where emotion control is overwhelmed (e.g., when trauma or stress has been intense or so continuous it overtaxes even those with good emotion control).*

Secondary Students

What kind of skill in reading others' emotions and regulating their own emotions do adolescents have? Let's explore what you can expect in a typical secondary classroom.

Reading Others' Emotions

Students' ability to talk about and read subtle emotions in others will continue to develop through high school (and on into old age; yours is still developing). That is part of what makes literary analysis so fascinating with adolescents. It also makes possible their greater skill in helping friends feel better, such as, "I know you are disappointed that you didn't make show choir, but now you have more time to do something else." It also makes possible their humanitarian interest in the plight of others in distant countries, such as gathering supplies for victims of natural disasters. Yet, ironically, research suggests that adolescents are not necessarily more empathic to those around them than younger children. Some studies even find a decrease in empathy in adolescents (Hastings, Zahn-Waxler, Robinson, Usher, & Bridges, 2000; Zahn-Waxler, Kochanska, Krupnick, & McKnew, 1990). Perhaps this is because, along with greater ability to understand others' emotions, also comes greater ability to be self-protective.

Regulating One's Own Emotions

If students have adult-like emotion regulation skills by age 10 years, why are adolescents so moody? Perhaps they are not. Research suggests this is mostly a myth. For example, one study found that when adults and children of various ages are asked to report how they feel at the very moment that beepers randomly went off throughout their day, most adolescents reported feeling happy most of the time (Larson & Richards, 1994). They also reported more often feeling *more bored and sleepy, as well as lonely and socially awkward,* compared to adults and younger children.

Teens do have a few forces working against their emotional well-being. They are overly tired (see Chapter 2!). They are hypersensitive to social evaluation, such as feeling embarrassment just because they think someone is looking at them. For example, in one study students were put in an fMRI machine and told that a peer could see them. Younger children, 6- to 9-year-olds, didn't care, but 15- to 18-year-olds felt embarrassed (Somerville, 2013). Teens also feel stressed out. This stress centers around friends, romances, parents, and feeling pressed to get good grades or test scores (Gutman & Eccles, 2007; Seiffge-Krenke et al., 2009). Nevertheless, in a diary study, teens reported feeling positive moods and having positive interactions with others more than negative moods or interactions (Flook, 2011).

The research suggests that if you have adolescent students who are moody in the sense that they are frequently angry, sad, or anxious, they need help. This is not due to puberty, nor is it a normal phase of development that will naturally be outgrown. Teens who have an abundance of stressors (e.g., parents' fighting, moving, family drug use) are more likely to fit the moody adolescent stereotype. Seek the help of a counselor for students who are chronically negative.

Emotions Can be Out of Control:
Depression and Anxiety Disorders

Some students are unable to contain their negative emotions or augment positive emotions, nor are they able to draw upon effective coping strategies (Bonanno & Burton, 2013; Gross & Jazaieri, 2014). When students are unable to regulate their emotions, they may act out in anger, or they may withdraw in sadness (Rhee, Lahey, & Waldman, 2015). They may have *emotional disorders*, which are disturbingly common. Almost one quarter of students will have an emotional disorder before reaching adulthood (Avenevoli, Swendsen, He, Burstein, & Merikangas, 2015; Merikangas et al., 2010). You can expect that some of your students have these emotional disorders.

The most common disorders are *depression*, *anxiety*, and *conduct disorder*. Your school probably commits substantial resources to addressing substance use and behavior problems, but depression and anxiety often go unaddressed, although they are more common and interfere with success at school. You may wonder whether your school can even make a difference in depression among students, but it can! A large national study found that which school a student attended predicted whether the student was depressed beyond other key factors (E. C. Dunn, Milliren, Evans, Subramanian, & Richmond, 2015). Later in this chapter, you'll learn what you can do to help your school become a place that promotes students' *emotional well-being*.

Most children do not get treatment, so it is important to advocate for your students who need help. Watch for these signs of depression (American Psychiatric Association, 2013):

Social withdrawal	Poor hygiene
Lack of interest in school	Frequent crying
Feeling worthless	Sleep problems
Changes in appetite	*Poor concentration
Self-criticism	*Unable to sit still (nail biting, hair
Irritability	twirling, lip chewing)

Clinical levels of anxiety can have some of the same symptoms, particularly the last two (marked *). Anxiety disorders are as prevalent as depression, and sometimes they occur together.

If you teach in a secondary school, you are more likely to see depression because rates peak in adolescence, but it can occur in preschoolers (and even infants). Teachers in the primary grades tend to overlook depression, as Olivia's teacher did:

> *In a kindergarten, the students are supposed to be transitioning to a new center. Olivia is supposed to get a book to look at, but instead grabs her backpack, pulls out a toy and hides under a table to play with it. Ms. Reid sees her and beckons for her to come out. Olivia begins sobbing. Ms. Reid asks her what is wrong. Olivia says that the other kids don't like her and she wants to stay under the table. Ms. Reid asks about any specific incidents that might have triggered the crying, but there don't seem to be any so she asks Olivia to sit in the safe seat until she calms down. Olivia sits by herself crying for a few minutes, but then somberly goes to a center to work. This behavior occurs occasionally with Olivia. Ms. Reid assumes she will outgrow it.*

Olivia might outgrow her depression symptoms in the sense that she might develop some constructive coping strategies on her own, but it is not likely. She would fare better if Ms. Reid would use the tools you'll learn about later in this chapter.

Anxiety disorders emerge earlier than depression, on average at age 6 years (Merikangas et al., 2010). Some studies find that as many as one third of children in kindergarten are anxious. However, many young children will outgrow their anxiety, unlike depression (Duchesne, Larose, Vitaro, & Tremblay, 2010). Still, if you teach young children, watch for those that are more anxious than their peers, because the earlier treatment occurs, the better the outcome (Luby, 2010).

Depression and anxiety are bad enough consequences in themselves; you do not want your students to be unhappy or worried. Yet these emotional disorders lead to other problems as well, such as ADHD and learning problems (Rhee et al., 2015). Students who are depressed and anxious have a hard time paying attention; they process information more slowly, are lonely, and are more prone to illness and drug abuse (Duchesne et al., 2010; Foersterling & Binser, 2002; Kochel, Ladd, & Rudolph, 2012; Pomerantz & Rudolph, 2003; Van Zalk, Kerr, Branje, Stattin, & Meeus, 2010; Verboom, Sijtsema, Verhulst, Penninx, & Ormel, 2014). Fortunately, not all depressed or anxious students will develop these problems.

> **"** Students unable to regulate their emotions may develop depression or anxiety disorder, which are very common. Both interfere with learning. Teachers, counselors, and schools can make a difference. **"**

You can make a difference. If you think a student may have an emotional disorder based on the symptoms above, or because the student seems chronically in a negative mood, notify a counselor. Counselors can arrange *interventions* that are effective (Muñoz, Beardslee, & Leykin, 2012). In addition, as you implement the suggestions in the next section, you will help all your students become more *emotionally competent*, including those with emotional disor-

Table 6.2 Summary of Age-Appropriate Emotional Competence

Toddlers & Preschoolers	Elementary Students	Secondary Students
• Toddlers may have tantrums. This behavior should disappear by age 5 years. • Being a little anxious is common, and not a concern. • Preschoolers mimic others' emotions and read them to see how to behave (social referencing). • They can talk about and understand basic emotions, but are poor at judging guilt. • They can regulate their own emotions a little, and even fake them sometimes, but often need your help to contain strong emotions.	• Elementary students can talk about and understand sophisticated emotions. • They have adult-like ability to regulate their own emotions by age 10 years. • Anxiety disorders emerge on average at age 6 years.	• Secondary students are capable of great empathy for distant others, yet are not more empathic to those around them. • Typical students are not moody, but are quick to feel embarrassment. • Depression rates tend to peak.

ders. In fact, in psychotherapy, parents are trained to do some of the same things to help their children overcome emotional disorders (Dougherty et al., 2015; Weisz, McCarty, & Valeri, 2006).

Help Your Students Become More Emotionally Competent

You can help your students become more emotionally competent. You'll learn about six key tools in this section. The first two are a review of tools you have already learned about in Chapters 3 and 5.

Develop Positive Relationships

The primary mechanism through which your students learned to regulate their emotions is the attachment relationship they have with their parents. Sensitive, responsive parents soothe their children when they experience overwhelming emotions. This happens when the children are upset, but also during play. For example, if they notice their child is getting too wound up during a tickling game, sensitive parents back off a little to allow the child time to get emotions under control before jumping in again. As children have thousands of daily experiences like this, their brains develop robust networks to regulate emotions (Blair et al., 2008; Braungart-Rieker, Hill-Soderlund, & Karrass, 2010). This is why children with secure attachment tend to have good emotion regulation ability (Morris, Silk, Steinberg, Myers, & Robinson, 2007). They are able to trust others, take on emotionally charged situations with confidence, and receive others' emotions. They are less likely to become depressed (Allen et al., 2007). They are better able to understand others' emotions and feel more sympathy compared to insecure students who are more likely to feel personal distress (Dykas & Cassidy, 2011; Mikulineer & Shaver, 2005).

❝Students learn to regulate emotions in attachment relationships.❞

In contrast, children whose parents are insensitive and intrusive tend to develop an angry emotional core and poor emotion regulation (Braungart-Rieker et al., 2010). Some parents may be inconsistently responsive and may not bother soothing the children until they are in a full-blown tantrum. As a result, their children's brains become trained to rapidly escalate intensity of emotions. Such children become more difficult to soothe over time and are often anxious (Thompson, 1990). Other parents may be hostile, intrusive, or emotionally unavailable. An intrusive parent is one who chronically overrides the child's agenda with their own agenda, when it is not necessary. For example, during parent-child storybook reading, the child may be carefully studying a picture, but the parent turns the page anyway. Children of such parents are often angry and frustrated, but they suppress emotions around their parents and do not seek their parents' help. While this might seem adaptive, it keeps the children from developing constructive coping strategies (Cassidy, 1994). They may avoid emotional closeness or seem hostile and detached by others. *Insecure attachment is the most common cause of depression and anxiety disorders at all ages* (Hammen, 2009; Madigan et al., 2013; Madigan et al., 2016).

The same principles apply to teachers. Students need teachers to be available to help them learn to regulate their emotions. *Students whose teachers are responsive become less anxious and more emotionally positive than students whose teachers are critical or detached* (Hestenes, Kontos, & Bryan, 1993). Sadly, students who have a double whammy of a negative relationship with both their parents and their teachers are the most likely to become depressed or delinquent (M.-T. Wang et al., 2013).

Use Effective Discipline

Power-assertive discipline harms relationships and creates angry students. When teachers use harsh, power-assertive discipline they escalate negative emotions in the encounter, causing the target students to be overwhelmed by emotion and unable to regulate their emotions. This often causes the situation to boil over. This is what happened to Shawn, the child who was reprimanded in one class and in the next, too. The detrimental effect of power-assertive discipline on students' ability to regulate their own emotions has been found for preschoolers through high schoolers (e.g., Lipscomb et al., 2011). That is, no matter what grade level you teach, if you use power-assertive discipline you may undermine your students' emotional competence. In contrast, if you use victim-centered induction you will be able to maintain positive relationships, *while also training empathy in students.* Recall that victim-centered induction focuses misbehaving students' attention on how their behavior affected others.

" Power-assertive discipline promotes anger in students. Induction keeps relationships positive and trains empathy in students.**"**

Respond Constructively to Students' Emotions

When your students express emotion, you can respond appropriately or inappropriately. Inappropriate responses include yelling at, threatening, belittling, shaming, dismissing, or placating students for their emotions. Students who receive these kinds of responses to their emotions tend to develop poor *emotion regulation*, become chronically angry, and act out at school (e.g., Leerkes et al., 2011; Lipscomb et al., 2011; Swanson, Valiente, Lemery-Chalfont, Bradley, & Eggum-Wilkens, 2014). In contrast, appropriate responses include respectfully acknowledging the students' emotions and responding with understanding and compassion. For example, your response to anger might be, "I can see you are upset. Tell me what is going on and let's see if we can find a solution." When you respond compassionately to your students' distress you become a model of empathy to them (Denham, Mitchell-Copeland, Strandberg, Auerbach, & Blair, 1997; Eisenberg, Fabes, Schaller, Carlo, & Miller, 1991). However, appropriate responses do not necessarily include accepting student outbursts if they hurt others' feelings. *While most genuine emotions should be accepted as legitimate, not all behaviors should be accepted.*

Express Your Emotions

Are you usually cheerful in class, or do you often appear angry, irritated, frustrated, or depressed? If you model poor emotion regulation, your students are likely to imitate you. They'll have fewer coping strategies and feel depressed or anxious themselves (Blandon et al., 2008; Stocker, Richmond, Rhoades, & Kuang, 2007). In addition, students learn less content from depressed teachers (McLean & Connor, 2015). In contrast, if you are mostly cheerful and warm with students, modeling good coping abilities, your students are likely to become better at regulating their own emotions and become more sympathetic toward others (Michalik et al., 2007).

---

66 Your response to your students' emotions and the emotions you model affect your students' ability to regulate their emotions, feel sympathy, and learn content.**"**

You do not need to be super human and overly cheerful all the time; students need to learn emotion regulation from models who cope with occasional negative emotions. For example, imagine that rather than Jerome's father figure being seriously ill, it was Mr. Pauling's father. If Mr. Pauling conveyed to his students that he was deeply sad, yet told them something about his coping strategies (e.g., "I sit with my dad every evening and tell him my favorite childhood memories"), he would be modeling emotional competence. So feel free to express a wide range of emotions, but be primarily positive over all. It's hard, but sometimes you have to act happy whether you feel it or not. As a result, you will probably feel your mood lifting.

Deliberately use *emotion contagion* to your students' advantage. Express enjoyment of your students and of the subject matter. Students read and catch emotions better if you convey them vividly and clearly (Zaki, Bolger, & Ochsner, 2008). They also catch negative emotions. For example, one study found that if students had a teacher with math anxiety, they were more likely to become math anxious as well. So be careful what emotions you convey about the content you teach (Beilock, Gunderson, Ramirez, & Levine, 2010).

Talk About Emotions

How often do you use words like surprised, angry, or guilty in your classroom? This may surprise you, but talking about emotions will help your students become more emotionally competent. For example, you might say, "Jenny is *angry* with you, because you are not sharing computer time" instead of just saying "You must share computer time." When you talk with students about emotions during an emotionally charged event, you are giving them several important gifts: (1) time to get their own emotions under control, (2) information about why people behave the way they do, (3) opportunity to learn coping strategies, (4) greater awareness of emotions, and (5) increased emotion vocabulary. This last gift is a big deal because the ability to correctly label emotions helps students regulate their emotions better. For example, one study found that students who were more precise in their "emotion talk" (e.g., "I felt sad at first, but then I became angry") compared to students who were less precise (e.g., "I felt bad") were better at regulating their own emotions (Kashdan, Barrett, & McKnight, 2015). Why might this be? The ability to talk about emotions allows students to step out of themselves long enough to look upon the emotion with some objectivity and get it under control (Bernstein et al., 2015).

❝ Talking about emotions with students and building their "emotion vocabulary" helps them become more emotionally competent.❞

You have opportunities to talk about emotions during everyday classroom events as well as in the flow of curriculum. Conflicts between students provide an especially rich context for talking about emotions, so do not shy away from them. Conversations around negative emotions tend to be richer than those around positive emotions because you are more likely to discuss the causes of emotions and use more emotion-related vocabulary (Lagattuta & Wellman, 2002). Conflict is a teaching moment! Reading literature and history can also provide a good context for talking about emotions and build empathy for people in other places and times (Kidd & Castano, 2013; Lysaker, Tonge, Gauson, & Miller, 2011). In one study, teachers of 5th and 6th graders asked "feeling" questions (e.g., "How would you feel if . . .") as they taught literature, in addition to critical thinking questions. Their students became more supportive of one another and said their classroom was a friendlier place, compared with a control group (Shechtman & Yaman, 2012). As a bonus, they also learned more of the subject matter!

Teach Emotion Coping Strategies

You can directly coach your students in coping strategies. Research has found that when students are coached in *coping strategies*, not only do they improve in emotion regulation, but also in attention, impulse control, and even their health (Abaied & Rudolph, 2011; Lunkenheimer, Shields, & Cortina, 2007; Morris et al., 2007).

Which strategies should you teach? Preferably the more constructive coping strategies listed in Table 6.1 above. Keep this table readily available in your classroom until you feel you have mastered it. Your students will fare better if they have at least a few different strategies that they can draw upon as the need arises (Bonanno & Burton, 2013; Gross, 2015). Try not to overemphasize avoidant strategies. Unfortunately, teachers generally prefer students who use avoidant strategies, such as backing out of angry encounters (Kliewer, 1991). This is understandable because such students are less likely to be in confrontations, which makes them easier to deal with. However, these are not always the best strategies because they do not lead to problem solving, or learning to stand up for oneself, and they can embolden bullies. An especially versatile strategy that you may want to equip your students with is reappraisal.

Reappraisal

As you learned above, how you interpret a situation has a large effect on the emotions you feel. Many emotion-provoking situations are ambiguous, so you can interpret them in different ways. Prosocial students tend to assume the best possible motives of others in ambiguous situations. If someone takes their seat in the lunchroom, they do not assume it was a deliberate attack on them. In contrast, aggressive students tend to take the opposite stance, assuming the worst possible motive on the part of others. They attend more carefully to possible hostile cues from others, assume it is okay to be aggressive toward others they decide deserve it, and they do not have good strategies to cope with anger (Arsenio, Adams, & Gold, 2009; Dodge, Godwin, & Group, 2013; Paciello, Fida, Tramontano, Lupinetti, & Caprara, 2008; Werner & Hill, 2010). An old adage is, "A foolish man takes offense when it is not intended; a wise man learns not to take offense when it is." When you coach students in *reappraisal*, you can help them behave more like the wise man. At what age can you start coaching reappraisal? Starting as early as preschool, students who are coached in reappraisal have better emotion regulation (Morris et al., 2011).

Volcano Myth

You may have heard some people assert that if you suppress your emotions they will eventually explode like a volcano, making things worse, so you should let your emotions out. Is this true? Charles Darwin (1965/1872), one of

---

❝Directly coaching students, especially in reappraisal, helps them regulate their emotions better. Suppressing emotions dampens them; expressing them augments them.**❞**

---

the most famous scientists in history, concluded quite the opposite after studying emotional expression in many different tribes of people and even animals. According to Darwin, expressing emotions intensifies them and suppressing emotions dampens them. Modern research has consistently supported his conclusion, and you have probably noticed it yourself. The emotions you express grow and the ones you suppress diminish. For example, imagine that you have had a bad day that left you feeling discouraged and sad. Parent-teacher conferences are that evening, so you muster the energy to smile at parent after parent, telling them how wonderful their child is. Soon, you will begin to actually feel happier. There is a physiological reason for this. As you fake a smile, your facial muscles send messages to your brain that alters the physiological component of your emotion, altering the emotion itself (Kraft & Pressman, 2012). I tell my university students, "Fake it 'til you make it" actually works. It is a great tool for teachers.

Summary

In this section you have learned six research-based tools for helping your students become more emotionally competent:

1. Develop positive teacher-student relationships.

2. Use effective discipline; avoid anger-causing, power-assertive discipline.

3. Respond constructively to students' emotions.

4. Express mostly positive emotions, but also model coping with negative emotions.

5. Seize opportunities to talk about emotions, even just briefly.

6. Teach constructive emotion-coping strategies, especially reappraisal.

If you use these tools, your students should increase in emotional competence. But better yet, try to get your school to implement these tools on a school-wide basis. Earlier, you learned that some schools promote depression in students. School-wide implementation of these tools will help ensure that your school is not one of them. I have been in many schools in my professional work and noted glaring differences in school climate. Some schools feel friendly and almost all students smile and greet others as they pass in the hallway, whereas other schools feel dismal.

I have personally experienced both friendly and dismal schools at each economic extreme from poor to wealthy. In fact, some of the most dismal have been in exclusive neighborhoods; those schools had uptight, pressure-cooker climates. However, the research suggests that in general if you teach in a school with many impoverished students you need to become especially skilled in using these tools. Students from low-income families tend to have greater difficulty regulating their emotions. This may be because they have more stressors to cope with in their lives that cascade on them. Before they have managed to cope with one crisis, another descends (Zimmer-Gembeck & Skinner, 2008). They also may have fewer supportive adults to help them cope. You can be the support they need. Such students who have adults in their lives who do the things you learned in this section develop good emotion regulation despite living with poverty (Raver, 2004).

Create an Emotionally Positive Classroom

Classroom climate is driven by three powerful forces. The first is the quality of the teacher-student relationship. You learned about this in Chapter 5. The second is the quality of student-student interaction; the more prosocial classmates are, the more positive the classroom climate. You have learned how to promote prosocial behavior among students throughout this book. The third force is the extent to which students feel and express positive emotions in the classroom. In this chapter, you learned how to promote student happiness and its importance. These forces are interrelated, as Figure 6.1 shows. Positive teacher-student relationships drive student happiness in the classroom. When students feel more positive emotions they earn higher grades and test scores and behave more prosocially toward each other, which makes them feel even more positive. Positive emotions also restore self-control after self-control is spent, which increases opportunity to learn (Baumeister, Vohs, & Tice, 2007). Thus, if you apply the tools you have learned in this book, you will create a positive classroom climate where greater learning occurs. There are two final strategies you can apply to create an emotionally positive classroom.

Simple Ways to Generate Positive Emotions in Students

You can easily induce positive emotions in your students that are strong enough to increase prosocial behavior (and increase content learning). In experiments, researchers find measurable increases in positive emotions from tasks as simple as asking people to think about a fond memory, giving them an unexpected reward, or playing upbeat, happy music. In your classroom you can tell happy stories or celebrate achievements. You can play games that make students think fast, which is fun and energizing and leads to better moods (Pronin & Jacobs, 2008). You can also help your stu-

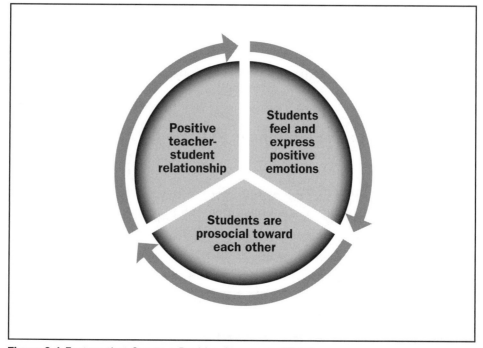

Figure 6.1 Factors that Create a Positive Classroom Climate

dents express *gratitude* in your classroom. Research on gratitude finds that it results in increased prosocial behavior toward others, whether they were the cause of the gratitude or not (Bartlett & DeSteno, 2006; McCullough, Kimeldorf, & Cohen, 2008). An intervention as simple as writing down three things they are grateful for each day can raise your students' level of happiness (Lyubomirsky, 2007).

Humor in the Classroom

> **❝**In addition to six tools to help your students become more emotionally competent, you can increase your students' positive emotions through quick interventions and by having more fun and humor in your classroom.**❞**

You can also induce positive emotions by interjecting a little fun and *humor* into your classroom. In Chapter 1 you learned that humor is part of being prosocial; some students use humor to make others feel better. Humor is also a coping strategy that helps you smooth over awkward situations and facilitates social interactions, bringing a positive climate to the classroom. Playful teasing that is good-natured strengthens social bonds, making students feel closer to each other (Keltner, Capps, Kring, Young, & Heerey, 2001). (Teasing that is hostile, ridiculing, or sexually charged has no place in schools.) Humor also facilitates learning, enhances attention, and makes learning fun (Banas et al., 2010; Fitzsimmons & McKenzie, 2003; D. Martin et al., 2006). Consider this experience of a teacher:

> *I was writing on the board when light from the window created a shadow that moved across the board. It looked like a giant rodent was outside. It was so bizarre that it caught my attention along with several of my students. Suddenly, I realized it was caused by the hair of a student in the front row, shifting at her desk. I chuckled briefly. A student said, "Mr. Rushton, that's the first time we've seen you smile." That made me*

> *realize that I was much too uptight with my classes. I started*
> *injecting a little humor into my lessons. Now my students are*
> *more receptive to my lessons and I feel like we are working*
> *together instead of in opposition. Classroom management has*
> *actually improved!*

You can build humor into your lessons, using jokes, props, or movie clips to illustrate a concept (Berk, 2002). One beloved 3rd grade teacher had students share jokes at the beginning of each day. This set a nice tone for the day, but also kept the humor under the bounds the teacher set. What kinds of jokes your students like depends on their age. Generally, students use and enjoy humor that is just at their level of cognitive understanding, or involves concepts they have recently mastered. This is why preschoolers find incongruities or distortions of the world (e.g., a cow who dances) and poop jokes funny. This is why 1st graders like knock-knock jokes (kudos to teachers who endure these for years on end!), riddles, and puns, because they are just coming to understand phonetics and how language works. This is why high school students enjoy jokes that involve witticism, innuendo, and larger social understandings. For example, they find double entendres funny.

You do not have to be a comedian extraordinaire, but if generating humor makes you uncomfortable, then simply give some latitude to your humorous students. Often it is your brightest students who are humorous and bring fun to the classroom because humor is related to intelligence, verbal ability, and creativity (Greengross & Miller, 2011; Ziv, 2013). You might also find that giving them this outlet for their creativity improves their behavior. Teachers tend to respond more positively to the humor of students they already like better, so you may have to take care to appreciate the humorous contributions of students with whom you have a difficult relationship (Fabrizi & Pollio, 1987). In addition, elementary teachers tend to be more accepting of humor than secondary teachers, such that humor occurs two to three times more often in elementary classrooms; secondary teachers may have more work to do here (Banas et al., 2010, Fabrizi & Pollio, 1987; McGhee, 2013).

You might assume that it is easier to create a positive classroom climate with younger students than in high school. After all, what's not to like about kindergarten? Actually, several large studies of early childhood classrooms found teachers' scored an average of 5 on a scale of 1 to 7 when they were rated on the quality of emotional support and teacher-student relationships in their classroom. That's good, but it suggests that even in early childhood classes there is some room for improvement using the tools you have learned in this book.

NOTE ABOUT AGGRESSIVE STUDENTS

The climate of your school affects aggression. Positive school climate reduces victimization and bullying (Harel-Fisch et al., 2011; Kowalski, Giumetti, Schroeder, & Lattanner, 2014). You can make a difference. For example, in one study, teachers were trained to successfully turn around a negative peer culture in which students pressured each other not to achieve academically. What were they trained to do? The same things you have learned in this chapter—become aware of the peer culture in the classroom and create a positive classroom climate (Hamm, Farmer, Lambert, & Gravelle, 2014).

FOR REFLECTION AND DISCUSSION

How would you describe the emotional climate of your classroom? Randomly choose six students to focus on. Are they happy to be in your classroom? Do they have more positive than negative emotions?

Can you identify any of your students who might have an emotional disorder that needs a counselors' help?

For each of the six prosocial enhancement methods in this chapter, rate yourself on a scale of 1 (low) to 5 (high) for how effective you are with each. What specific practices do you already have in place that lead to your highest score? Write a plan for how you will improve in one of those areas where you need the most improvement in the next two weeks.

APPENDIX

Case Study for Review

A case study is presented here for you to use to review the information you have learned through this book, and to provide a common case to discuss in your peer learning group. This is an authentic composite of cases in real classrooms. Names are changed to protect anonymity.

Review Case Study: 6th Grade Math

Liam, a 6th grader, and his younger brother have been removed from their mother's custody due to criminal neglect. She is a drug user and does not make the boys go to school, feed them, clean the house, nor supervise them. Children's protective services place them in the custody of their father, whom they hate. Protective services are called because the father beats the boys using "the belt." The boys are not removed from their father's custody, but they are in family counseling. Liam doesn't have friends at school; the other students avoid him and stay away. He was been suspended for hitting other students when he is angry.

Liam was moved from a different math class into Ms. Baird's class because the former math teacher could not control his behavior. During a parent conference, Liam's father argued that Liam should stay in the original classroom and "get his stuff done in there. He shouldn't be rewarded for not doing what the math teacher wants him to do." The father was more focused on punishing Liam than getting him into a setting where Liam could be more successful.

Ms. Baird works to build a trusting relationship with Liam, who seems to soak up positive attention. However, occasionally he misbehaves as though he is unable to take all the positive attention and wants Ms. Baird to yell at him. She does not give in. She simply makes her expectations clear, gives him reasons for why his behavior needs to change, and restates directives until he complies, but without getting angrier. He usually (but not always) comes round. She is trying to model good emotion regulation.

Ms. Baird goes out of her way to chat with Liam. She follows his lead when he is interested in something. He is interested in the two lizards in the room, so she puts Liam in charge. He checks on them and mists their cages. He uses this as an excuse to visit her classroom often.

Ms. Baird uses cooperative learning often. The other students initially do not want to work with Liam. One day he asks a pair of prosocial girls if he can work with them. To Ms. Baird's relief, they say yes. Still, she keeps a careful eye on them in case there is conflict. She provides a lot of structure to the groups to try to prevent any problems. Things go smoothly.

One day, in Mr. Reynolds' class, Liam refuses to do a worksheet. Mr. Reynolds threatens to send him to the office if he does not cooperate. Liam defies the teacher, so Mr. Reynolds addresses the whole class, "How many of you feel that Liam should be sent to the office and not come back to class today?" All hands go up. He tells Liam to go to the office, but Liam refuses. Mr. Reynolds calls the office.

The principal, a juvenile court officer, and a P.E. teacher arrive in the classroom. Liam runs out the back door. The principal threatens Liam, saying that if he does not come back, she will call his father and the police. He refuses, so the principal goes to make the calls. The P.E. teacher walks out back to talk with Liam, explaining that things would get worse for him if Liam does not go to the office. Liam has a trusting relationship with the P.E. teacher, so he goes to the office with him.

Liam is very angry. He calls the principal a b---h. The principal feels threatened by him, so Liam is suspended for three days.

Three days later when Liam returns to school, a student in first period makes a snide remark about having him back. Ms. Baird immediately stops the class, and tells the students to gather around. As they sit in a group she asks them, "How would you feel if you were Liam?" She says, "When somebody makes a mistake, It is not your role to hold it over their head and say things that make them feel bad. It is your role to model better behavior and help others do the same." The group talk only takes about 5 minutes, and then students go back to their work. No more negative comments are made about Liam.

Liam hangs out in Ms. Baird's class whenever he can. He helps her by running errands, cutting things out, straightening tables, or putting books away. One day he comes to her for advice about conflict he was having with another student, instead of bullying his way through it. Ms. Baird feels this is momentous improvement!

Suggested Discussion Questions:

1. What type of discipline does Ms. Baird use? Is it effective? Why or why not?

2. What opportunities for practicing prosocial behavior did Ms. Baird provide to Liam?

3. What principles of attachment might be at work in Liam's life? What type of relationship does Ms. Baird have with Liam? What strategies discussed in the book did Ms. Baird implement? Were they successful?

4. What parenting style do Liam's parents have? What styles do Ms. Baird and Mr. Reynolds have? What kinds of student behavior could you expect based on each teacher's behavior?

5. Does Liam have age-appropriate emotional competence? What behaviors lead you to this conclusion?

6. What factors that lead to emotional competence are operating in Liam's life, and what factors are harmful? What additional strategies might Ms. Baird use to strengthen Liam's emotional competence?

7. Reflect on students in your classroom and your own teaching practices. Are there commonalities with the students and teachers in this example? What lessons from this example can you take away to try in your own classroom?

ENDNOTES

[1] This has created some controversy about making yet another domain ripe for high-stakes testing (Duckworth, 2016). Clearly these non-academic factors matter, and schools should be looking at their data. Yet, this is a difficult area to measure well, so the Department of Education has released an online toolbox to help administrator's better understand and measure non-academic factors, such as school climate.

[2] If you want to have a few charming "feel good" minutes to boost your faith in mankind, search on the internet Warneken or Tomasello with "toddler altruism" or a similar phrase. They have posted videos of toddlers spontaneously helping adults in need. The "cabinet task" is one of my favorites.

[3] Names have been changed to protect students and teachers.

[4] One exception is that some "friendships" are negative. That is, students encourage misbehavior in each other. These friendships should not be promoted.

[5] The WWC is a service provided by the U.S. Department of Education. It reviews programs and studies that receive media attention to determine the scientific rigor and trustworthiness of their results.

[6] The National Center for Education Statistics conducts a survey every few years of teachers and principals called the "Schools and Staffing Survey." This statistic is taken from the 2011–12 administration, Table 230.95.

[7] Maslow was a professor of psychology in New York, but he didn't start out

that way. He started out as a child and, like many other children, he was mediocre in school and initially a disappointment to his Russian, Jewish immigrant parents. You may want to know this because teachers need an arsenal of inspirational stories for their mediocre students. Albert Einstein cannot bear all the weight of hopeful parents. (Claims of Einstein's laziness, dyslexia, ADHD, Asperger's syndrome, and flunking math are all probably myths, anyway.)

[8] Bobo was an inflatable clown doll that was weighted in the bottom so that it bounced back up if it was punched down. Some children watched an adult actor yell at, punch, kick and hit Bobo with a mallet (Bandura, 1965). Later the children were given the chance to play alone with Bobo. Children who had watched the aggressive adult were more aggressive toward the Bobo doll compared to children who had not seen the adult. In fact, they were aggressive in the very same ways as the adult. This study showed that although the children had not been reinforced for their behavior, they had learned specific aggressive acts from a model. You can find videos of the experiment online.

[9] Principals' values were tested by asking which of the following statements they were most likely to endorse: (1) helping the people around him; caring for their well-being, (2) being loyal to her friends; devoting herself to people close to her, (3) being very successful; having his achievements recognized, (4) showing her abilities; being admired, (5) having adventure and excitement, (6) making her own decisions; being free and not dependent on others, (7) caring for nature and the environment, (8) treating everyone equally; giving everyone equal opportunities in life (Berson & Oreg, 2016). Which would your principal be most likely to endorse?

[10] The negative effect of tangible rewards does not apply to situations where the child has no intrinsic interest in the activity. You cannot undermine motivation when there is none to begin with. This is why offering treats to some toddlers helps with potty training, if the toddler has no initial interest in it, without undermining motivation to use the potty. In addition, rewards may not undermine motivation if they are unexpected. They may also be useful sometimes to help very shy children overcome reticence to help others.

REFERENCES

Abaied, J. L., & Rudolph, K. D. (2011). Maternal influences on youth responses to peer stress. *Developmental Psychology, 47*(6), 1776–1785. doi: 10.1037/a0025439

Achenbach, T. M., Dumenci, L., & Rescorla, L. A. (2003). Are American children's problems still getting worse? A 23-year comparison. *Journal of Abnormal Child Psychology, 31*(1), 1–11.

Adams, J. W., Snowling, M. J., Hennessy, S. M., & Kind, P. (1999). Problems of behaviour, reading and arithmetic: Assessments of comorbidity using the Strengths and Difficulties Questionnaire. *British Journal of Educational Psychology, 69,* 571–585.

Ainsworth, M. D. (1973). The development of infant-mother attachment. In B. Caldwell & H. Ricciuti (Eds.), *Review of child development research* (Vol. 3, pp. 1–94). Chicago: University of Chicago Press.

Ainsworth, M. D. (1979). Infant-mother attachment. *American Psychologist, 34*(10), 932–937. doi: 10.1037//0003-066x.34.10.932

Akiba, M., LeTendre, G. K., & Scribner, J. P. (2007). Teacher quality, opportunity gap, and national achievement in 46 countries. *Educational Researcher, 36*(7), 369–387.

Aknin, L. B., Hamlin, J. K., & Dunn, E. W. (2012). Giving leads to happiness in young children. *PLoS One, 7*(6), e39211.

Alink, L. R., Mesman, J., van Zeijl, J., Stolk, M., Juffer, F., Koot, H. M., . . . van IJzendoorn, M. H. (2006). The early childhood aggression curve: Development of physical aggression in 10- to 50-month-old children. *Child Development, 77*(4), 954–966.

Allen, J., Pianta, R. C., Gregory, A., Mikami, A. Y., & Lun, J. (2011). An interaction-based approach to enhancing secondary school instruction and student achievement. *Science, 333*(6045), 1034–1037.

Allen, J., Porter, M., McFarland, C., McElhaney, K. B., & Marsh, P. (2007). The relation of attachment security to adolescents' paternal and peer relationships, depression, and externalizing behavior. *Child Development, 78*(4), 1222–1239.

American Psychiatric Association. (2013). Diagnostic and statistical manual of mental disorders (5th ed.). Arlington, VA: Author.

Anderson, C. A. (2001). Heat and violence. *Current Directions in Psychological Science, 10*(1), 33–38.

Appleton, J. J., Christenson, S. L., Kim, D., & Reschly, A. L. (2006). Measuring cognitive and psychological engagement: Validation of the Student Engagement Instrument. *Journal of School Psychology, 44*(5), 427–445. doi: 10.1016/j.jsp.2006.04.002

Arnold, D. H., McWilliams, L., & Arnold, E. H. (1998). Teacher discipline and child misbehavior in day care: Untangling causality with correlational data. *Developmental Psychology, 34*, 276–287.

Arsenio, W. F., Adams, E., & Gold, J. (2009). Social information processing, moral reasoning, and emotion attributions: Relations with adolescents' reactive and proactive aggression. *Child Development, 80*(6), 1739–1755.

Arsenio, W. F., Cooperman, S., & Lover, A. (2000). Affective predictors of preschoolers' aggression and peer acceptance: Direct and indirect effects. *Developmental Psychology, 36*(4), 438–448.

Ashby, F. G., Isen, A. M., & Turken, A. U. (1999). A neuropsychological theory of positive affect and its influence on cognition. *Psychological Review, 106*(3), 529–550.

Atwater, J., & Morris, E. (1988). Teachers' instruction and children's compliance in preschool classrooms: A descriptive analysis. *Journal of Applied Behavior Analysis, 21*, 157–167.

Autor, D., Figlio, D., Karbownik, K., Roth, J., & Wasserman, M. (2015). *Family disadvantage and the gender gap in behavioral and educational outcomes. Working Paper 15–16*. Evanston, IL: Institute for Policy Research, Northwestern University.

Avenevoli, S., Swendsen, J., He, J.-P., Burstein, M., & Merikangas, K. (2015). Major depression in the National Comorbidity Survey-Adolescent Supplement: Prevalence, correlates, and treatment. *Journal of the American Academy of Child and Adolescent Psychiatry, 54*(1), 37–44.

Aviezer, O., Sagi, A., Resnick, G., & Gini, M. (2002). School competence in young adolescence: Links to early attachment relationships beyond concurrent self-perceived competence and representations of relationships. *International Journal of Behavioral Development, 26*(5), 387–409. doi: 10.1080/01650250143000328

Baillargeon, R., Morisset, A., Keenan, K., Norman, C., Jeyaganth, S., Boiivin, M., & Tremblay, R. (2011). The development of prosocial behaviors in young children: A propsective population-based cohort study. *Journal of Genetic Psychology, 172*(3), 221–251.

Baillargeon, R., Zoccolillo, M., Keenan, K., Cote, S., Perusse, D., Wu, H.-Z., . . . Tremblay, R. E. (2007). Gender differences in physical aggression: A prospective population-based survey of children before and after 2 years of age. *Developmental Psychology, 43*(1), 13–26.

Bakermans-Kranenburg, M., van IJzendoorn, M., & Juffer, F. (2003). Less is more: Meta-analyses of sensitivity and attachment interventions in early childhood. *Psychological Bulletin, 129*(2), 195–215.

Bamford, C., & Lagattuta, K. H. (2012). Looking on the bright side: Children's knowledge about the benefits of positive versus negative thinking. *Child Development, 83*(2), 667–682.

Banas, J. A., Dunbar, N., Rodriguez, D., & Liu, S.-J. (2010). A review of humor in educational settings: Four decades of research. *Communication Education, 60*(1), 115–144. doi: 10.1080/03634523.2010.496867

Bandura, A. (1965). Influence of models' reinforcement contingencies on the acquisition of imitative responses. *Journal of Personality and Social Psychology, 1*(6), 589–595.

Bandura, A., Barbaranelli, C., Caprara, G., & Pastorelli, C. (1996). Multifaceted impact of self-efficacy beliefs on academic functioning. *Child Development, 67*, 1206–1222.

Barber, B. K., Stolz, H., & Olsen, J. (2005). Parental support, psychological control, and behavioral control: Assessing relevance across time, method, and culture. *Monographs of the Society for Research in Child Development, 70*(4). doi: 10.1111/j.1540-5834.2005.00365.x

Barber, B. K., Xia, M., Olsen, J. A., McNeely, C. A., & Bose, K. (2012). Feeling disrespected by parents: Refining the measurement and understanding of psychological control. *Journal of Adolescence, 35*(2), 273–287. doi: 10.1016/j.adolescence.2011.10.010

Bartlett, M. Y., & DeSteno, D. (2006). Gratitude and prosocial behavior: Helping when it costs you. *Psychological Science, 17*(4), 319–325.

Bates, J., Viken, R., Alexander, D., Beyers, J., & Stockton, L. (2002). Sleep and adjustment in preschool children: Sleep diary reports by mothers related to behavior reports by teachers. *Child Development, 73*(1), 62–74.

Batson, C. D., Coke, J. S., Chard, F., Smith, D., & Taliaferro, A. (1979). Generality of the "glow of goodwill": Effects of mood on helping and information acquisition. *Social Psychology Quarterly,* 176–179.

Batson, C. D., & Powell, A. A. (2003). Altruism and prosocial behavior. *Handbook of Psychology.* Wiley Online Library. doi: 10.1002/0471264385.wei0519

Baumeister, R. F., Vohs, K. D., & Tice, D. (2007). The strength model of self-control. *Current Directions in Psychological Science, 16*(6), 351–355.

Baumrind, D. (1971). Current patterns of parental authority. *Developmental Psychology Monographs, 4*(1 part 2), 1–103.

Baumrind, D. (1973). The development of instrumental competence through socialization. In A. Pick (Ed.), *Minnesota symposium on child psychology* (Vol. 7, pp. 3–46). Minneapolis: University of Minneapolis Press.

Becker, D. V., & Srinivasan, N. (2014). The vividness of the happy face. *Current Directions in Psychological Science, 23*(3), 189–194. doi: 10.1177/0963721414533702

Behrens, K. Y., Hesse, E., & Main, M. (2007). Mothers' attachment status as determined by the adult attachment interview predicts their 6-year-olds' reunion responses: A study conducted in Japan. *Developmental Psychology, 43*(6), 1553–1567.

Beijersbergen, M. D., Bakermans-Kranenburg, M. J., van IJzendoorn, M. H., & Juffer, F. (2008). Stress regulation in adolescents: Physiological reactivity during the adult attachment interview and conflict interaction. *Child Development, 79*(6), 1707–1720.

Beilock, S. L., Gunderson, E. A., Ramirez, G., & Levine, S. C. (2010). Female teachers' math anxiety affects girls' math achievement. *Proceedings of the National Academy of Sciences, 107*(5), 1860–1863. doi: 10.1073/pnas.0910967107

Belfield, C., Bowden, B., Klapp, A., Levin, H., Shand, R. & Zander, S. (2015). The economic value of social and emotional learning. New York: Center for Benefit-Cost Studies of Education, Teachers College, Columbia University.

Bellmore, A. (2011). Peer rejection and unpopularity: Associations with GPAs across the transition to middle school. *Journal of Educational Psychology, 103*(2), 282–295. doi: 10.1037/a0023312

Bender, H. L., Allen, J. P., McElhaney, K. B., Antonishak, J., Moore, C. M., Kelly, H. O., & Davis, S. M. (2007). Use of harsh physical discipline and developmental outcomes in adolescence. *Development and Psychopathology, 19*, 227–242.

Berger, R. H., Miller, A. L., Seifer, R., Cares, S. R., & LeBourgeois, M. K. (2011). Acute sleep restriction effects on emotion responses in 30- to 36-month-old children. *Journal of Sleep Research*, 1–12. doi: 10.1111/j.1365–2869.2011.00962.x

Bergin, C. (1987). Prosocial development in toddlers: The patterning of mother-infant interactions. In M. E. Ford & D. H. Ford (Eds.), *Humans as self-constructing living systems: Putting the framework to work* (pp. 121–143). Hillsdale, NJ: Erlbaum.

Bergin, C. (2014). Educating students to be prosocial at school. In L. M. Padilla-Walker & G. Carlo (Eds.), *Prosocial development: A multidimensional approach* (pp. 279–301): Oxford University Press.

Bergin, C., & Bergin, D. A. (1999). Classroom discipline that promotes self-control. *Journal of Applied Developmental Psychology, 20*(2), 189–206.

Bergin, C., & Bergin, D. A. (2009). Attachment in the classroom. *Educational Psychology Review, 21*(2), 141–170. doi: 10.1007/s10648-009-9104-0

Bergin, C., & Bergin, D. A. (2010). Sleep: The E-Z-Z-Z Intervention. *Educational Leadership, 67*(4), 44–47.

Bergin, C., & Bergin, D. A. (2015). *Child and adolescent development in your classroom* (2nd ed.). Belmont, CA: Wadsworth Cengage.

Bergin, C., Bergin, D. A., & French, E. (1995). Preschoolers' prosocial repertoires: Parents' perspectives. *Early Childhood Research Quarterly, 10*, 81–103.

Bergin, C., Talley, S., & Hamer, L. (2003). Prosocial behaviours of young adolescents: A focus group study. *Journal of Adolescence, 26*, 13–32.

Berk, R. A. (2002). *Humor as an instructional defibrillator.* Sterling, VA: Stylus Publishing.

Berkowitz, R., Moore, H., Astor, R. A., & Benbenishty, R. (2017). A research synthesis of the associations between socioeconomic background, inequality, school climate, and academic achievement. *Review of Educational Research, 87*(2), 425–469. doi: 10.3102/0034654316669821

Berndt, T. J., Hawkins, J., & Jiao, Z. (1999). Influences of friends and friendships on adjustment to junior high school. *Merrill-Palmer Quarterly, 45*(1), 13–41.

Bernier, A., Matte-Gagné, C., Bélanger, M.-È., & Whipple, N. (2014). Taking stock of two decades of attachment transmission gap: Broadening the assessment of maternal behavior. *Child Development, 85*(5), 1852–1865. doi: 10.1111/cdev.12236

Bernier, A., Matte-Gagné, C., & Bouvette-Turcot, A.-A. (2014). Examining the interface of children's sleep, executive functioning, and caregiving relationships: A plea against silos in the study of biology, cognition, and relationships. *Current Directions in Psychological Science, 23*(4), 284–289. doi: 10.1177/0963721414534852

Bernier, A., & Meins, E. (2008). A threshold approach to understanding the origins of attachment disorganization. *Developmental Psychology, 44*(4), 969–982.

Bernstein, A., Hadash, Y., Lichtash, Y., Tanay, G., Shepherd, K., & Fresco, D. M. (2015). Decentering and related constructs: A critical review and meta-cognitive processes model. *Perspectives on Psychological Science, 10*(5), 599–617. doi: 10.1177/1745691615594577

Berson, Y., & Oreg, S. (2016). The role of school principals in shaping children's values. *Psychological Science.* doi: 10.1177/0956797616670147

Bierman, K. L., Torres, M. M., Domitrovich, C. E., Welsh, J. A., & Gest, S. D. (2009). Behavioral and cognitive readiness for school: Cross-domain associations for children attending Head Start. *Social Development, 18*(2), 305–323.

Bjorklund, D. F., & Pellegrini, A. (2000). Child development and evolutionary psychology. *Child Development, 71*(6), 1687–1708.

Blair, C., Granger, D. A., Kivlighan, K. T., Mills-Koonce, W. R., Willoughby, M., Greenberg, M. T., . . . Family Life Project Investigators. (2008). Maternal and child contributions to cortisol response to emotional arousal in young children from low-income, rural communities. *Developmental Psychology, 44*(1), 1095–1109.

Blandon, A., Calkins, S. D., Keane, S. P., & O'Brien, M. (2008). Individual differences in trajectories of emotion regulation processes: The effects of maternal depressive symptomatology and children's physiological regulation. *Developmental Psychology, 44*(4), 1110–1123.

Bohlin, G., Hagekull, B., & Rydell, A. (2000). Attachment and social functioning: A longitudinal study from infancy to middle childhood. *Social Development, 9,* 24–39. doi: 10.1111/1467-9507.00109

Bokhorst, C., Bakermans-Kranenburg, M., Fearon, P., van IJzendoorn, M., Fonagy, P., & Schuengel, C. (2003). The importance of shared environment in mother-infant attachment security: A behavioral genetic study. *Child Development, 74*(6), 1769–1782.

Bonanno, G. A., & Burton, C. L. (2013). Regulatory flexibility: An individual differences perspective on coping and emotion regulation. *Perspectives on Psychological Science, 8*(6), 591–612. doi: 10.1177/1745691613504116

Bouchard, T. (2004). Genetic influence on human psychological traits. *Current Directions in Psychological Science, 13*(4), 148–151.

Bowlby, J. (1969). *Attachment* (Vol. I). New York: Basic Books.

Bradshaw, C. P., Mitchell, M. M., O'Brennan, L. M., & Leaf, P. J. (2010). Multilevel exploration of factors contributing to the overrepresentation of black students in office disciplinary referrals. *Journal of Educational Psychology, 102*(2), 508–520. doi: 10.1037/a0018450

Braungart-Reiker, J. M., Garwood, M. M., Powers, B. P., & Wang, X. (2001). Parental sensitivity, infant affect, and affect regulation: Predictors of later attachment. *Child Development, 72*(1), 252–270.

Braungart-Rieker, J. M., Hill-Soderlund, A. L., & Karrass, J. (2010). Fear and anger reactivity trajectories from 4 to 16 months: The roles of temperament, regulation, and maternal sensitivity. *Developmental Psychology, 46*(4), 791–804.

Brendgen, M., Boivin, M., Dionne, G., Barker, E. D., Vitaro, F., Girard, A., . . . Pérusse, D. (2012). Gene-environment processes linking aggression, peer victimization, and the teacher-child relationship. *Child Development, 82*(6), 2021–2036.

Brock, L. L., Rimm-Kaufman, S. E., Nathanson, L., & Grimm, K. J. (2009). The contributions of "hot" and "cool" executive function to children's academic achievement, learning-related behaviors, and engagement in kindergarten. *Early Childhood Research Quarterly, 24*(3), 337–349.

Bronfenbrenner, U., & Ceci, S. J. (1994). Nature-nurture reconceptualized in developmental perspective: A bioecological model. *Psychological Review, 101*(4), 568–586.

Bryan, C., Master, A., & Walton, G. (2014). "Helping" versus "Being a Helper": Invoking the self to increase helping in young children. *Child Development, 85*(5), 1836–1842. doi: 10.1111/cdev.12244

Buckhalt, J. A., El-Sheikh, M., Keller, P., & Kelly, R. J. (2009). Concurrent and longitudinal relations between children's sleep and cognitive functioning: The moderating role of parent education. *Child Development, 80*(3), 875–892.

Bus, A. G., & van IJzendoorn, M. H. (1997). Affective dimension of mother-infant picturebook reading. *Journal of School Psychology, 35*(1), 47–60.

Caldarella, P., & Merrell, K. W. (1997). Common dimensions of social skills of children and adolescents: A taxonomy of positive behaviors. *School Psychology Review, 26*(2), 264–278.

Caplan, M., & Hay, D. F. (1989). Preschoolers' responses to peers' distress and beliefs about bystander intervention. *Journal of Child Psychology & Psychiatry & Allied Disciplines, 30*(2), 231–242.

Caprara, G., Barbaranelli, C., & Pastorelli, C. (2001). Prosocial behavior and aggression in childhood and pre-adolescence. In A. Bohart & D. Stipek (Eds.), *Constructive and destructive behavior: Implications for family, school, and society* (pp. 187–203). Washington, DC: APA.

Caprara, G., Barbaranelli, C., Pastorelli, C., Bandura, A., & Zimbardo, P. (2000). Prosocial foundations of children's academic achievement. *Psychological Science, 11*(4), 302–306.

Card, N. A., Stucky, B. D., Sawalani, G. M., & Little, T. D. (2008). Direct and indirect aggression during childhood and adolescence: A meta-analytic review of gender differences, intercorrelations, and relations to maladjustment. *Child Development, 79*(5), 1185–1229.

Carlo, G., Crockett, L., Wilinson, J., & Beal, S. (2011). The longitudinal relationships between rural adolescents' prosocial behaviors and young adult substance use. *Journal of Youth and Adolescence, 40*, 1192–1202.

Carlo, G., Crockett, L. J., Wolff, J. M., & Beal, S. J. (2012). The role of emotional reactivity, self-regulation, and puberty in adolescents' prosocial behaviors. *Social Development, 21*(4), 667–685. doi: 10.1111/j.1467-9507.2012.00660.x

Carlo, G., Padilla-Walker, L. M., & Nielson, M. G. (2015). Longitudinal bidirectional relations between adolescents' sympathy and prosocial behavior. *Developmental Psychology, 51*(12), 1771–1777. doi: 10.1037/dev0000056

Carlo, G., Samper, P., Malonda, E., Tur-Porcar, A., & Davis, A. (2016). The effects of perceptions of parents' use of social and material rewards on prosocial behaviors in Spanish and U.S. youth. *Journal of Early Adolescence*, 1–23. doi: 10.1177/0272431616665210

Carlsmith, J., Lepper, M., & Landauer, T. (1974). Children's obedience to adult requests: Interactive effects of anxiety arousal and apparent punitiveness of the adult. *Journal of Personality and Social Psychology, 30*, 822–828.

CASEL. (2013). Social and emotional learning policy agenda. Report available at: CASEL.org.

Casner-Lotto, J., & Barrington, L. (2006). Are they really ready to work? Employers' perspectives on the basic knowledge and applied skills of new entrants to the 21st century U.S. workforce: The Conference Board, Inc., the Partnership for 21st Century Skills, Corporate Voices for Working Families, and the Society for Human Resource Management.

Cassidy, J. (1994). Emotion regulation: Influences of attachment relationships. In N. A. Fox (Ed.), *Emotion regulation: Behavioral and biological considerations. Monographs for the Society for Research in Child Development* (Vol. 59, pp. 228–249).

Champagne, F. A., & Mashoodh, R. (2009). Genes in context: Gene-environment interplay and the origins of individual differences in behavior. *Current Directions in Psychological Science, 18*(3), 127–131.

Chernyak, N., & Kushnir, T. (2013). Giving preschoolers choice increases sharing behavior. *Psychological Science, 24*(10), 1971–1979. doi: 10.1177/0956797613482335

Clarke, L., Ungerer, J., Chahoud, K., Johnson, S., & Stiefel, I. (2002). Attention deficit hyperactivity disorder is associated with attachment insecurity. *Clinical Child Psychology and Psychiatry, 7*(2), 1359–1045.

Coie, J. D., & Dodge, K. A. (1998). Aggression and antisocial behavior. In N. Eisenberg (Ed.), *Handbook of child psychology: Social, emotional, and personality development* (5th ed., Vol. 3, pp. 779–862). New York: Wiley.

Cole, P. M., Luby, J., & Sullivan, M. W. (2008). Emotions and the development of childhood depression: Bridging the gap. *Child Development Perspectives,* *2*(3), 141–148.

Compton, R. J., Robinson, M. D., Ode, S., Quandt, L., Fineman, S. L., & Carp, J. (2008). Error monitoring ability predicts daily stress regulation. *Psychological Science, 19*(7), 702–708.

Coolahan, K., Fantuzzo, J., Mendez, J., & McDermott, P. (2000). Preschool peer interactions and readiness to learn: Relationships between classroom peer play and learning behaviors and conduct. *Journal of Educational Psychology, 92*(3), 458–465.

Cornelius-White, J. (2007). Learner-centered teacher-student relationships are effective: A meta-analysis. *Review of Educational Research, 77*(1), 113–143.

Crittenden, P. M., & DiLalla, D. L. (1988). Compulsive compliance: The development of an inhibitory coping strategy in infancy. *Journal of Abnormal Child Psychology, 16*, 585–599.

Crone, D. A., Hawken, L. S., & Horner, R. H. (2015). *Building positive behavior support systems in schools: Functional behavioral assessment* (2nd ed.). New York: Guilford.

Crowell, J., Treboux, D., Gao, Y., Fyffe, C., Pan, H., & Waters, E. (2002). Assessing secure base behavior in adulthood: Development of a measure, links to adult attachment representations, and relations to couples' communication and reports of relationships. *Developmental Psychology, 38*(5), 679–693.

Curby, T. W., Rimm-Kaufman, S. E., & Ponitz, C. C. (2009). Teacher-child interactions and children's achievement trajectories across kindergarten and first grade. *Journal of Educational Psychology, 101*(4), 912–925.

Dahl, A. (2015). The developing social context of infant helping in two U.S. samples. *Child Development, 86*(4), 1080–1093. doi: 10.1111/cdev.12361

Dahl, R., & Lewin, D. (2002). Pathways to adolescent health: Sleep regulation and behavior. *Journal of Adolescent Health, 31*(6), 175–184.

Darwin, C. (1965/1872). *The expression of the emotions in man and animals.* Chicago: University of Chicago Press.

Davidov, M., & Grusec, J. (2006). Untangling the links of parental responsiveness to distress and warmth to child outcomes. *Child Development, 77*(1), 444–458.

Davies, P., Cicchetti, D., & Hentges, R. F. (2015). Maternal unresponsiveness and child disruptive problems: The interplay of uninhibited temperament and dopamine transporter genes. *Child Development, 86*(1), 63–79. doi: 10.1111/cdev.12281

Davis, C., Brady, M. P., Williams, R. E., & Hamilton, R. (1992). Effects of high-probability requests on the acquisition and generalization of responses to requests in young children with behavior disorders. *Journal of Applied Behavior Analysis, 25*, 905–916.

Davis, E., Levine, L., Lench, H., & Quas, J. (2010). Metacognitive emotion regulation strategies: Children's awareness that changing thoughts and goals can alleviate negative emotions. *Emotion, 10*, 498–510. doi: 10.1037/a0018428

Decety, J., & Cowell, J. M. (2014). Friends or foes: Is empathy necessary for moral behavior? *Perspectives on Psychological Science, 9*(5), 525–537. doi: 10.1177/1745691614545130

Deci, E. L., Vallerand, R. J., Pelletier, L. G., & Ryan, R. M. (1991). Motivation and education: The self-determination perspective. *Educational Pyschologist, 26*(3 & 4), 325–346.

DeMulder, E., Denham, S., Schmidt, M., & Mitchell, J. (2000). Q-sort assessment of attachment security during the preschool years: Links from home to school. *Developmental Psychology, 36*(2), 274–282.

Denham, S. A., Blair, K., DeMulder, E., Levitas, J., Sawyer, K., Auerbach-Major, S., & Queenan, P. (2003). Preschool emotional competence: Pathway to social competence? *Child Development, 74*(1), 238–256.

Denham, S. A., Mason, T. & Couchoud, E. (1995). Scaffolding young children's prosocial responsiveness: Preschooler's responses to adult sadness, anger, and pain. *International Journal of Behavioral Development, 18*, 489–504.

Denham, S. A., McKinley, M., Couchoud, E. A., & Holt, R. (1990). Emotional and behavioral predictors of preschool peer ratings. *Child Development, 61*, 1145–1152.

Denham, S. A., Mitchell-Copeland, J., Strandberg, K., Auerbach, S., & Blair, K. (1997). Parental contributions to preschoolers' emotional competence: Direct and indirect effects. *Motivation and Emotion, 21*(1), 65–86.

Dennis, T., & Kelemen, D. (2009). Preschool children's views on emotion regulation: Functional associations and implications for social-emotional adjustment. *International Journal of Behavioral Development, 33*(3), 243–252. doi: 10.1177/0165025408098024

DiCerbo, P., Anstrom, K., Baker, L., & Rivera, C. (2014). A review of the literature on teaching academic English to English language learners. *Review of Educational Research, 20*(10), 1–37.

Diener, M. L., Isabella, R. A., Behunin, M., & Wong, M. S. (2007). Attachment to mothers and fathers during middle childhood: Association with child gender, grade, and competence. *Social Development, 17*(1), 84–101.

Dinh, J. E., & Lord, R. G. (2013). Current trends in moral research: What we know and where to go from here. *Current Directions in Psychological Science, 22*(5), 380–385. doi: 10.1177/0963721413486147

Doctoroff, G. L., Greer, J. A., & Arnold, D. H. (2006). The relationship between social behavior and emergent literacy among preschool boys and girls. *Journal of Applied Developmental Psychology, 27*(1), 1–13.

Dodge, K. A., Godwin, J., & The Conduct Problems Prevention Research Group (2013). Social-information-processing patterns mediate the impact of preventive intervention on adolescent antisocial behavior. *Psychological Science.* doi: 10.1177/0956797612457394

Domitrovich, C. E., Durlak, J. A., Staley, K. C., & Weissberg, R. P. (2017). Social-emotional competence: An essential factor for promoting positive adjustment and reducing risk in school children. *Child Development, 88*(2), 408–416. doi: 10.1111/cdev.12739

Dougherty, L. R., Leppert, K. A., Merwin, S. M., Smith, V. C., Bufferd, S. J., & Kushner, M. R. (2015). Advances and directions in preschool mental health research. *Child Development Perspectives, 9*(1), 14–19. doi: 10.1111/cdep.12099

Douglas, E. M. (2006). Familial violence socialization in childhood and later life approval of corporal punishment: A cross-cultural perspective. *American Journal of Orthopsychiatry, 76*(1), 23–30.

Dowling, J. (2013). School-age children talking about humor: Data from focus groups. *Humor, 27*(1), 121–139. doi: 10.1515/humor-2013-0047

Doyle, A., Lawford, H., & Markiewicz, D. (2009). Attachment style with mother, father, best friend, and romantic partner during adolescence. *Journal of Research on Adolescence, 19*(4), 690–714.

Ducharme, J. M., Pontes, E., Guger, S., Crozier, K., Lucas, H., & Popynick, M. (1994). Errorless compliance to parental requests II: Increasing clinical practicality through abbreviation of treatment parameters. *Behavior Therapy, 25*, 469–487.

Duchesne, S., Larose, S., Vitaro, F., & Tremblay, R. E. (2010). Trajectories of anxiety in a population sample of children: Clarifying the role of children's behavioral characteristics and maternal parenting. *Development and Psychopathology, 22*(2), 361–373. doi: doi:10.1017/S0954579410000118

Duckworth, A. (2016, March 26). Don't grade schools on grit, *New York Times.*

Dunfield, K., & Kuhlmeier, V. (2010). Intention-mediated selective helping in infancy. *Psychological Science, 21*(4), 523–527.

Dunfield, K., & Kuhlmeier, V. (2013). Classifying prosocial behavior: Children's responses to instrumental need, emotional distress, and material desire. *Child Development, 84*(5), 1766–1776. doi: 10.1111/cdev.12075

Dunn, E. C., Milliren, C. E., Evans, C. R., Subramanian, S. V., & Richmond, T. K. (2015). Disentangling the relative influence of schools and neighborhoods on adolescents' risk for depressive symptoms. *American Journal of Public Health, 105*(4), 732–740. doi: 10.2105/AJPH.2014.302374

Dunn, E. W., Aknin, L. B., & Norton, M. I. (2008). Spending money on others promotes happiness. *Science, 319*(5870), 1687–1688.

Durlak, J. A., Weissberg, R. P., Dymnicki, A. B., Taylor, R. D., & Schellinger, K. B. (2011). The impact of enhancing students' social and emotional learning: A meta-analysis of school-based universal interventions. *Child Development, 82*(1), 405–432. doi: 10.1111/j.1467-8624.2010.01564.x

Dusenbury, L., Zadrazil, J., Mart, A., & Weissberg, R. P. (2011). State learning standards to advance social and emotional learning: University of Illinois at Chicago, Social and Emotional Learning Research Group.

Dykas, M. J., & Cassidy, J. (2011). Attachment and the processing of social information across the life span: Theory and evidence. *Psychological Bulletin, 137*(1), 19–46.

Dynarski, M., Clarke, L., Cobb, B., Finn, J., Rumberger, R., & Smink, J. (2008). Dropout prevention: A practice guide (NCEE 2008–4025). Washington, DC: Department of Education National Center for Education Evaluation and Regional Assistance, Institute of Education Sciences, U.S. Department of Education.

Eberly, M. B., & Montemayor, R. (1998). Doing good deeds: An examination of adolescent prosocial behavior in the context of parent-adolescent relationships. *Journal of Adolescent Research, 13*(4), 403–432.

Eisenberg-berg, N., & Geisheker, E. (1979). Content of preachings and power of the model/preacher: The effect on children's generosity. *Developmental Psychology, 15,* 168–175.

Eisenberg, N., Fabes, R. A., Karorn, M., Murphy, B. C., Wosinski, M., Polazzi, L., . . . Juhnke, C. (1996). The relations of children's dispositional prosocial behavior to emotionality, regulation and social functioning. *Child Development, 67,* 974–992.

Eisenberg, N., Fabes, R. A., Schaller, M., Carlo, G., & Miller, P. A. (1991). The relations of parental characteristics and practices to children's vicarious emotional responding. *Child Development, 62,* 1393–1408.

Eisenberg, N., Fabes, R. A., Shepard, S. A., Murphy, B. C., Guthrie, I. K., Jones, S., . . . Maszk, P. (1997). Contemporaneous and longitudinal prediction of children's social functioning from regulation and emotionality. *Child Development, 68*(4), 642–664.

Eisenberg, N., Fabes, R. A., & Spinrad, T. L. (2006). Prosocial development. In W. Damon, R. M. Lerner & N. Eisenberg (Eds.), *Handbook of child psychology; Social, emotional, and personality development.* (6th ed., Vol. 3, pp. 646–718). New Jersey: Wiley.

Eisenberg, N., Hofer, C., Sulik, M. J., & Liew, J. (2014). The development of prosocial moral reasoning and a prosocial orientation in young adulthood: Concurrent and longitudinal correlates. *Developmental Psychology, 50*(1), 58–70. doi: 10.1037/a0032990

Eisenberg, N., & Miller, P. (1987). The relation of empathy to prosocial and related behaviors. *Psychology Bulletin, 101,* 91–119.

Eisenberg, N., VanSchyndel, S. K., & Spinrad, T. L. (2016). Prosocial motivation: Inferences from an opaque body of work. *Child Development, 87*(6), 1668–1678. doi: 10.1111/cdev.12638

Eisenberg, N., Wolchik, S., Goldberg, L., & Engle, I. (1992). Parental values, reinforcement, and young children's prosocial behavior: A longitudinal study. *Journal of Genetic Psychology, 153*(1), 19–36.

El-Sheikh, M., Bub, K. L., Kelly, R. J., & Buckhalt, J. A. (2013). Children's sleep and adjustment: A residualized change analysis. *Developmental Psychology, 49*(8), 1591–1601. doi: 10.1037/a0030223

Ellis, B. J., Volk, A. A., Gonzalez, J.-M., & Embry, D. D. (2015). The Meaningful Roles Intervention: An evolutionary approach to reducing bullying and increasing prosocial behavior. *Journal of Research on Adolescence, 26*(4), 622–637. doi: 10.1111/jora.12243

Emmer, E., & Gerwels, M. (2002). Cooperative learning in elementary classrooms: Teaching practices and lesson characteristics. *Elementary School Journal, 103*(1), 75–91.

Emmer, E., Sabornie, E., Evertson, C. M., & Weinstein, C. S. (2013). *Handbook of Classroom Management: Research, Practice, and Contemporary Issues.* London: Routledge.

Englund, M., Kuo, S., Puig, J., & Collins, W. (2011). Early roots of adult competence: The significance of close relationships from infancy to early adulthood. *International Journal of Behavioral Development, 35*, 490–496. doi: 10.1177/0165025411422994

Erath, S. A., El-Sheikh, M., & Cummings, E. M. (2009). Harsh parenting and child externalizing behavior: Skin conductance level reactivity as a moderator. *Child Development, 80*(2), 578–592.

Erkman, F., & Rohner, R. P. (2006). Youths' perceptions of corporal punishment, parental acceptance, and psychological adjustment in a Turkish metropolis. *Cross-Cultural Research, 40*(3), 250–267.

Ettekal, I., & Ladd, G. W. (2015). Costs and benefits of children's physical and relational aggression trajectories on peer rejection, acceptance, and friendships: Variations by aggression subtypes, gender, and age. *Developmental Psychology, 51*(12), 1756–1770. doi: 10.1037/dev0000057

Evans, G. W. (2004). The environment of childhood poverty. *American Psychologist, 59*(2), 77–92.

Evertson, C. M., Emmer, E. T., & Worsham, M. E. (2000). *Classroom management for elementary teachers* (5th ed.). Boston: Allyn and Bacon.

Fabes, R. A., Carlo, G., Kupanoff, K., & Laible, D. (1999). Early adolescence and prosocial/moral behavior I: The role of individual processes. *Journal of Early Adolescence, 19*(1), 5–16.

Fabes, R. A., Eisenberg, N., Hanish, L., & Spinrad, T. L. (2001). Preschoolers' spontaneous emotion vocabulary: Relations to likability. *Early Education and Development, 12*, 11–27.

Fabes, R. A., Eisenberg, N., Jones, S., Smith, M., Guthrie, I., Poulin, R., . . . Friedman, J. (1999). Regulation, emotionality, and preschoolers' socially competent peer interactions. *Child Development, 70*(2), 432–442.

Fabes, R. A., Fultz, J., Eisenberg, N., May-Plumlee, T., & Christopher, F. S. (1989). Effects of rewards on children's prosocial motivation: A socialization study. *Developmental Psychology, 25,* 509–515.

Fabrizi, M., & Pollio, H. (1987). A naturalistic study of humorous activity in a third, seventh, and eleventh grade classroom. *Merrill-Palmer Quarterly, 33*(1), 107–128.

Fearon, R. P., Bakermans-Kranenburg, M. J., van Ijzendoorn, M. H., Lapsley, A.-M., & Roisman, G. I. (2010). The significance of insecure attachment and disorganization in the development of children's externalizing behavior: A meta-analytic study. *Child Development, 81*(2), 435–456.

Feldman, R., & Klein, P. (2003). Toddlers' self-regulated compliance to mothers, caregivers, and fathers: Implications for theories of socialization. *Developmental Psychology, 39*(4), 680–692.

Felner, R. D., Seitsinger, A. M., Brand, S., Burns, A., & Bolton, N. (2007). Creating small learning communities: Lessons from the Project on High-Performing Learning Communities about "what works" in creating productive, developmentally enhancing, learning contexts. *Educational Psychologist, 42*(4), 209–221.

Feshbach, N. D., & Feshbach, S. (1982). Empathy training and the regulation of aggression: Potentialities and limitations. *Academic Psychology Bulletin, 4,* 399–413.

Fitzsimmons, P., & McKenzie, B. (2003). Play on words: Humor as the means of developing authentic learning. In D. Lytle (Ed.), *Play and educational theory and practice* (Vol. 5, pp. 197–211). Westport, CT: Praeger.

Fletcher, A. C., Darling, N. E., Steinberg, L., & Dornbusch, S. M. (1995). The company they keep: Relations of adolescents' adjustment and behavior to their friends' perceptions of authoritative parenting in the social network. *Developmental Psychology, 31,* 300–310.

Fletcher, A. C., Walls, J. K., Cook, E. C., Madison, K. J., & Bridges, T. H. (2008). Parenting style as a moderator of associations between maternal disciplinary strategies and child well-being. *Journal of Family Issues, 29*(1?), 1724–1744.

Flook, L. (2011). Gender differences in adolescents' daily interpersonal events and well-being. *Child Development, 82*(2), 454–461.

Flournoy, J. C., Pfeifer, J. H., Moore, W. E., Tackman, A. M., Masten, C. L., Mazziotta, J. C., . . . Dapretto, M. (2016). Neural reactivity to emotional faces may mediate the relationship between childhood empathy and adolescent prosocial behavior. *Child Development, 87*(6), 1691–1702. doi: 10.1111/cdev.12630

Foersterling, F., & Binser, M. (2002). Depression, school performance and the veridicality of perceived grades and causal attributions. *Personality and Social Psychology Bulletin, 28*(10), 1441–1449.

Forgas, J. P. (2013). Don't worry, be sad! On the cognitive, motivational, and interpersonal benefits of negative mood. *Current Directions in Psychological Science, 22*(3), 225–232. doi: 10.1177/0963721412474458

Fredrickson, B. L. (2001). The role of positive emotions in positive psychology: The broaden-and-build theory of positive emotions. *American Psychologist, 56*(3), 218–226.

Fredrickson, B. L., & Losada, M. (2005). Positive affect and the complex dynamics of human flourishing. *American Psychologist, 60*(7), 678–686.

Fredriksen, K., Rhodes, J., Reddy, R., & Way, N. (2004). Sleepless in Chicago: Tracking the effects of adolescent sleep loss during the middle school years. *Child Development, 75*(1), 84–95.

Freiberg, H. J., Huzinec, C. A., & Templeton, S. M. (2009). Classroom management—a pathway to student achievement: A study of fourteen inner-city elementary schools. *Elementary School Journal, 110*(1), 63–80.

Friedlaender, D., Burns, D., Lewis-Charp, H., Cook-Harvey, C. M., & Darling-Hammond, L. (2014). Student-centered schools: Closing the opportunity gap. Stanford Center for Opportunity Policy in Education.

Fuchs, L. S., Fuchs, D., Kazdan, S., Karns, K., Calhoon, M. B., Hamlett, C. L., & Hewlitt, S. (2000). Effects of workgroup structure and size on student productivity during collaborative work on complex tasks. *Elementary School Journal, 100*(3), 183–212.

Gable, P. A., & Harmon-Jones, E. (2008). Approach-motivated positive affect reduces breadth of attention. *Psychological Science, 19*(5), 476–482.

Galindo, C., & Fuller, B. (2010). The social competence of Latino kindergartners and growth in mathematical understanding. *Developmental Psychology, 46*(3), 579–592.

Ganiban, J. M., Saudino, K. J., Ulbricht, J., Neiderhiser, J. M., & Reiss, D. (2008). Stability and change in temperament during adolescence. *Journal of Personality and Social Psychology, 95*(1), 222–236.

Gee, D. G., Gabard-Durnam, L., Telzer, E. H., Humphreys, K. L., Goff, B., Shapiro, M., . . . Tottenham, N. (2014). Maternal buffering of human amygdala-prefrontal circuitry during childhood but not during adolescence. *Psychological Science, 25*(11), 2067-2078. doi: 10.1177/0956797614550878

Gershoff, E. T. (2010). More harm than good: A summary of scientific research on the intended and unintended effects of corporal punishment on children. *Law & Contemporary Problems, 73*(2), 31–56.

Gillen-O'Neel, C., Huynh, V. W., & Fuligni, A. J. (2013). To study or to sleep? The academic costs of extra studying at the expense of sleep. *Child Development, 84*(1), 133–142. doi: 10.1111/j.1467-8624.2012.01834.x

Gillies, R. (2003). The behaviors, interactions, and perceptions of junior high students during small-group learning. *Journal of Educational Psychology, 95*(1), 137–147.

Goldwyn, R., Stanley, C., Smith, V., & Green, J. (2000). The Manchester Child Attachment Story Task: Relationship with parental AAI, SAT and child behaviour. *Attachment & Human Development, 2*(1), 71–84.

Goleman, D. (1995). *Emotional Intelligence.* New York, NY: Bantam Books.

Granot, D., & Mayseless, O. (2001). Attachment security and adjustment to school in middle childhood. *International Journal of Behavioral Development, 25*(6), 530–541.

Green, G., Rhodes, J., Hirsch, A. H., Suarez-Orozco, C., & Camic, P. M. (2008). Supportive adult relationships and the academic engagement of Latin American immigrant youth. *Journal of School Psychology, 46*, 393–412.

Green, J., Whitney, P. G., & Potegal, M. (2011). Screaming, yelling, whining, and crying: Categorical and intensity differences in vocal expressions of anger and sadness in children's tantrums. *Emotion, 11*(5), 1124–1133. doi: 10.1037/a0024173

Greene, R.. (2011). Collaborative problem solving can transform school discipline. *Phi Delta Kappan, 93*(2), 25–29. doi: 10.1177/003172171109300206

Greener, S., & Crick, N. R. (1999). Normative beliefs about prosocial behavior in middle childhood: What does it mean to be nice? *Social Development,* *8*(3), 349–363. doi: 10.1111/1467-9507.00100

Greengross, G., & Miller, G. (2011). Humor ability reveals intelligence, predicts mating success, and is higher in males. *Intelligence, 39*(4), 188–192. doi: 10.1016/j.intell.2011.03.006

Gregory, A., Cornell, D., & Fan, X. (2011). The relationship of school structure and support to suspension rates for Black and White high school students. *American Educational Research Journal, 48*(4), 904–934. doi: 10.3102/0002831211398531

Gregory, A., Cornell, D., Fan, X., Sheras, P., Shih, T.-H., & Huang, F. (2010). Authoritative school discipline: High school practices associated with lower bullying and victimization. *Journal of Educational Psychology, 102*(2), 483–496. doi: 10.1037/a0018562

Gregory, A., & Ripski, M. B. (2008). Adolescent trust in teachers: Implications for behavior in the high school classroom. *School Psychology Review, 37*(3), 337–353.

Gregory, A., & Weinstein, R. S. (2008). The discipline gap and African Americans: Defiance or cooperation in the high school classroom. *Journal of School Psychology, 46*, 455–475.

Gregory, A. M., Light-Häusermann, J. H., Rijsdijk, F., & Eley, T. C. (2009). Behavioral genetic analyses of prosocial behavior in adolescents. *Developmental Psychology, 12*(1), 165–174.

Griffith, J. (2002). A multilevel analysis of the relation of school learning and social environments to minority achievement in public elementary schools. *Elementary School Journal, 102*, 349–366.

Grimm, K. J., Steele, J. S., Mashburn, A. J., Burchinal, M., & Pianta, R. C. (2010). Early behavioral associations of achievement trajectories. *Developmental Psychology, 46*(5), 976–983.

Grolnick, W. S. (2003). *The psychology of parental control: How well-meant parenting backfires.* Mahwah, NJ: Lawrence Erlbaum.

Grolnick, W. S., Deci, E. L., & Ryan, R. M. (1997). Internalization within the family: The self-determination theory perspective. In J. E. Grusec & L. Kuczynski (Eds.), *Parenting and children's internalization of values: A handbook of contemporary theory* (pp. 135–161). New York: Wiley.

Grolnick, W. S., & Pomerantz, E. M. (2009). Issues and challenges in studying parental control: Toward a new conceptualization. *Child Development Perspectives, 3*(3), 165–170.

Gross, J. (2015). Emotion regulation: Current status and future prospects. *Psychological Inquiry, 26*(1), 1–26. doi: 10.1080/1047840X.2014.940781

Gross, J., & Jazaieri, H. (2014). Emotion, emotion regulation, and psychopathology: An affective science perspective. *Clinical Psychological Science, 2*(4), 387–401. doi: 10.1177/2167702614536164

Gruman, D., Harachi, T. W., Abbott, R. D., Catalano, R. F., & Fleming, C. B. (2008). Longitudinal effects of student mobility on three dimensions of elementary school engagement. *Child Development, 79*(6), 1833–1852.

Grusec, J. (1982). The socialization of altruism. In N. Eisenberg (Ed.), *The development of prosocial behavior* (pp. 139–166). New York: Academic Press.

Grusec, J., & Goodnow, J. J. (1994). The impact of parental discipline methods on the child's internalization of values: A reconceptualization of current points of view. *Developmental Psychology, 30*, 4–19.

Grusec, J., & Kuczynski, L. (Eds.). (1997). *Parenting and children's internalization of values: A handbook of contemporary theory.* New York: Wiley.

Grusec, J., & Redler, E. (1980). Attribution, reinforcement, and altruism: A developmental analysis. *Developmental Psychology, 16*, 525–534. doi: 10.1037/0012-1649.16.5.525

Gueguen, N., & De Gail, M. A. (2003). The effect of smiling on helping behavior: Smiling and good Samaritan behavior. *Communication reports, 16*(2), 133–140.

Gunderson, E. A., Gripshover, S. J., Romero, C., Dweck, C. S., Goldin-Meadow, S., & Levine, S. C. (2013). Parent praise to 1- to 3-year-olds predicts children's motivational frameworks 5 years later. *Child Development, 84*(5), 1526–1541. doi: 10.1111/cdev.12064

Gutman, L. M., & Eccles, J. S. (2007). Stage-environment fit during adolescence: Trajectories of family relations and adolescent outcomes. *Developmental Psychology, 43*(2), 522–537.

Hallinan, M. T. (2008). Teacher influences on students' attachment to school. *Sociology of Education, 81*, 271–283.

Hamm, J., Farmer, T., Lambert, K., & Gravelle, M. (2014). Enhancing peer cultures of academic effort and achievement in early adolescence: Promotive effects of the SEALS intervention. *Developmental Psychology, 50*(1), 216–228. doi: 10.1037/a0032979

Hammen, C. (2009). Adolescent depression: Stressful interpersonal contexts and risk for recurrence. *Current Directions in Psychological Science, 18*(4), 200–204.

Hamre, B., Hatfield, B., Pianta, R., & Jamil, F. (2014). Evidence for general and domain-specific elements of teacher–child interactions: Associations with preschool children's development. *Child Development, 85*(3), 1257–1274. doi: 10.1111/cdev.12184

Hardman, E. L., & Smith, S. W. (2003). An analysis of discipline-related content in elementary education journals. *Behavioral Disorders, 28*, 173–186.

Hardy, S. A., Carlo, G., & Roesch, S. C. (2010). Links between adolescents' expected parental reactions and prosocial behavioral tendencies: The mediating role of prosocial values. *Journal of Youth & Adolescence, 39*(1), 84–95.

Hardy, S. A., Walker, L. J., Olsen, J. A., Woodbury, R. D., & Hickman, J. R. (2014). Moral identity as moral ideal self: Links to adolescent outcomes. *Developmental Psychology, 50*(1), 45–57. doi: 10.1037/a0033598

Harel-Fisch, Y., Walsh, S. D., Fogel-Grinvald, H., Amitai, G., Pickett, W., Mocho, M., . . . Members of the HBSC Violence and Injury Prevention Focus Group. (2011). Negative school perceptions and involvement in school bullying: A universal relationship across 40 countries. *Journal of Adolescence, 34*, 639–652.

Hart, D., Donnelly, T. M., Youniss, J., & Atkins, R. (2007). High school community service as a predictor of adult voting and volunteering. *American Educational Research Journal, 44*(1), 197–219.

Hartup, W. W., & Abecassis, M. (2002). Friends and enemies. In P. Smith & C. Hart (Eds.), *Blackwell handbook of childhood social development* (pp. 285–306). Oxford: Blackwell.

Hastings, P., Zahn-Waxler, C., Robinson, J., Usher, B., & Bridges, D. (2000). The development of concern for others in children with behavior problems. *Developmental Psychology, 36*, 531–546.

Hay, D. F. (1994). Prosocial development. *Journal of Child Psychology & Psychiatry & Allied Disciplines, 35*(1), 29–71.

Hay, D. F. (2009). The roots and branches of human altruism. *British Journal of Psychology, 100*(3), 473–479.

Hay, D. F., Caplan, M., Castle, J., & Stimson, C. A. (1991). Does sharing beome increasingly "rational" in the second year of life? *Developmental Psychology, 27*(6), 987–993.

Hay, D. F., Castle, J., & Davies, L. (2000). Toddlers' use of force against familiar peers: A precursor of serious aggression? *Child Development, 71,* 457–467.

Hay, D. F., & Pawlby, S. (2003). Prosocial development in relation to children's and mother's psychological problems. *Child Development, 74*(5), 1314–1327.

Hay, D. F., Waters, C. S., Perra, O., Swift, N., Kairis, V., Phillips, R., . . . van Goozen, S. (2014). Precursors to aggression are evident by 6 months of age. *Developmental Science, 17*(3), 471–480. doi: 10.1111/desc.12133

Helwig, C., To, S., Wang, Q., Liu, C., & Yang, S. (2014). Judgments and reasoning about parental discipline involving induction and psychological control in China and Canada. *Child Development, 85*(3), 1150–1167. doi: 10.1111/cdev.12183

Henderlong, J., & Lepper, M. R. (2002). The effects of praise on children's intrinsic motivation: A review and synthesis. *Psychological Bulletin, 128*(5), 774–795.

Hepach, R. (2017). Prosocial arousal in children. *Child Development Perspectives, 11*(1), 50–55. doi: 10.1111/cdep.12209

Hepach, R., Vaish, A., Grossmann, T., & Tomasello, M. (2016). Young children want to see others get the help they need. *Child Development, 87*(6), 1703–1714. doi: 10.1111/cdev.12633

Hepach, R., Vaish, A., & Tomasello, M. (2013). Young children sympathize less in response to unjustified emotional distress. *Developmental Psychology, 49*(6), 1132–1139. doi: 10.1037/a0029501

Hesse, E. (1999). The adult attachment interview: Historical and current perspectives. In J. Cassidy & P. Shaver (Eds.), *Handbook of attachment: Theory, research, and clinical applications.* (pp. 395–433). New York: Guilford.

Hestenes, L., Kontos, S., & Bryan, Y. (1993). Children's emotional expressions in childcare centers varying in quality. *Early Childhood Research Quarterly, 8,* 295 307.

Heyman, G., Gee, C., & Giles, J. (2003). Preschool children's reasoning about ability. *Child Development, 74*(2), 516–534.

Ho, C., Bluestein, D. N., & Jenkins, J. M. (2008). Cultural differences in the relationship between parenting and children's behavior. *Developmental Psychology, 44*(2), 507–522.

Hodges, E., Finnegan, R., & Perry, D. (1999). Skewed autonomy-relatedness in preadolescents' conceptions of their relationships with mother, father, and best friend. *Developmental Psychology, 35*(3), 737–748.

Hoffman, D. (2009). Reflecting on social emotional learning: A critical perspective on trends in the United States. *Review of Educational Research, 79*(2), 533–556.

Hoffman, M. (1975). Altruistic behavior and the parent-child relationship. *Journal of Personality and Social Psychology, 31*, 937–943.

Hoffman, M.., & Saltzstein, H. (1967). Parent discipline and the child's moral development. *Journal of Personality and Social Psychology, 5*, 45–57.

Hofmann, W., De Houwer, J., Perugini, M., Baeyens, F., & Crombez, G. (2010). Evaluative conditioning in humans: A meta-analysis. *Psychological Bulletin, 136*(3), 390–421. doi: 10.1037/a0018916

Hoglund, W., & Leadbeater, B. (2004). The effects of family, school, and classroom ecologies on changes in children's social competence and emotional and behavioral problems in first grade. *Developmental Psychology, 40*(4), 533–544.

Honig, A. A., & Pollack, B. (1990). Effects of a brief intervention program to promote prosocial behaviors in young children. *Early Education and Development, 1*, 438–444.

Houltberg, B. J., Morris, A., Cui, L., Henry, C. S., & Criss, M. M. (2016). The role of youth anger in explaining links between parenting and early adolescent prosocial and antisocial behavior. *Journal of Early Adolescence, 36*(3), 297–318. doi: 10.1177/0272431614562834

Howes, C., & Ritchie, S. (1999). Attachment organizations in children with difficult life circumstances. *Development and Psychopathology, 11*, 251–268.

Hughes, J. N., Luo, W., Kwok, O.-M., & Loyd, L. K. (2008). Teacher-student support, effortful engagement, and achievement: A 3-year longitudinal study. *Journal of Educational Psychology, 100*(1), 1-14.

Hughes, J. N., Wu, J., Kwok, O., Villarreal, V., & Honson, A. (2012). Indirect effects of child reports of teacher-student relationship on achievement. *Journal of Educational Psychology, 104*(2), 350–365. doi: 10.1037/a0026339

Huntsinger, J. R. (2013). Does emotion directly tune the scope of attention? *Current Directions in Psychological Science, 22*(4), 265–270. doi: 10.1177/0963721413480364

Iacoboni, M. (2009). Imitation, empathy, and mirror neurons. *Annual Review of Psychology, 60*, 653–670.

Igel, C. (2015). *The effect of cooperative learning on student achievement: A meta-analysis.* Paper presented at the American Educational Research Association, Chicago.

Imuta, K., Henry, J. D., Slaughter, V., Selcuk, B., & Ruffman, T. (2016). Theory of mind and prosocial behavior in childhood: A meta-analytic review. *Developmental Psychology, 52*(8), 1192–1205. doi: 10.1037/dev0000140

Isen, A. M., & Levin, P. F. (1972). Effect of feeling good on helping: Cookies and kindness. *Journal of Personality and Social Psychology, 21*(3), 384.

Izard, C. E., Fine, S., Schultz, D., Mostow, A., Ackerman, B., & Youngstrom, E. (2001). Emotion knowledge as a predictor of social behavior and academic competence in children at risk. *Psychological Science, 12*(1), 18–23.

James, J. H. (2012). Caring for "others": Examining the interplay of mothering and deficit discourses in teaching. *Teaching and Teacher Education, 28*(2), 165–173. doi: http://dx.doi.org/10.1016/j.tate.2011.09.002

Jeffrey, A., Auger, R., & Pepperell, J. (2013). If we're ever in trouble they're always there: A qualitative study of teacher-student caring. *Elementary School Journal, 114*(1), 100–117.

Jennings, J., & DiPrete, T. A. (2010). Teacher effects on social and behavioral skills in early elementary school. *Sociology of Education, 83*(2), 135–159.

Jia, Y., Way, N., Ling, G., Yoskihawa, H., Chen, X., Hughes, D., . . . Lu, Z. (2009). The influence of student perceptions of school climate on socioemotional and academic adjustment: A comparison of Chinese and American adolescents. *Child Development, 80*(5), 1514–1530.

Johnson, M., Crosnoe, R., & Elder, G. H. (2001). Students' attachment and academic engagement: The role of race and ethnicity. *Sociology of Education, 74*(October), 318–340.

Johnson, N. A., Smith, J. J., Pobiner, B., & Schrein, C. (2012). Why are chimps still chimps? *American Biology Teacher, 74*(2), 74–80. doi: 10.1525/abt.2012.74.2.3

Johnson, S. R., Seidenfeld, A. M., Izard, C. E., & Kobak, R. (2013). Can classroom emotional support enhance prosocial development among children with depressed caregivers? *Early Childhood Research Quarterly, 28*(2), 282–290.

Jones, D. E., Greenberg, M., & Crowley, M. (2015). Early social-emotional functioning and public health: The relationship between kindergarten social competence and future wellness. *American Journal of Public Health*, e1–e8. doi: 10.2105/AJPH.2015.302630

Joussemet, M., Vitaro, F., Barker, E. D., Cote, S., Nagin, D. S., Zoccolillo, M., & Tremblay, R. E. (2008). Controlling parenting and physical aggression during elementary school. *Child Development, 79*(2), 411–425.

Juvonen, J. (2007). Reforming middle schools: Focus on continuity, social connectedness, and engagement. *Educational Psychologist, 42*(4), 197–208.

Kahn, A., Van de Merckt, C., Rebauffat, E., Mozin, M., Sottiaux, M., Blum, D., & Hennart, P. (1989). Sleep problems in healthy preadolescents. *Pediatrics, 84*(3), 542–546.

Kärtner, J., Keller, H., & Chaudhary, N. (2010). Cognitive and social influences on early prosocial behavior in two sociocultural contexts. *Developmental Psychology, 46*(4), 905–914.

Kashdan, T. B., Barrett, L. F., & McKnight, P. E. (2015). Unpacking emotion differentiation: Transforming unpleasant experience by perceiving distinctions in negativity. *Current Directions in Psychological Science, 24*(1), 10–16. doi: 10.1177/0963721414550708

Kazdin, A. (1993). Treatment of conduct disorder: Progress and directions in psychotherapy research. *Development and Psychopathology, 5*, 277–310.

Keen, R. (2011). The development of problem solving in young children: A critical cognitive skill. *Annual Review of Psychology, 62*, 1–21. doi: 10.1146/annurev.psych.031809.130730

Keltner, D., Capps, L., Kring, A. M., Young, R. C., & Heerey, E. A. (2001). Just teasing: A conceptual analysis and empirical review. *Psychological Bulletin, 83*(1), 229–248.

Kensinger, E. A. (2007). Negative emotion enhances memory accuracy: Behavioral and neuroimaging evidence. *Current Directions in Psychological Science, 16*(4), 213–218.

Kerns, K. A., & Brumariu, L. E. (2014). Is insecure parent–child attachment a risk factor for the development of anxiety in childhood or adolescence? *Child Development Perspectives, 8*(1), 12–17. doi: 10.1111/cdep.12054

Kerr, D. C., Lopez, N. L., Olson, S. L., & Sameroff, A. J. (2004). Parental discipline and externalizing behavior problems in early childhood. The roles of moral regulation and child gender. *Journal of Abnormal Child Psychology, 32*(4), 369–383.

Kidd, D., & Castano, E. (2013). Reading literary fiction improves theory of mind. *Science, 342*(6156), 377–380. doi: 10.1126/science.1239918

Kienbaum, J. (2001). The socialization of compassionate behavior by child care teachers. *Early Education and Development, 12*(1), 139–153.

Kim-Cohen, J., & Gold, A. L. (2009). Measured gene-environment interactions and mechanisms promoting resilient development. *Current Directions in Psychological Science, 18*(3), 138–142.

Kim-Spoon, J., Cicchetti, D., & Rogosch, F. A. (2013). A longitudinal study of emotion regulation, emotion lability-negativity, and internalizing symptomatology in maltreated and nonmaltreated children. *Child Development, 84*(2), 512–527. doi: 10.1111/j.1467–8624.2012.01857.x

Klassen, R. M., Perry, N. E., & Frenzel, A. C. (2012). Teachers' relatedness with students: An underemphasized component of teachers' basic psychological needs. *Journal of Educational Psychology, 104*(1), 150–165. doi: 10.1037/a0026253

Kliewer, W. (1991). Coping in middle childhood: Relations to competence, Type A behavior, monitoring, blunting, and locus of control. *Developmental Psychology, 27,* 689–697.

Klimes-Dougan, B., & Kistner, J. (1990). Physically abused preschoolers' responses to peers' distress. *Developmental Psychology, 26*(4), 599–602.

Kochanska, G. (1997). Mutually responsive orientation between mothers and their young children: Implications for early socialization. *Child Development, 68,* 94–112.

Kochanska, G., Aksan, N., & Joy, M. E. (2007). Children's fearfulness as a moderator of parenting in early socialization: Two longitudinal studies. *Developmental Psychology, 43*(1), 222–237.

Kochanska, G., Aksan, N., & Koenig, A. L. (1995). A longitudinal study of the roots of preschoolers' conscience: Committed compliance and emerging internalization. *Child Development, 66*, 1752–1769.

Kochanska, G., Koenig, J. L., Barry, R. A., Kim, S., & Yoon, J. E. (2010). Children's conscience during toddler and preschool years, moral self, and a competent, adaptive developmental trajectory. *Developmental Psychology, 46*(5), 1320–1332. doi: 10.1037/a0020381

Kochel, K. P., Ladd, G. W., & Rudolph, K. D. (2012). Longitudinal associations among youth depressive symptoms, peer victimization, and low peer acceptance: An interpersonal process perspective. *Child Development, 83*(2), 637–650. doi: 10.1111/j.1467-8624.2011.01722.x

Köster, M., Ohmer, X., Nguyen, T. D., & Kärtner, J. (2016). Infants understand others' needs. *Psychological Science, 27*(4), 542–548. doi: 10.1177/0956797615627426

Kowalski, R. M., Giumetti, G. W., Schroeder, A. N., & Lattanner, M. R. (2014). Bullying in the digital age: A critical review and meta-analysis of cyberbullying research among youth. *Psychological Bulletin, 140*(4), 1073–1137. doi: 10.1037/a0035618

Kraft, T., & Pressman, S. (2012). Grin and bear it: The influence of manipulated facial expression on the stress response. *Psychological Science, 23*(1), 1372–1378. doi: 10.1177/0956797612445312

Krevans, J., & Gibbs, J. C. (1996). Parents' use of inductive discipline: Relations to children's empathy and prosocial behavior. *Child Development, 67*(6), 3263–3277.

Kromm, H., Färber, M., & Holodynski, M. (2015). Felt or false smiles? Volitional regulation of emotional expression in 4-, 6-, and 8-year-old children. *Child Development, 86*(2), 579–597. doi: 10.1111/cdev.12315

Kuhn, D. (2015). Thinking together and alone. *Educational Researcher, 44*(1), 46–53. doi: 10.3102/0013189X15569530

Ladd, G., Kochenderfer-Ladd, B., Visconti, K., Ettekal, I., Sechler, C., & Cortes, K. (2014). Grade-school children's social collaborative skills: Links with partner preference and achievement. *American Educational Research Journal, 51*(1), 152–183. doi: 10.3102/0002831213507327

LaFontana, K., & Cillessen, A. (2002). Children's perceptions of popular and unpopular peers: A multimethod assessment. *Developmental Psychology, 38*(5), 635–647.

Lagattuta, K. H., & Wellman, H. (2002). Differences in early parent-child conversations about negative versus positive emotions: Implications for the development of psychological understanding. *Developmental Psychology, 38*(4), 564–580.

Laible, D., Panfile, T., & Makariev, D. (2008). The quality and frequency of mother-toddler conflict: Links with attachment and temperament. *Child Development, 79*(2), 426–443. doi: 10.1111/j.1467–8624.2007.01134.x

Lamont, J. H., Devore, C. D., Allison, M., Ancona, R., Barnett, S. E., Gunther, R., . . . Young, T. (2013). Policy Statement. Out-of-school suspension and expulsion. *Pediatrics, 131*(3), e1000–e1007. doi: 10.1542/peds.2012-3932

Lansford, J. E., Skinner, A. T., Sorbring, E., Di Giunta, L., Deater-Deckard, K., Dodge, K. A., . . . Chang, L. (2012). Boys' and girls' relational and physical aggression in nine countries. *Aggressive Behavior, 38*, 298–308.

Larson, R., & Richards, M. H. (1994). *Divergent realities: The emotional lives of mothers, fathers, and adolescents.* New York: Basic Books.

Laursen, B., Pulkkinen, L., & Adams, R. (2002). The antecedents and correlates of agreeableness in adulthood. *Developmental Psychology, 38*(4), 591–603.

Lee, D. L. (2005). Increasing compliance: A quantitative synthesis of applied research on high-probability request sequences. *Exceptionality, 13*(3), 141–154.

Leerkes, E. M., Parade, S. H., & Gudmundson, J. A. (2011). Mothers' emotional reactions to crying pose risk for subsequent attachment insecurity. *Journal of Family Psychology, 25*(5), 635–643. doi: 10.1037/a0023654

Leppanen, J. M., Moulson, M. C., Vogel-Farley, V. K., & Nelson, C. A. (2007). An ERP study of emotional face processing in the adult and infant brain. *Child Development, 78*(1), 232–245.

Lepper, M. R. (1983). Social-control processes and the internalization of social values: An attributional perspective. In E. T. Higgins, D. Ruble & W. Hartup (Eds.), *Social cognition and social development: A sociocultural perspective* (pp. 294–330). Cambridge, UK: Cambridge University Press.

Lepper, M. R., Greene, D., & Nisbett, R. E. (1973). Undermining children's intrinsic interest with extrinsic reward: A test of the "overjustification" hypothesis. *Journal of Personality and Social Psychology, 28,* 129–137.

Lepper, M. R., Keavney, M., & Drake, M. (1996). Intrinsic motivation and extrinsic rewards: A commentary on Cameron and Pierce's meta-analysis. *Review of Educational Research, 66*(1), 5–32.

Leyva, D., Weiland, C., Barata, M., Yoshikawa, H., Snow, C., Treviño, E., & Rolla, A. (2015). Teacher–child interactions in Chile and their associations with prekindergarten outcomes. *Child Development, 86*(3), 781–799. doi: 10.1111/cdev.12342

Lindquist, K. A., Satpute, A. B., & Gendron, M. (2015). Does language do more than communicate emotion? *Current Directions in Psychological Science, 24*(2), 99–108. doi: 10.1177/0963721414553440

Lipscomb, S. T., Leve, L. D., Harold, G. T., Neiderhiser, J. M., Shaw, D., Ge, Z., & Reiss, D. (2011). Trajectories of parenting and child negative emotionality during infancy and toddlerhood: A longitudinal analysis. *Child Development, 82*(5), 1661–1675.

Lisonbee, J. A., Mize, J., Payne, A. L., & Granger, D. A. (2008). Children's cortisol and the quality of teacher-child relationships in child care. *Child Development, 79*(6), 1818–1832.

Liu, Y., & Wang, Z. (2014). Positive affect and cognitive control: Approach-motivation intensity influences the balance between cognitive flexibility and stability. *Psychological Science, 25,* 1116–1123. doi: 10.1177/0956797614525213

Losoya, S. H., & Eisenberg, N. (2000). Affective empathy. In J. Hall & F. J. Bernieri (Eds.), *Interpersonal sensitivity: Theory and measurement* (pp. 21–44). Mahwah, NJ: Erlbaum.

Luby, J. L. (2010). Preschool depression. *Current Directions in Psychological Science, 19*(2), 91–95. doi: 10.1177/0963721410364493

Lunkenheimer, E. S., Shields, A. M., & Cortina, K. S. (2007). Parental emotion coaching and dismissing in family interactions. *Social Development, 16*(2), 232–248.

Lysaker, J., Tonge, C., Gauson, D., & Miller, A. (2011). Reading and social imagination: What relationally oriented reading insruction can do for children. *Reading Psychology, 32*(6), 520–566.

Lytton, H. (1980). *Parent-child interaction: The socialization process observed in twin and singleton families.* New York: Plenum.

Lyubomirsky, S. (2007). *The how of happiness: A scientific approach to getting the life you want.* New York: Penguin Press.

Maag, J. W. (2001). Rewarded by punishment: Reflections on the disuse of positive reinforcement in schools. *Exceptional Children, 67*(2), 173–186. doi: 10.1177/001440290106700203

Maccoby, E. E. (1992). The role of parents in the socialization of children: An historical overview. *Developmental Psychology, 28*(6), 1006–1017.

Maccoby, E. E., & Martin, J. A. (1983). Socialization in the context of the family: Parent-child interaction. In P. H. Mussen (Ed.), *Handbook of child psychology: Vol. 4. Socialization, personality, and social development* (4th ed., Vol. He, pp. 1–101). New York: Wiley.

Madigan, S., Atkinson, L., Laurin, K., & Benoit, D. (2013). Attachment and internalizing behavior in early childhood: A meta-analysis. *Developmental Psychology, 49*(4), 672–689. doi: 10.1037/a0028793

Madigan, S., Brumariu, L. E., Villani, V., Atkinson, L., & Lyons-Ruth, K. (2016). Representational and questionnaire measures of attachment: A meta-analysis of relations to child internalizing and externalizing problems. *Psychological Bulletin, 142*(4), 367–399. doi: 10.1037/bul0000029

Malecki, C., & Elliot, S. (2002). Children's social behaviors as predictors of academic achievement: A longitudinal analysis. *School Psychology Quarterly, 17*(1), 1–23.

Mali, T. (2012). *What teachers make: In praise of the greatest job in the world.* New York: G. P. Putnam's Sons.

Malti, T., & Krettenauer, T. (2013). The relation of moral emotion attributions to prosocial and antisocial behavior: A meta-analysis. *Child Development, 84*(2), 397-412. doi: 10.1111/j.1467-8624.2012.01851.x

Malti, T., Ongley, S. F., Peplak, J., Chaparro, M. P., Buchmann, M., Zuffianò, A., & Cui, L. (2016). Children's sympathy, guilt, and moral reasoning in helping, cooperation, and sharing: A 6-year longitudinal study. *Child Development, 87*(6), 1783–1795. doi: 10.1111/cdev.12632

Manucia, G. K., Baumann, D. J., & Cialdini, R. B. (1984). Mood influences on helping: Direct effects or side effects? *Journal of Personality and Social Psychology, 46*(2), 357.

Manuck, S. B., & McCaffery, J. M. (2014). Gene-environment interaction. *Annual Review of Psychology, 65*(1), 41–70. doi: 10.1146/annurev-psych-010213-115100

Markiewicz, D., Lawford, H., Doyle, A., & Haggart, N. (2006). Developmental differences in adolescents' and young adults' use of mothers, fathers, best friends, and romantic partners to fulfill attachment needs. *Journal of Youth and Adolescence, 35*(1), 127–140.

Martin, A., Lin, K., & Olson, K. R. (2016). What you want versus what's good for you: Paternalistic motivation in children's helping behavior. *Child Development, 87*(6), 1739–1746. doi: 10.1111/cdev.12637

Martin, A., & Olson, K. R. (2015). Beyond good and evil: What motivations underlie children's prosocial behavior? *Perspectives on Psychological Science, 10*(2), 159–175. doi: 10.1177/1745691615568998

Martin, D. , Preiss, R. W., Gayle, B. M., & Allen, M. (2006). A meta-analytic assessment of the effect of humorous lectures on learning. In B. M. Gayle, R. W. Preiss, N. Burrell & M. Allen (Eds.), *Classroom communication and instructional processes*. Mahwah, NJ: Erlbaum.

Marzano, R. J., Marzano, J., & Pickering, D. (2003). *Classroom management that works*. Alexandria, VA: ASCD.

Mashburn, A. J., Pianta, R. C., Hamre, B., Downer, J. T., Barbarin, O. A., Bryant, D., . . . Howes, C. (2008). Measures of classroom quality in prekindergarten and children's development of academic, language, and social skills. *Child Development, 79*(3), 732–749.

Maslow, A. (1970). *Motivation and personality* (2nd ed.). New York: Harper & Row.

Matthews, J. S., Kizzie, K. T., Rowley, S. J., & Cortina, K. (2010). African Americans and boys: Understanding the literacy gap, tracing academic trajectories, and evaluating the role of learning-related skills. *Journal of Educational Psychology, 102*(3), 757–771. doi: 10.1037/a0019616

Maunder, R. G., & Hunter, J. J. (2001). Attachment and psychosomatic medicine: Developmental contributions to stress and disease. *Psychosomatic Medicine, 63*(4), 556–567.

McClelland, M., & Morrison, F. (2003). The emergence of learning-related social skills in preschool children. *Early Childhood Research Quarterly, 18*, 206–224.

McCullough, M. E., Kimeldorf, M. B., & Cohen, A. D. (2008). An adaptation for altruism? The social causes, social effects, and social evolution of gratitude. *Current Directions in Psychological Science, 17*(4), 281–285.

McDowell, D., O'Neil, R., & Parke, R. D. (2000). Display rule application in a disappointing situation and children's emotional reactivity: Relations with social competence. *Merrill-Palmer Quarterly, 46*, 306–324.

McElwain, N. L., Booth-LaForce, C., Lansford, J. E., Wu, X., & Dyer, W. J. (2008). A process model of attachment-friend linkages: Hostile attribution biases, language ability, and mother-child affective mutuality as intervening mechanisms. *Child Development, 79*(6), 1891–1906.

McElwain, N. L., Holland, A. S., Engle, J. M., & Ogolsky, B. G. (2014). Getting acquainted: Actor and partner effects of attachment and temperament on young children's peer behavior. *Developmental Psychology, 50*(6), 1757–1770. doi: 10.1037/a0036211

McGhee, P. (Ed.). (2013). *Humor and children's development: A guide to practical applications.* London: Routledge.

McGuigan, N., Fisher, R., & Glasgow, R. (2016). The influence of receiver status on donor prosociality in 6- to 11-year-old children. *Child Development, 87*(3), 855–869. doi: 10.1111/cdev.12517

McLean, L., & Connor, C. M. (2015). Depressive symptoms in third-grade teachers: Relations to classroom quality and student achievement. *Child Development, 86*(3), 945–954. doi: 10.1111/cdev.12344

Meaney, M. (2010). Epigenetics and the biological definition of gene X environment interactions. *Child Development, 81*(1), 41–79.

Meehan, B., Hughes, J., & Cavell, T. (2003). Teacher-student relationships as compensatory resources for aggressive children. *Child Development, 74*(4), 1145–1157.

Melis, A. P., Grocke, P., Kalbitz, J., & Tomasello, M. (2016). One for you, one for me: Humans' unique turn-taking skills. *Psychological Science, 27*(7), 987–996. doi: 10.1177/0956797616644070

Merikangas, K. R., He, J.-p., Burstein, M., Swanson, S. A., Avenevoli, S., Cui, L., . . . Swendsen, J. (2010). Lifetime prevalence of mental disorders in U.S. adolescents: Results from the National Comorbidity Survey Replication - Adolescent Supplement (NCS-A). *Journal of the American Academy of Child & Adolescent Psychiatry, 49*(10), 980–989.

Merrell, K., Guelderner, B., Ross, A., & Isava, D. (2008). How effective are school bullying intervention programs? *School Psychology Quarterly, 23*, 26–42.

Michalik, N. M., Eisenberg, N., Spinrad, T. L., Ladd, B., Thompson, M., & Valiente, C. (2007). Longitudinal relations among parental emotional expressivity and sympathy and prosocial behavior in adolescence. *Social Development, 16*(2), 286–309.

Mikulineer, M., & Shaver, P. (2005). Attachment security, compassion, and altruism. *Current Directions in Psychological Science, 14*(1), 34–38.

Miles, S., & Stipek, D. (2006). Contemporaneous and longitudinal associations between social behavior and literacy achievement in a sample of low-income elementary school children. *Child Development, 77*(1), 103–117.

Milgram, S. (1974). *Obedience to authority: An experimental view.* New York: Harper & Row.

Miller, J. G., Kahle, S., & Hastings, P. D. (2015). Roots and benefits of costly giving: Children who are more altruistic have greater autonomic flexibility and less family wealth. *Psychological Science, 26*(7), 1038–1045. doi: 10.1177/0956797615578476

Miller, J. G., Nuselovici, J. N., & Hastings, P. D. (2016). Nonrandom acts of kindness: Parasympathetic and subjective empathic responses to sadness predict children's prosociality. *Child Development, 87*(6), 1679–1690. doi: 10.1111/cdev.12629

Mischel, W., Shoda, Y., & Mendoza-Denton, R. (2002). Situation-behavior profiles as a locus of consistency in personality. *Current Directions in Psychological Science, 11*(2), 50–54.

Mitchell-Copeland, Denham, S., & DeMulder, E. (1997). Q-sort assessment of child-teacher attachment relationships and social competence in the preschool. *Early Education and Development, 8*(1), 27–39.

Molano, A., Jones, S., & Willett, J. (2014). *Peer effects in the elementary school classroom: Socialization of aggressive and prosocial behavior and its consequences for academic achievement.* Dissertation. Harvard.

Moore, B. S., Underwood, B., & Rosenhan, D. L. (1973). Affect and altruism. *Developmental Psychology, 8*, 99–104.

Morawska, A., & Sanders, M. (2011). Parental use of time out revisited: A useful or harmful parenting strategy? *Journal of Child and Family Studies, 20*(1), 1–8. doi: 10.1007/s10826-010-9371-x

Morris, A. S., Silk, J. S., Morris, M. D., Steinberg, L., Aucoin, K. J., & Keyes, A. W. (2011). The influence of mother-child emotion regulation strategies on children's expression of anger and sadness. *Developmental Psychology, 47*(1), 213–225.

Morris, A. S., Silk, J. S., Steinberg, L., Myers, S. S., & Robinson, L. R. (2007). The role of the family context in the development of emotion regulation. *Social Development, 16*(2), 361–388.

Moss, E., & St-Laurent, D. (2001). Attachment at school age and academic performance. *Developmental Psychology, 37*(6), 863–874.

Muñoz, R., Beardslee, W. R., & Leykin, Y. (2012). Major depression can be prevented. *American Psychologist, 67*(4), 285–295.

Murray, C. (2009). Parent and teacher relationships as predictors of school engagement and functioning among low-income urban youth. *Journal of Early Adolescence, 29*(3), 376–404. doi: 10.1177/0272431608322940

Mussen, P., & Eisenberg, N. (2001). Prosocial development in context. In A. Bohart & D. Stipek (Eds.), *Constructive and destructive behavior: Implications for family, school, and society* (pp. 103–126). Washington, DC: APA.

Nadler, R. T., Rabi, R., & Minda, J. P. (2010). Better mood and better performance: Learning rule-described categories is enhanced by positive mood. *Psychological Science, 21*(12), 1770–1776.

Naparstek, N. (1990). Children's conceptions of prosocial behavior. *Child study journal, 20*, 207–220.

Neal, J. W., Neal, Z. P., & Cappella, E. (2014). I know who my friends are, but do you? Predictors of self-reported and peer-inferred relationships. *Child Development, 85*(4), 1366–1372. doi: 10.1111/cdev.12194

Newton, E. K., Thompson, R. A., & Goodman, M. (2016). Individual differences in toddlers' prosociality: Experiences in early relationships explain variability in prosocial behavior. *Child Development, 87*(6), 1715–1726. doi: 10.1111/cdev.12631

Noddings, N. (1992). *The challenge to care in schools: An alternative approach to education.* New York: Teachers College Press.

Noltemeyer, A. L., Marie, R., McLoughlin, C., & Vanderwood, M. (2015). Relationship between school suspension and student outcomes: A meta-analysis. *School Psychology Review, 44*(2), 224–240.

Normandeau, S., & Guay, F. (1998). Preschool behavior and first-grade school achievement: The mediational role of cognitive self-control. *Journal of Educational Psychology, 90*(1), 111–121.

O'Connor, E., Dearing, E., & Collins, B. A. (2011). Teacher-child relationship and behavior problem trajectories in elementary school. *American Educational Research Journal, 48*(1), 120–162.

O'Connor, E., & McCartney, K. (2007). Examining teacher-child relationships and achievement as part of an ecological model of development. *American Educational Research Journal, 44*(2), 340–369.

Okonofua, J. A., Walton, G. M., & Eberhardt, J. L. (2016). A vicious cycle: A social–psychological account of extreme racial disparities in school discipline. *Perspectives on Psychological Science, 11*(3), 381–398. doi: 10.1177/1745691616635592

Olweus, D. (1993). *Bullying at school: What we know and what we can do.* Oxford, UK: Blackwell.

Osher, D., Kidron, Y., Brackett, M., Dymnicki, A., Jones, S., & Weissberg, R. P. (2016). Advancing the science and practice of social and emotional learning. *Review of Research in Education, 40*(1), 644–681. doi: doi:10.3102/0091732X16673595

Osterman, K. (2000). Students' need for belonging in the school community. *Review of Educational Research, 70*(3), 323–367.

Ottmar, E. R., Rimm-Kaufman, S. E., Larsen, R. A., & Berry, R. Q. (2015). Mathematical knowledge for teaching, standards-based mathematics teaching practices, and student achievement in the context of the Responsive Classroom approach. *American Educational Research Journal, 52*(4), 787–821. doi: 10.3102/0002831215579484

Owens, J., & AAP Adolescent Sleep Working Group. (2014). Insufficient sleep in adolescents and young adults: An update on causes and consequences. *Pediatrics, 134*(3), e921–932. doi: 10.1542/peds.2014-1696

Paciello, N., Fida, R., Tramontano, C., Lupinetti, C., & Caprara, G. V. (2008). Stability and change of moral disengagement and its impact on aggression and violence in late adolescence. *Child Development, 79*(5), 1288–1309.

Padilla-Walker, L. M., Carlo, G., Christensen, K. J., & Yorgason, J. B. (2012).

Bidirectional relations between authoritative parenting and adolescents' prosocial behaviors. *Journal of Research on Adolescence, 22*(3), 400–408. doi: 10.1111/j.1532-7795.2012.00807.x

Pagani, L., Tremblay, R. E., Vitaro, F., Boulerice, B., & McDuff, P. (2001). Effects of grade retention on academic performance and behavioral development. *Development and Psychopathology, 13*, 297–315.

Parker, J. G., & Asher, S. R. (1993). Friendship and friendship quality in middle childhood: Links with peer group acceptance and feelings of loneliness and social dissatisfaction. *Developmental Psychology, 29*(4), 611–621.

Patterson, G. R., & Bank, C. L. (1989). Some amplifying mechanisms for pathologic processes in families. In M. Gunnar & E. Thelen (Eds.), *Systems and development: Symposia on child psychology* (pp. 167–210). Hillsdale, NJ: Erlbaum.

Pauli-Pott, U., Haverkock, A., Pott, W., & Beckmann, D. (2007). Negative emotionality, attachment quality, and behavior problems in early childhood. *Infant Mental Health Journal, 28*(1), 39–53.

Paulus, M. (2014). The emergence of prosocial behavior: Why do infants and toddlers help, comfort, and share? *Child Development Perspectives, 8*(2), 77–81. doi: 10.1111/cdep.12066

Paulussen-Hoogeboom, M. C., Stams, G. J., Hermanns, J. M., & Peetsma, T. T. (2007). Child negative emotionality and parenting from infancy to preschool: A meta-analytic review. *Developmental Psychology, 43*(2), 438–453.

Paunesku, D., Walton, G. M., Romero, C., Smith, E. N., Yeager, D. S., & Dweck, C. S. (2015). Mind-set interventions are a scalable treatment for academic underachievement. *Psychological Science, 26*(6), 784–793. doi: 10.1177/0956797615571017

Pellegrini, A. (2011). "In the eye of the beholder": Sex bias in observations and ratings of children's aggression. *Educational Researcher, 40*(6), 281–286.

Penela, E. C., Walker, O. L., Degnan, K. A., Fox, N. A., & Henderson, H. A. (2015). Early behavioral inhibition and emotion regulation: Pathways toward social competence in middle childhood. *Child Development, 86*(4), 1227–1240. doi: 10.1111/cdev.12384

Pianta, R. (1999). *Enhancing relationships between children and teachers* Washington, DC: American Psychological Association.

Pianta, R. (2001). Student-teacher relationship scale–short form. Lutz, FL: Psychological Assessment Resources.

Pianta, R., Mashburn, A., Downer, J., Hamre, B., & Justice, L. (2008). Effects of web-mediated professional development resources on teacher-child interactions in pre-kindergarten classrooms. *Early Childhood Research Quarterly, 23*, 431–451. doi: 10.1016/j.ecr-esq.2008.02.001

Pianta, R., Nimetz, S., & Bennett, E. (1997). Mother-child relationships, teacher-child relationships, and school outcomes in preschool and kindergarten. *Early Childhood Research Quarterly, 12*, 263–280.

Planty, M., Bozick, R., & Regnier, M. (2006). Helping because you have to or helping because you want to? Sustaining participation in service work from adolescence through young adulthood. *Youth & Society, 38*(2), 177–202. doi: 10.1177/0044118x06287961

Plötner, M., Over, H., Carpenter, M., & Tomasello, M. (2015). Young children show the bystander effect in helping situations. *Psychological Science, 26*(4), 499–506. doi: 10.1177/0956797615569579

Polderman, T. J. C., Benyamin, B., de Leeuw, C. A., Sullivan, P. F., van Bochoven, A., Visscher, P. M., & Posthuma, D. (2015). Meta-analysis of the heritability of human traits based on fifty years of twin studies. *Nature Genetics, 47*(7), 702–709. doi: 10.1038/ng.3285

Pomerantz, E. M., & Rudolph, K. (2003). What ensues from emotional distress? Implications for competence estimation. *Child Development, 74*(2), 329–345.

Pronin, E., & Jacobs, E. (2008). Thought speed, mood, and the experience of mental motion. *Perspectives on Psychological Science, 3*(6), 461–485.

Putallaz, M., Grimes, C. L., Foster, K. J., Kupersmidt, J. B., Coie, J. D., & Dearing, K. (2007). Overt and relational aggression and victimization: Multiple perspectives within the school setting. *Journal of School Psychology, 45*, 523–547.

Qin, L., Pomerantz, E. M., & Wang, Q. (2009). Are gains in decision-making autonomy during early adolescence beneficial for emotional functioning? The case of the United States and China. *Child Development, 80*(6), 1705–1721.

Quartz, S., & Sejnowski, T. (2002). *Liars, lovers, and heroes: What the new brain science reveals about how we become who we are.* New York: Morrow.

Radke-Yarrow, M., Zahn-Waxler, C., Richardson, D., Susman, A., & Martinez, P. (1994). Caring behavior in children of clinically depressed and well mothers. *Child Development, 65*, 1405–1414.

Rakow, A., Forehand, R., Haker, K., McKee, L. G., Champion, J. E., Potts, J., . . . Compas, B. E. (2011). Use of parental guilt induction among depressed parents. *Journal of Family Psychology, 25*(1), 147–151. doi: 10.1037/a0022110

Ramaswamy, V., & Bergin, C. C. (2009). Do reinforcement and induction increase prosocial behavior? Results of a teacher-based intervention in preschools. *Journal of Research in Childhood Education, 23*(4), 525–536.

Rand, D. G. (2016). Cooperation, fast and slow: Meta-analytic evidence for a theory of social heuristics and self-interested deliberation. *Psychological Science.* doi: 10.1177/0956797616654455

Raposa, E. B., Laws, H. B., & Ansell, E. B. (2015). Prosocial behavior mitigates the negative effects of stress in everyday life. *Clinical Psychological Science.* doi: 10.1177/2167702615611073

Rasch, B., & Born, J. (2008). Reactivation and consolidation of memory during sleep. *Current Directions in Psychological Science, 17*(3), 188–192.

Raudenbush, S. W. (2009). The Brown legacy and the O'Connor challenge: Transforming schools in the images of children's potential. *Educational Researcher, 38*, 169–180.

Raver, C. C. (2004). Placing emotional self-regulation in sociocultural and socioeconomic contexts. *Child Development, 75*(2), 346–353.

Readdick, C. A., & Chapman, P. (2000). Young children's perceptions of time out. *Journal of Research in Childhood Education, 15*(1), 81–87.

Reardon, S. F. (2011). The widening academic achievement gap between the rich and the poor: New evidence and possible explanations. In G. J. Duncan & R. Murnane (Eds.), *Whither opportunity* (pp. 91–116). New York: Russell Sage.

Reardon, S. F. (2013). The widening income achievement gap. *Educational Leadership, 70*(8), 10–16.

Recchia, H. E., Wainryb, C., Bourne, S., & Pasupathi, M. (2014). The construction of moral agency in mother–child conversations about helping and hurting across childhood and adolescence. *Developmental Psychology, 50*(1), 34–44. doi: 10.1037/a0033492

Reid, J. B. (1993). Prevention of conduct disorder before and after school entry: Relating interventions to developmental findings. *Development and Psychopathology, 5*, 243–262.

Reinke, W., Herman, K., & Newcomer, L. (2016). The Brief Student-Teacher Classroom Interaction Observation: Using dynamic indicators of behaviors in the classroom to predict outcomes and inform practice. *Assessment for Effective Intervention, preprint*, 1–11. doi: 10.1177/1534508416641605

Resetar, J. L., & Noell, G. H. (2008). Evaluating preference assessments for use in the general education population. *Journal of Applied Behavior Analysis, 41*(3), 447–451.

Restorative Practices Working Group. (2014). Restorative practices: Fostering healthy relationships and promoting positive discipline in schools: Advancement project, American Federation of Teachers, National Education Association, and National Opportunity to Learn Campaign.

Rhee, S. H., Lahey, B. B., & Waldman, I. D. (2015). Comorbidity among dimensions of childhood psychopathology: Converging evidence from behavior genetics. *Child Development Perspectives, 9*(1), 26–31. doi: 10.1111/cdep.12102

Rodkin, P., Ryan, A., Jamison, R., & Wilson, T. (2013). Social goals, social behavior, and social status in middle childhood. *Developmental Psychology, 49*(6), 1139–1150. doi: 10.1037/a0029389

Roehrs, T., & Roth, T. (2008). Caffeine: Sleep and daytime sleepiness. *Sleep Medicine Reviews, 12*, 153–162.

Rollins, B. C., & Thomas, D. L. (1979). Parental support, power, and control techniques in the socialization of children. In W. Burr, R. Hill, F. I. Nye & I. L. Reiss (Eds.), *Contemporary theories about the family* (pp. 317–364). New York: Free Press.

Romano, E., Babchishin, L., Pagani, L. S., & Kohen, D. (2010). School readiness and later achievement: Replication and extension using a nationwide Canadian survey. *Developmental Psychology, 46*(5), 995–1007.

Roorda, D. L., Koomen, H. M. Y., Spilt, J. L., & Oort, F. J. (2011). The influence of affective teacher–student relationships on students' school engagement and achievement. *Review of Educational Research, 81*(4), 493–529. doi: 10.3102/0034654311421793

Rose, S. A., Futterweit, L. R., & Jankowski, J. J. (1999). The relation of affect to attention and learning in infancy. *Child Development, 70*(3), 549–559.

Roseth, C. J., Johnson, D. W., & Johnson, R. T. (2008). Promoting early adolescents' achievement and peer relationships: The effects of cooperative, competitive, and individualistic goal structures. *Psychological Bulletin, 134*(2), 223–246.

Roth, G. (2008). Perceived parental conditional regard and autonomy support as predictors of young adults' self-versus other-oriented prosocial tendencies. *Journal of Personality, 76*(3), 513–533. doi: 10.1111/j.1467-6494.2008.00494.x

Roth, G., Kanat-Maymon, Y., & Bibi, U. (2011). Prevention of school bullying: The important role of autonomy-supportive teaching and internalization of pro-social values. *British Journal of Educational Psychology, 81*(4), 654–666. doi: 10.1348/2044-8279.002003

Rushton, J. (1982). Social learning theory and the development of prosocial behavior. In N. Eisenberg (Ed.), *The development of prosocial behavior* (pp. 77–108). New York: Academic Press.

Ryan, R. M., & Deci, E. L. (1996). Intrinsic motivation and extrinsic rewards: A commentary on Cameron and Pierce's meta-analysis. *Review of Educational Research, 66*, 33–38.

Rydell, A. M., Berlin, L., & Bohlin, G. (2003). Emotionality, emotion regulation, and adaptation among 5- to 8-year-old children. *Emotion, 3*(1), 30–47.

Saarni, C. (1999). *The development of emotional competence.* New York: Guilford.

Sadeh, A., Gruber, R., & Raviv, A. (2003). The effects of sleep restriction and extension on school-age children: What a difference an hour makes. *Child Development, 74*(2), 444–455.

Saudino, K. J., & Micalizzi, L. (2015). Emerging trends in behavioral genetic studies of child temperament. *Child Development Perspectives, 9*(3), 144–148. doi: 10.1111/cdep.12123

Savitz-Romer, M., Rowan-Kenyon, H., Zhang, X., & Fancsali, C. (2014). Social-emotional and affective skills landscape analysis: IMPAQ International.

Scher, A., & Mayseless, O. (2000). Mothers of anxious/ambivalent infants: Maternal characteristics and child-care context. *Child Development, 71*(6), 1629–1639.

Schnall, S., Roper, J., & Fessler, D. M. T. (2010). Elevation leads to altruistic behavior. *Psychological Science, 21*(3), 315–320.

Scourfield, J., John, B., Martin, N., & McGuffin, P. (2004). The development of prosocial behavior in children and adolescents: A twin study. *Journal of Child Psychology and Psychiatry, 45*(5), 927–935.

Seiffge-Krenke, I., Aunola, K., & Nurmi, J.-E. (2009). Changes in stress perception and coping during adolescence: The role of situational and personal factors. *Child Development, 80*(1), 259–279.

Shaw, A., Choshen-Hillel, S., & Caruso, E. M. (2016). The development of inequity aversion. *Psychological Science, 27*(10), 1352–1359. doi: doi:10.1177/0956797616660548

Shechtman, Z., & Yaman, M. A. (2012). SEL as a component of a literature class to improve relationships, behavior, motivation and content knowledge. *American Educational Research Journal, 49*(3), 546–567.

Shin, H., & Ryan, A. M. (2017). Friend influence on early adolescent disruptive behavior in the classroom: Teacher emotional support matters. *Developmental Psychology, 53*(1), 114–125. doi: 10.1037/dev0000250

Short, M., Gradisar, M., Lack, L., & Wright, H. (2013). The impact of sleep on adolescent depressed mood, alertness, and academic performance. *Journal of Adolescence, 36*, 1025–1033. doi: org/10.1016/j.adolescence.2013.08.007

Sigel, I. E. (1960). Influence techniques: A concept used to study parental behaviors. *Child Development, 31*, 799–806.

Skinner, E. A., Furrer, C., Marchand, G., & Kindermann, T. A. (2008). Engagement and disaffection in the classroom: Part of a larger motivational dynamic? *Journal of Educational Psychology, 100*(4), 765–781.

Sletta, O., Sobstad, F., & Valas, H. (1995). Humour, peer acceptance and perceived social competence in preschool and school-aged children. *British Journal of Educational Psychology, 65*, 179–195.

Smith, D., Schneider, B., Smith, P., & Ananiadou, K. (2004). The effectiveness of whole school programs: A synthesis of evaluation research. *School Psychology Review, 33*, 547–560.

Smith, R.., & Rose, A. J. (2011). The "cost of caring" in youths' friendships: Considering associations among social perspective taking, co-rumination, and empathetic distress. *Developmental Psychology, 47*(6), 1792–1803. doi: 10.1037/a0025309

Smith, T. (1983). Adolescent reactions to attempted parental control and influence techniques. *Journal of Marriage and the Family, 45*(3), 533–542.

Snell, E. K., Adam, E. K., & Duncan, G. (2007). Sleep and the body mass index and overweight status of children and adolescents. *Child Development, 78*(1), 309–323.

Snow, C. E., Lawrence, J. F., & White, C. (2010). Generating knowledge of academic language among urban middle school students. *Journal of Educational Effectiveness, 2*(4), 325–344.

Social and Character Development Research Consortium. (2010). Efficacy of schoolwide programs to promote social and character development and reduce problem behavior in elementary school children (NCER 2011–2001). Washington, DC: National Center for Education Research, Institute of Education Sciences.

Solomon, D., Battistich, V., Watson, M., Schaps, E., & Lewis, C. (2000). A six-district study of educational change: Direct and mediated effects of the Child Development Project. *Social Psychology of Education, 41*(1), 3–51.

Somerville, L. H. (2013). The teenage brain: Sensitivity to social evaluation. *Current Directions in Psychological Science, 22*(2), 121–127. doi: 10.1177/0963721413476512

Spera, C. (2005). A review of the relationship among parenting practices, parenting styles, and adolescent school achievement. *Educational Psychology Review, 17*(2), 125–146.

Spilt, J., Hughes, J., Wu, J.-Y., & Kwok, O.-M. (2012). Dynamics of teacher-student relaitonships: Stability and change across elementary school and the influence on children's academic success. *Child Development, 83*(4), 1180–1195. doi: 10.1111/j.1467-8624.2012.01761.x

Spivak, A. L., White, S. S., Juvonen, J., & Graham, S. (2015). Correlates of prosocial behaviors of students in ethnically and racially diverse middle schools. *Merrill-Palmer Quarterly, 61*(2), 236–263.

Sroufe, L. A. (1996). *Emotional development: The organization of emotional life in the early years.* Cambridge, UK: Cambridge University Press.

Sroufe, L. A., Fox, N., & Pancake, V. (1983). Attachment and dependency in developmental perspective. *Child Development, 54,* 1615–1627.

Steinberg, L., Blatt-Eisengart, I., & Cauffman, E. (2006). Patterns of competence and adjustment among adolescents from authoritative, authoritarian, indulgent, and neglectful homes: A replication in a sample of serious juvenile offenders. *Journal of Research on Adolescence, 16*(1), 47–58.

Steinberg, L., Dornbusch, S., & Brown, B. B. (1992). Ethnic differences in adolescent achievement: An ecological perspective. *American Psychologist, 47,* 723–729.

Steinberg, L., & Silk, J. S. (2002). Parenting adolescents. In M. H. Bornstein (Ed.), *Handbook of parenting* (2nd ed., Vol. 1, pp. 103–133). Mahwah, NJ: Erlbaum.

Stevenson-Hinde, J., & Verschueren, K. (2002). Attachment in childhood. In P. Smith & C. Hart (Eds.), *Blackwell handbook of childhood social development* (pp. 182–204). Oxford, UK: Blackwell.

Stipek, D., & Miles, S. (2008). Effects of aggression on achievement: Does conflict with the teacher make it worse? *Child Development, 79*(6), 1721–1735.

Stocker, C. M., Richmond, M. K., Rhoades, G. K., & Kuang, L. (2007). Family emotional proesses and adoelscents' adjustment. *Social Development, 16*(2), 310–325.

Strayer, J., & Roberts, W. (1989). Children's empathy and role-taking: Child and parental factors and relations to prosocial behavior. *Journal of Applied Developmental Psychology, 10,* 227–239.

Strickgold, R., & Walker, M. (2004). To sleep, perchance to gain creative insight? *Trends in Cognitive Sciences, 8*(5), 191–192.

Strough, J., Berg, C., & Meegan, S. (2001). Friendship and gender differences in task and social interpretations of peer collaborative problem solving. *Social Development, 10,* 1–22.

Sussman, T. J., Heller, W., Miller, G. A., & Mohanty, A. (2013). Emotional distractors can enhance attention. *Psychological Science, 24*(11), 2322–2338. doi: 10.1177/0956797613492774

Swanson, J., Valiente, C., Lemery-Chalfont, K., Bradley, R., & Eggum-Wilkens, N. (2014). Longitudinal relations among parents' reactions to children's negative emotions, effortful control, and math achievement in early elementary school. *Child Development, 85*(5), 1932–1947. doi: 10.1111/cdev.12260

Szynal-Brown, C., & Morgan, R. (1983). The effects of reward on tutor's behavior in a cross-age tutoring context. *Journal of Experimental Child Psychology, 36*(2), 196–208.

Tang, C. S.-k. (2006). Corporal punishment and physical maltreatment against children: A community study on Chinese parents in Hong Kong. *Child Abuse & Neglect, 30,* 893–907.

Tarabulsy, G. M., Bernier, A., Provost, M. A., Maranda, J., Larose, S., Moss, E., . . .

Tessier, R. (2005). Another look inside the gap: Ecological contributions to the transmission of attachment in a sample of adolescent mother-infant dyads. *Developmental Psychology, 41*(1), 212–234.

Thomas, D. E., Bierman, K. L., & Powers, C. J. (2011). The influence of class-room aggression and classroom climate on aggressive-disruptive behavior. *Child Development, 82*(3), 751–757.

Thompson, R. A. (1990). Emotion and self-regulation. *Nebraska Symposium on Motivation*, 367–467.

Thompson, R. A. (2012). Whither the preconventional child? Toward a life-span moral development theory. *Child Development Perspectives, 6*(4), 423–429. doi: 10.1111/j.1750-8606.2012.00245.x

Thorkildsen, T., Reese, D., & Corsino, A. (2002). School ecologies and attitudes about exclusionary behavior among adolescents and young adults. *Merrill-Palmer Quarterly, 48*(1), 25–51.

Trzesniewski, K., Moffitt, T., Caspi, A., Taylor, A., & Maughan, B. (2006). Revis-iting the association between reading achievement and antisocial behavior: New evidence of an environmental explanation from a twin study. *Child Development, 77*(1), 72–88.

Turkheimer, E., Pettersson, E., & Horn, E. E. (2014). A phenotypic null hypoth-esis for the genetics of personality. *Annual Review of Psychology, 65*(1), 515–540. doi:10.1146/annurev-psych-113011-143752

Ulber, J., Hamann, K., & Tomasello, M. (2016). Extrinsic rewards diminish costly sharing in 3-year-olds. *Child Development, 87*(4), 1192–1203. doi: 10.1111/cdev.12534

Underwood, M. (2002). Sticks and stones and social exclusion: Aggression among girls and boys. In P. Smith & C. Hart (Eds.), *Blackwell handbook of childhood social development* (pp. 533–548). Oxford, UK: Blackwell.

Ursache, A., Blair, C., & Raver, C. C. (2012). The promotion of self-regulation as a means of enhancing school readiness and early achievement in children at risk for school failure. *Child Development Perspectives, 6*(2), 122–128.

U.S. Department of Education. (2016). The state of racial diversity in the edu-cator workforce. Washington, DC: USDE Office of Planning, Evaluation and Policy Development, Policy and Program Studies Service.

U.S. Department of Health and Human Services. (2014). Policy statement on expulsion and suspension policies in early childhood settings. Washington, DC: U.S. Department of Education.

Vaish, A., Carpenter, M., & Tomasello, M. (2009). Sympathy through affective perspective taking and its relation to prosocial behavior in toddlers. *Developmental Psychology, 45*(2), 534–543.

Vaish, A., Carpenter, M., & Tomasello, M. (2016). The early emergence of guilt-motivated prosocial behavior. *Child Development, 87*(6), 1772–1782. doi: 10.1111/cdev.12628

Valiente, C., Lemery-Chalfant, K., & Swanson, J. (2010). Prediction of kindergartners' academic achievement from their effortful control and emotionality: Evidence for direct and moderated relations. *Journal of Educational Psychology, 102*(3), 550–560.

Valiente, C., Swanson, J., & Eisenberg, N. (2012). Linking students' emotions and academic achievement: When and why emotions matter. *Child Development Perspectives, 6*(2), 129–135.

van den Berg, Y., & Cillessen, A. (2015). Peer status and classroom seating arrangements: A social relations analysis. *Journal of Experimental Child Psychology, 130*, 19–34. doi: 10.1016/j.jecp.2014.09.007

van Goethem, A., van Hoof, A., Orobio de Castro, B., Van Aken, M., & Hart, D. (2014). The role of reflection in the effects of community service on adolescent development: A meta-analysis. *Child Development, 85*(6), 2114–2130. doi: 10.1111/cdev.12274

van Hoorn, J., van Dijk, E., Meuwese, R., Rieffe, C., & Crone, E. A. (2016). Peer Influence on prosocial behavior in adolescence. *Journal of Research on Adolescence, 26*(1), 90–100. doi: 10.1111/jora.12173

van IJzendoorn, M. H., Rutgers, A. H., Bakermans-Kranenburg, M. J., Swinkels, S. H., van Daalen, E., Dietz, C., Naber, F., Buitelaar, J., & van Engeland, H. (2007). Parental sensitivity and attachment in children with autism spectrum disorder: Comparison with children with mental retardation, with language delays, and with typical development. *Child Development, 78*(2), 597–608.

van Rijsewijk, L., Dijkstra, J. K., Pattiselanno, K., Steglich, C., & Veenstra, R. (2016). Who helps whom? Investigating the development of adolescent prosocial relationships. *Developmental Psychology, 52*(6), 894–908. doi: 10.1037/dev0000106

Van Ryzin, M. J., Leve, L. D., Neiderhiser, J. M., Shaw, D. S., Natsuaki, M. N., & Reiss, D. (2015). Genetic influences can protect against unresponsive parenting in the prediction of child social competence. *Child Development, 86*(3), 667–680. doi: 10.1111/cdev.12335

Van Zalk, M., Kerr, M., Branje, S., Stattin, H., & Meeus, W. (2010). It takes three: Selection, influence, and de-selection processes of depression in adolescent friendship networks. *Developmental Psychology, 46*(4), 927–938.

Verboom, C., Sijtsema, J., Verhulst, F., Penninx, B., & Ormel, J. (2014). Longitudinal associations between depressive problems, academic performance, and social functioning in adolescent boys and girls. *Developmental Psycholoy, 50*(1), 247–257. doi: 10.1037/a0032547

Verhage, M. L., Schuengel, C., Madigan, S., Fearon, R. M. P., Oosterman, M., Cassibba, R., . . . van Ijzendoorn, M. H. (2016). Narrowing the transmission gap: A synthesis of three decades of research on intergenerational transmission of attachment. *Psychological Bulletin, 142*(4), 337–366. doi: 10.1037/bul0000038

Viljaranta, J., Aunola, K., Mullola, S., Virkkala, J., Hirvonen, R., Pakarinen, E., & Nurmi, J.-E. (2015). Children's temperament and academic skill development during first grade: Teachers' interaction styles as mediators. *Child Development, 86*(4), 1191–1209. doi: 10.1111/cdev.12379

Vincent, P., & Grove, D. (2012). Character education: A primer on history, research, and effective practices. In P. M. Brown, M. W. Corrigan & A. Higgins-D'Alessandro (Eds.), *Handbook of prosocial education* (Vol. 1, pp. 115–136). Lanham, MD: Rowman & Littlefield.

Vlachou, M., Andreou, E., Botsoglou, K., & Didaskalou, E. (2011). Bully/victim problems among preschool children: A review of current research evidence. *Educational Psychology Review, 23*, 329–358.

Wakschlag, L. S., Choi, S. W., Carter, A. S., Hullsiek, H., Burns, J., McCarthy, K., . . . Briggs-Gowan, M. J. (2012). Defining the developmental parameters of temper loss in early childhood: Implications for developmental psychopathology. *Journal of Child Psychology and Psychiatry, 53*(11), 1099–1108. doi: 10.1111/j.1469-7610.2012.02595.x

Wang, M.-T., Brinkworth, M., & Eccles, J. (2013). Moderating effects of teacher-student relationship in adolescent trajectories of emotional and behavioral adjustment. *Developmental Psychology, 49*(4), 690–705. doi: 10.1037/a0027916

Wang, M.-T., & Fredricks, J. A. (2014). The reciprocal links between school engagement, youth problem behaviors, and school dropout during adolescence. *Child Development, 85*(2), 722–737. doi: 10.1111/cdev.12138

Wang, Q., Pomerantz, E. M., & Chen, H. (2007). The role of parents' control in early adolescents' psychological functioning: A longitudinal investigation in the United States and China. *Child Development, 78*(5), 1592–1610.

Wang, Z., Bergin, C., & Bergin, D. A. (2014). Measuring engagement in fourth to twelfth grade classrooms: The Classroom Engagement Inventory. *School Psychology Quarterly, 29*(4), 517–535. doi: 10.1037/spq0000050

Warden, D., & Mackinnon, S. (2003). Prosocial children, bullies and victims: An investigation of their sociometric status, empathy and social problem-solving strategies. *British Journal of Developmental Psychology, 21*, 367–385.

Warneken, F. (2015). Precocious Prosociality: Why do young children help? *Child Development Perspectives, 9*(1), 1–6. doi: 10.1111/cdep.12101

Warneken, F., Lohse, K., Melis, A. P., & Tomasello, M. (2011). Young children share the spoils after collaboration. *Psychological Science, 22*(2), 267–273.

Warneken, F., & Tomasello, M. (2008). Extrinsic rewards undermine altruistic tendencies in 20-month-olds. *Developmental Psychology, 44*(6), 1785–1788.

Warneken, F., & Tomasello, M. (2009). The roots of human altruism. *British Journal of Psychology, 100*(3), 455–471.

Warneken, F., & Tomasello, M. (2012). Parental presence and encouragement do not influence helping in young children. *Infancy, 18*, 345–368. doi: 10.1111/j.1532-7078.2012.00120.x

Watkins, D. E., & Wentzel, K. R. (2008). Training boys with ADHD to work collaboratively: Social and learning outcomes. *Contemporary Educational Psychology, 33*(4), 625–646.

Webster-Stratton, C., & Reid, J. (2008). Strengthening social and emotional competence in young children who are socioeconomically disadvantaged. In W. Brown, S. Odom & M. R. (Eds.), *Social competence of young children: Risk, disability, and intervention* (pp. 185–203). Baltimore, MD: Brookes.

Wegener, D. T., & Petty, R. E. (1994). Mood management across affective states:

The hedonic contingency hypothesis. *Journal of Personality and Social Psychology, 66*(6), 1034.

Weiner, B. (1985). An attributional theory of achievement motivation and emotion. *Psychological Review, 92*(4), 548–573.

Weinfield, N. S., Sroufe, A., Egeland, B., & Carlson, E. (1999). The nature of individual differences in infant-caregiver attachment. In J. Cassidy & P. Shaver (Eds.), *Handbook of attachment: Theory, research, and clinical applications.* (pp. 68–88). New York: Guilford.

Weisz, J. R., McCarty, C. A., & Valeri, S. M. (2006). Effects of psychotherapy for depression in children and adolescents: A meta-analysis. *Psychological Bulletin, 132*(1), 132–149. doi: 10.1037/0033-2909.132.1.132

Wentzel, K. R. (1993). Does being good make the grade? Social behavior and academic competence in middle school. *Journal of Educational Psychology, 85*, 357–364.

Wentzel, K. R. (1997). Student motivation in middle school: The role of perceived pedagogical caring. *Journal of Educational Psychology, 89*(3), 411–419.

Wentzel, K. R. (2002). Are effective teachers like good parents? Teaching styles and student adjustment in early adolescence. *Child Development, 73*(1), 287–301.

Wentzel, K. R. (2006). A social motivation perspective for classroom management. In C. M. Evertson & C. S. Weinstein (Eds.), *Handbook of classroom management* (pp. 619–643). Mahwah, NJ: LEA.

Wentzel, K. R., Barry, C., & Caldwell, K. (2004). Friendships in middle school: Influences on motivation and school adjustment. *Journal of Educational Psychology, 96*(2), 195–203.

Wentzel, K. R., Filisetti, L., & Looney, L. (2007). Adolescent prosocial behavior: The role of self-processes and contextual cues. *Child Development, 78*(3), 895–910.

Wentzel, K. R., Muenks, K., McNeish, D., & Russell, S. (2017). Peer and teacher supports in relation to motivation and effort: A multi-level study. *Contemporary Educational Psychology, 49*, 32–45. doi: http://dx.doi.org/10.1016/j.cedpsych.2016.11.002

Werner, N. E., & Hill, L. G. (2010). Individual and peer group normative beliefs about relational aggression. *Child Development, 81*(3), 826–836. doi: 10.1111/j.1467-8624.2010.01436.x

What Works Clearinghouse. (2007). Caring School Community *WWC Intervention Report*: U.S. Department of Education Institute of Education Sciences.

Whiting, B. B. (1983). The genesis of prosocial behavior. In D. Bridgeman (Ed.), *The nature of prosocial development: Interdisciplinary theories and strategies.* (pp. 221–242). London: Academic Press.

Widen, S. (2013). Children's interpretation of facial expressions: The long path from valence-based to specific discrete categories. *Emotion Review, 5,* 72–77.

Wiebe, S. A., Espy, K. A., Stopp, C., Respass, J., Stewart, P., Jameson, T., . . . Huggenvik, J. I. (2009). Gene-environment interactions across development: Exploring DRD2 genotype and prenatal smoking effects on self-regulation. *Developmental Psychology, 45*(1), 31–44.

Williams, C. A., & Forehand, R. (1984). An examination of predictor variables for child compliance and noncompliance. *Journal of Abnormal Child Psychology, 12,* 491–503.

Wilson, J. (2012). Volunteerism research: A review essay. *Nonprofit and Voluntary Sector Quarterly, 41*(2), 176–212. doi: 10.1177/0899764011434558

Witkow, M. R., & Fuligni, A. J. (2010). In-school versus out-of-school friendships and academic achievement among an ethnically diverse sample of adolescents. *Journal of Research on Adolescence, 20*(3), 631–650.

Wolfgang, C. (1995). *Solving discipline problems: Methods and models for today's teachers.* Boston: Allyn & Bacon.

Wolfson, A., & Carskadon, M. (1998). Sleep schedules and daytime functioning in adolescents. *Child Development, 69*(4), 875–887.

Xie, H., Drabick, D. A., & Chen, D. (2011). Developmental trajectories of aggression from late childhood through adolescence: Similarities and differences across gender. *Aggressive Behavior, 37*(5), 387–404.

Yarrow, M., Scott, P., & Waxler, C. (1973). Learning concern for others. *Developmental Psychology, 8,* 240–260.

Yeager, D. S., & Dweck, C. S. (2012). Mindsets that promote resilience: When students believe that personal characteristics can be developed. *Educational Psychologist, 47*(4), 302–314. doi: 10.1080/00461520.2012.722805

Youniss, J., McLellan, J. A., Su, Y., & Yates, M. (1999). The role of community service in identity development: Normative, unconventional, and deviant orientations. *Journal of Adolescent Research, 14*(2), 248–261.

Zahn-Waxler, C., Kochanska, G., Krupnick, J., & McKnew, D. (1990). Patterns of guilt in children of depressed and well mothers. *Developmental Psychology, 26*(1), 51–59.

Zaki, J., Bolger, N., & Ochsner, K. (2008). It takes two: The interpersonal nature of empathic accuracy. *Psychological Science, 19*(4), 399–404.

Zanna, M., Lepper, M., & Abelson, R. (1973). Attentional mechanisms in children's devaluation of a forbidden activity in a forced-compliance situation. *Journal of Personality and Social Psychology, 28*, 355–359.

Zeller, M., Vannatta, K., Schafer, J., & Noll, R. (2003). Behavioral reputation: A cross-age perspective. *Developmental Psychology, 39*(1), 129-139.

Zimmer-Gembeck, M. J., & Skinner, E. A. (2008). Adolescents coping with stress: Development and diversity. *Prevention Researcher, 15*(4), 3–7.

Ziv, A. (2013). Using humor to develop creative thinking. In P. McGhee (Ed.), *Humor and children's development: A guide to practical applications* (pp. 99–115). London: Routledge.

INDEX

Note: Italicized page locators indicate figures; tables are noted with t.